TRIPLE
CROWN

TRIPLE CROWN

WINNING CANADA'S ENERGY FUTURE

JIM PRENTICE

with JEAN-SÉBASTIEN RIOUX

HarperCollins*Publishers*Ltd

Published by HarperCollins Publishers Ltd

First edition

HarperCollins books may be purchased for educational, business,
or sales promotional use through our Special Markets Department.

HarperCollins Publishers Ltd
2 Bloor Street East, 20th Floor
Toronto, Ontario, Canada
M4W 1A8

www.harpercollins.ca

Library and Archives Canada Cataloguing in Publication
information is available upon request.

ISBN 978-1-44342-491-2

Printed and bound in the United States of America

LSC/H   10   9   8   7   6   5   4   3   2   1

To Karen and Zoë
To our children and grandchildren
And, of course, to Julio

CONTENTS

PREFACE

On the afternoon of Wednesday, October 12, 2016, Jim Prentice and I worked on this book in his home office in Calgary, as we had done countless times over the previous 15 months. He sat at his computer at the large glass table, and I sat across from him with my laptop. We had recently received a final, "light" copyedit and were making our way through each of the editorial comments.

That day Jim and I completed our review of the first 86 pages of the manuscript. At 4:48 p.m. I saved our work before we called it a day, both of us happy and relieved that the book was just a few days from being complete and returned to the publisher one last time. Jim was looking forward to a golfing trip to British Columbia the following day, and we planned to meet again on Sunday.

As we now know, the next evening, Jim and his travelling companions, Dr. Ken Gellatly and Sheldon Reid, together with pilot Jim Kruk, died when the Cessna Citation they were in on their return home crashed just outside Kelowna. Karen Prentice lost the love of her life; his daughters lost their bedrock. I believe that Alberta and Canada lost one of their greatest public servants. And I lost a close friend, mentor and former boss.

Jim put his heart and his soul into this book, which represented the culmination of years of thinking about and acting upon energy, the environment and indigenous issues. I wrote this preface—with the encouragement of Jim's family—to give readers a sense of how the book came to be published posthumously.

After Jim's tragic passing, I consulted with Karen Prentice, editor Jim Gifford and literary agent Michael Levine, and we agreed that I would not alter anything after the end of Chapter 4, which is where we had left off. Therefore, I added no new words and I changed nothing, with two exceptions. First, I responded to the copyeditor's and proofreader's questions and approved the house style changes. Second, on November 8, 2016, Donald Trump was elected president of the United States, so I included this information in the two passages where it applied; the book's arguments did not change with the identity of the new president. We all agreed that with these minor changes, the book should be published just as it was when I left Jim and Karen's home shortly after 4:48 p.m. on Wednesday, October 12, 2016. It should stand as one of his lasting legacies.

Rest in peace, Jim. I hope this book provokes the thoughtful debate and discussion you were so keen to spark. I know you were eager to defend these ideas, and I am so sad that you won't have the opportunity to do so. I am proud to have known you, to have worked with you and to have been your friend.

Jean-Sébastien Rioux
Calgary, Alberta
November 19, 2016

INTRODUCTION

Under the Bins

I am the descendant of a long line of Canadian hockey players and underground miners.

I spent the better part of seven long summers breaking rocks "under the bins" in the coal mines of southern Alberta. While it would be an exaggeration to say that I loved the work, I have no regrets. It was a tough and dirty job. But I needed the money to pay for university, and coal mines were booming in those years. The men who were prepared to work under the bins would be well paid and so, not surprisingly, most of us were university students or recent immigrants.

The working conditions were awful and wouldn't be tolerated today. Visualize a long underground tunnel, dusty and illuminated by naked light bulbs. A conveyor belt ran down the middle of this long chamber carrying the pit run—the raw coal and rock from the mine on its way into the coal preparation plant, known as the "tipple." We were truly under the bins because the ceiling of this underground chamber consisted of a kilometre-long line of massive steel funnels, known as "bins," which were designed to vibrate, shaking the coal, rock and chewed-up timbers onto the conveyor belt. We worked in the noisy chamber beneath these massive bins.

The work wasn't complicated: The essential job was to break big rocks into small rocks. (I suppose it was good training for politics.) Tipples cannot handle big rocks or broken timbers, and so the job of the workers under the bins was to stop the conveyor belt when the rocks got too big, roll them off the belt, and use screeching pneumatic jackhammers to break them into smaller pieces and lift them back onto the conveyor belt. It wasn't glamorous work and, when the pit run was bad, we knew we were in for eight noisy hours of dust and confusion. Even by the standards of those days, it wasn't especially safe—no goggles, no ear muffs, no dust masks. What it was, however, in addition to pounding noise and choking dust, was a good wage and almost endless opportunities for double shifts (at twice the hourly rate), which is how I earned enough to pay my way through university.

Every man under the bins knew that we were at the bottom of Canada's industrial economy, but every one of us took pride in our work. The coal that we were mining was Canada's best metallurgical coal. We knew it was being exported to Japanese steel producers who were paying premium prices for it, and we were proud of that fact. And we knew intuitively—even though we were at the very bottom of the Canadian industrial economy—that, if we weren't competitive and if the bosses who ran the company and the politicians who ran the country didn't develop the right trade agreements, relationships and infrastructure to get that coal to Japan, we would be out of our jobs.

* * *

This book is about Canada's energy future—a future that once seemed bright, limitless and impossibly prosperous but which today is uncertain and clouded on many fronts. Historically speaking, we have been one of the world's most successful producers of energy in all its forms. Yet we now seem to have lost our way. I am writing about the opportunities that lie ahead and about the choices we need to make to regain the dream of converting Canada's vast energy resources into a secure, prosperous and environmentally responsible future. This book is about what we need to do to reassert that vision. It is also about the risks and the pitfalls we will face along this road back to a more confident future.

The past many years have seen Canada repeatedly stumble in our attempts to pursue a future as a powerful global player in the energy world. Only a few short years ago, then–prime minister Stephen Harper described Canada as an energy superpower. In the years since, however, we have proven amateurish. We have played checkers, while others played chess. We have been negligent in our failure to advance our own global interests, both as an energy exporter and as a country with a record of sound environmental achievement. We seem blithely unaware of the ability we have to work with the United States to exercise our collective expertise to export natural gas and oil into the world marketplace and, in the process, weaken OPEC's grip on world oil supplies and prices.

Our amateurism is evident in our quest to broaden our market access globally. It is also evident in our attempts to define a new relationship with indigenous peoples. It is true of our attempts to work with the United States on pipelines. It is true of our attempts to craft an energy partnership with new investors and markets, including the Chinese. And, certainly, it is true of our missteps in the areas that should have been Canadian strengths: the protection of the environment and climate change policies.

It also remains true of our attempts to build a liquefied natural gas (LNG) industry on Canada's west coast, where we have been embarrassed by the comparative success of Australia and the United States. In all these respects, we have reaped what we have sown. The past several years have been tumultuous, marred by setback after setback for Canada's energy economy.

We are not alone in this respect. Other countries have their own problems with pipelines and climate change; with fiscal policies, regulatory suffocation and indigenous land claims. And certainly, the ill wind of the 2015/16 commodity price collapse has shaken even the strongest energy-producing countries. But still . . . Canada used to be good at this kind of thing and today we struggle. Our governments have collectively lost sight of the need to improve our competitiveness, and our many setbacks have now begun to reverberate across the country, affecting Canada's economic performance, job markets, trade balance, public finances and even the value of our currency. Sadly, the worst is yet to come as a 20-year period of capital investment in Canada's energy economy winds down, accelerated by government carelessness in the oversight of public policy choices that are critical to our ability to develop and export our resources.

This book covers many aspects of Canada's energy future and focuses on the need for Canada to act strategically. It examines our energy security interests and our complex relationship with the United States. We consider that relationship special; whether the United States does is unclear. The rise of protectionist sentiment in the US during the 2016 presidential race underscores Canada's vulnerability. Certainly, though, the United States remains our largest customer, our most vocal critic and, more concerning, our most aggressive competitor. I examine how Canada and the United States, by working together and harnessing our collective resources—including the Canadian oil sands, North American natural gas and Canadian hydro power—can achieve North American energy sufficiency, allowing us to weaken the geo-economic and geopolitical power of OPEC. To do that, Canada must increase its export capacity to the US Gulf coast and, simultaneously, expand our reach to new markets in the Asia Pacific. China is, as we will see, of obvious consequence in that calculation.

Energy and the environment are inextricably linked, so this book is also about the environment and climate change, and how we must lead again—both in the protection of the former and in the battle against the latter. I devote attention to how we can fulfill our obligations while simultaneously preserving our ability to compete with others who are less earnest about the environment. We must lead, but we must also avoid a repetition of Kyoto. For Canada, an integrated and pragmatic approach to energy, climate change and the environment represents the best way forward.

This book is about more than oil and natural gas because renewable energy in general and hydroelectricity in particular are important in Canada's past and future. It therefore addresses all the infrastructure that we desperately need—the pipelines, ports, hydroelectric facilities and power lines. Without them, we undercut our standard of living by isolating ourselves from new markets for both our renewable and non-renewable energy. In the long term, hydroelectricity, rather than oil, may be Canada's greatest energy endowment.

Some will be surprised that this book also examines Canada's relationship with First Nations and explores how we might define new partnerships with them. The country faces no greater challenge and also has no more obvious an opportunity. Canada's indigenous peoples have always been an inspiration for me, and the chapters that follow attempt to clear some of the confusion in Canada over how our First Nations think about their inherent jurisdiction, the environment and energy. The Pacific Northwest coast is Canada's gateway to Asia, and Canada's energy ambitions will be realized only if First Nations lead as full economic partners in the pipelines, ports and marine infrastructure that are needed to get there. I will outline a new future that fulfills Canada's promise for oil exports to Asia via a pipeline and port that are owned, in part, by Canada's indigenous peoples.

The book is also about the strength of the industrial, financial and scientific ecosystems that underpin our resource industries and about our continuing need to innovate and invest in those areas. There is a practical aspect to all this since Canada's ability to continue to create world class, high-paying jobs depends, at least in part, on our ability to maintain our position as a favoured investment destination and a world leader in the responsible development of natural resources. It is really about the legacy that we pass on to future generations. In tomorrow's world, renewable and non-renewable energies will share the same ecosystems, driven by the same market needs, financed by the same intermediaries, and drawing on the same technically skilled workers. The real question for Canada is whether we wish to lead or follow in the transformation that this work entails, and whether we wish to reassert ourselves as a global leader in the energy world.

* * *

In some respects, I am an unlikely candidate to write this book. I am neither a geologist nor a petroleum engineer, and I never worked for an energy company.

My first career was in law and, in the 20 years I practised, I never once represented an oil company; indeed, my biggest successes involved my advocacy for farmers and ranchers *against* oil companies. In the first of those cases, I represented a small group of ranchers from a remote valley in southern Alberta who took on the energy giant Amoco over the company's right to drill for natural gas in an ecologically sensitive area in the foothills of that area. That confrontation, known as the battle over the "Whaleback,"[1] stunned the energy world when the Alberta Energy Resources Conservation Board (ERCB) ruled in our favour, agreed with the ranchers and rejected Amoco's application for drilling licences. Nothing like it had ever happened before in Alberta.

A few years later, just before I entered federal politics, I represented the residents of the Calgary community of Lynnwood in their lawsuit against Imperial Oil, a subsidiary of ExxonMobil and the owner of a pre-war oil tank yard that had been "cleaned up" but which continued to leach hydrocarbons. Neither case endeared me to Alberta's energy industry, and I don't recall one company ever asking me to represent it. We weren't close.

I set aside my law career in 2003 and was elected to the House of Commons in 2004 as a Conservative Member of Parliament. In 2006, a new Conservative government was elected: Stephen Harper became Canada's prime minister, and I found myself as one of his most influential ministers. Years later he would describe me as his chief operating officer through the Conservative minority governments. In practice, I chaired the Operations Committee of Cabinet, which controlled the day-to-day operations of the government and coordinated its response on difficult political files. I chaired that committee for six years, longer than anyone else in its history. I sat beside the prime minister in the House of Commons, and I served as the senior minister, or "political minister," for Alberta and, initially, the Yukon, the Northwest Territories and Nunavut. Those were heady days. I was also sent in to successive portfolios to solve problems. I was the Harper government's first minister of Indian affairs and northern development, later became the minister of industry, and finally the minister of environment, thrust into the cauldron of the climate change negotiations that culminated in the Copenhagen Climate Change Conference of 2009.

In the years between 2006 and 2011, through these successive portfolios, I maintained involvement in the government's energy, climate change and pipeline files. I was able to do so because I was the senior political minister from Alberta and because I held the chairmanship of both the Operations Committee of Cabinet and the Special Cabinet Committee on the Environment and Energy Security. Throughout my time in government, I also held the pipeline file and headed up our trilateral working relationship with the Americans and the Mexicans during the later years of the George W. Bush administration—the so-called Security and Prosperity Partnership. During President Barack Obama's first term, I served as the Canadian representative on the Clean Energy Dialogue. I was also Canada's negotiator in the many discussions leading to Copenhagen.

During those years, I began to work more closely with Canada's energy industry. Being a hands-on minister, I insisted on a personal presence at the table and soon was engaged in the complex negotiations surrounding our policies on Aboriginal issues, pipelines, the environment, climate change, market access and foreign investment—all the things that this book is about. Through those years, I developed close working relationships with stakeholders on all sides, including those from across the energy industry. I became Canada's environment minister in 2008, responsible for the carriage of the energy and climate change negotiations that would eventually culminate at Copenhagen. I didn't especially want the job but, as the prime minister put it, "You're the only one at the table who understands this climate change stuff . . . or wants to."

I left federal politics in November 2010 to work in the private sector but returned to politics a few years later; from September 2014 to May 2015, I served as premier of Alberta, a position that propelled me once again into the fray of energy and environment policy-making, and pipeline and climate change debates.

My former chief of staff, Jean-Sébastien Rioux, assisted me in writing this book from the beginning. He is now a professor at the University of Calgary's School of Public Policy and has been closely involved in energy policy issues for the past several years. We were close collaborators in Ottawa, and we are good friends today.

* * *

Canada has now reached the point of no return. The status quo is no longer an option. The absence of national leadership has brought us to a crossroads that will see us either up our game and emerge as a global energy player or falter and slip farther into the background as a captive supplier of discounted resources to the United States. The United States is well positioned to take advantage of our incompetence by importing Canadian oil and natural gas and then exporting it from their LNG terminals and port facilities, creating American jobs, American profits and American tax revenues. It will do this, not because it is greedy but because we share a continental marketplace that allows for the free flow of energy molecules and the creation of economic gain by those who seize opportunity. The United States is seizing it. We are not.

If we do nothing, there will be measurable economic losses. The current malaise in the energy sector, brought on by the worldwide decline in oil prices of 2015 and 2016, provides a glimpse of what those consequences will look like: declining capital investment, declining foreign investment, declining employment, declining royalties, declining exports and, ultimately, declining government revenue in every part of Canada since every province and territory is tied to the energy economy. Over time, the quantum of those losses will be catastrophic for all Canadians because the energy industry accounts for more of Canada's investment, exports and job creation than any other industry.

But that isn't the only point. Perhaps it isn't even the most important point. The real point is that we are better than this. We are one of the most respected democracies in the world. We have excelled throughout our history in balancing our stewardship over the environment with the advancement of our economy. Our record of environmental achievement, whether in conservation or in the development of new technologies, is the best in the world.

Canada has always led, and we should lead again. In the 21st century, the world faces the dual challenge of advancing the living standards of billions of new citizens who seek access to energy while simultaneously protecting the planet from the worst consequences of climate change and escalating carbon emissions. Canadians should not retreat in the face of that challenge. We should lead. We should not abdicate the field to the long list of undemocratic regimes that currently control the world's energy marketplace. Instead, Canada should be the country that the world looks to for responsible energy development.

That's what this book is about. It is about where we are going and what we need to do to get back on our game.

PART ONE

Our Resources and Our Strategic Interests

CHAPTER 1

Canada's Global Opportunity:
Our Energy Resources and Markets

Imagine a country whose proven energy reserves are among the largest in the world—its oil reserves alone larger than all but two of the OPEC states' and five times the size of those of the next closest industrial democracy. Suppose, too, that this nation also has massive natural gas reserves that are several hundred times larger than it can itself consume. Visualize, too, that it has frontier energy basins, offshore reserves and Arctic resources that are still largely unexplored and which hold even greater energy reserves. And, aspiring to a lower-carbon future, imagine that its hydroelectric potential exceeds that of any other country on the globe. Consider that its uranium reserves are among the world's largest and more than sufficient to fuel the nuclear energy ambitions of the entire planet. And, recognizing that this country occupies one-eighth of the world's land mass, imagine the expanse of opportunity for its renewable energies—wind, tidal, geothermal and solar. In fact, such a country actually exists. We call it Canada.

Unfortunately, Canadians seem unaware of our own potential. I have always been taken aback by the diffidence—even embarrassment—that many Canadians seem to feel about Canada's natural resource wealth. This sentiment is more pronounced in some parts of the country than in others, but I am continually surprised by the lack of understanding among Canadians everywhere about the sheer magnitude of our resource opportunities, especially our renewable and non-renewable energy resources.

Equally concerning is the lack of appreciation of the extent to which our standard of living and the high quality of the public and private goods that we enjoy is tied to the extraction, processing and export of those resources. The Canadian economy is largely resource-driven, and the strength of that economy, the health of our trade balance and the resiliency of our public finances, and even our currency, are inextricably connected to the development of those resources.

At the 2016 annual meeting of the World Economic Forum in Davos, Switzerland, Prime Minister Justin Trudeau observed that Canada is a "resourceful" economy rather than a "resource" economy. This was a clever turn of phrase, and I understand the importance of Canada marketing itself more deeply. However, it would be a mistake to let Canadians lose sight of the reality that our standard of living is strongly correlated to the development of our natural resources, especially our energy resources. According to Statistics Canada, about 10 percent of the Canadian economy is predicated on the extraction, processing and export of our natural resources—oil, natural gas, minerals, and agricultural and forest products. Those very products comprise 53 percent of our exports, and the companies engaged in those industries represent the lion's share of capital investment in Canada and much of the value of the Toronto Stock Exchange. The natural resource and energy industries are our "family business"—and, frankly, our history is that we are good at it.

I am not suggesting that we don't excel at other things, too. We are very good at manufacturing, and both Ontario and Quebec are known for their excellence in the manufacture and assembly of the most complex of modern products, including automobiles, smart phones and airplanes. Our capital markets and financial services industries are also world class. So, too, are our activities in pharmaceuticals. Our universities are consistently good, and a half-dozen are among the best research institutions in the world. We also are a leading agricultural producer, known for our developing excellence in biotechnology. All these are important pillars of our economy, and we should be justifiably proud of what we have achieved and optimistic about the future.

But we seem especially reluctant to acknowledge our position in the area of natural resources. Among many there seems to be a quiet embarrassment about our efforts to wrestle oil, natural gas, uranium, potash, aluminum, gold, silver, iron, zinc, nickel and countless other minerals from the ground, or about our efforts to produce hydroelectricity, lumber, and pulp and paper. Some appear to feel that these activities are somehow beneath us, even though they have always been mainstays of the Canadian economy.

In today's world, the jobs created in these industries are rarely at the end of a shovel or under the bins, but are instead technically demanding, highly skilled and well-paying positions. These industries also hold continuing potential for innovation, given the advanced products, processes and systems they rely on. The spinoffs from them also drive other Canadian successes, in technology, manufacturing and the training and service industries.

Those indirect benefits drive our success both at home and abroad. Canada's highly successful capital markets, for example, are known worldwide as one of the best places to raise equity or debt to finance resource projects and energy projects, whether the physical resources are located here or elsewhere. Skilled Canadian workers, entrepreneurs and executives can be found in every corner of the world where the extraction and development of natural resources are under way.

Perhaps Canadians were once—in the words of historian Harold Innis—"hewers of wood and drawers of water." This description may have been accurate for the 19th century, but it doesn't begin to describe the modern complexity of Quebec's James Bay complex, which lights the eastern seaboard of North America; or that of the Irving refinery in New Brunswick, the largest supplier of refined petroleum products into the eastern seaboard of the United States; or the stunning scale of Alberta's oil sands installations, which produce 3.5 million barrels of oil a day; or the magnitude and complexities of the Shell or Petronas LNG facilities under consideration on the west coast of British Columbia.

Canadians need bear in mind that there is no shame in mining, in forestry, or in the oil and gas industry, as long as we are the best in the world at it and as long as our practices are environmentally sustainable.

Canada's Energy Reserves—Vast and Diversified

Canada's energy wealth is staggering in scale. In a world where the availability of energy separates those who are industrialized from those who are not and those who are rich from those who are poor, Canada stands out as one of the very few countries that is rich in virtually every form of renewable and non-renewable energy. Put simply, no other democracy in the world possesses a comparable set of energy opportunities.

Canada's proven oil reserves are the third-largest in the world, ranking behind only Saudi Arabia and Venezuela. Reserves are said to be "proven" if they can be recovered under existing economic conditions, using existing technology.[1] Those oil reserves include the oil sands together with both conventional and non-conventional reserves and significant off-shore reserves on Canada's east coast. Our resource base in the Arctic is also large but remains to be fully explored.

The oil sands are a significant part of Canada's reserve base, comprising 170 billion barrels of recoverable resource using current technologies. In fact, our oil sands deposits are, by a wide margin, the largest petroleum reserves in the Western democratic world. Few appreciate the size and potential longevity of Canada's 170 billion barrels of proven oil sands reserves. To put that quantum in perspective, it represents more than 120 years of production at current levels, using current technologies—that's five generations! Frankly, the real limitation in our ability to produce from the oil sands is the environmental sustainability of our production, not the resource's size.

Canada also possesses enormous natural gas reserves. The true quantum of our reserves is unknown since we have not even begun to assess the natural gas potential of Canada's more remote Arctic Basin, or even the Beaufort or the frontier basin of the Mackenzie Valley. Our proven reserves amount to 72 trillion cubic feet, and even those volumes vastly exceed Canada's own future needs by many hundred-fold. It needs to be said, however, that the world has a lot of natural gas, and Canada is not unique in this respect. In fact, our proven reserves are 18th in the world, dwarfed by those of Russia, the OPEC powers and even the United States. Nonetheless, newer Canadian natural gas plays such as the Montney, Duvernay, Horn River and Liard are world class resources that are cost competitive for both North American pipeline and global LNG markets.

Canada's hydroelectric potential is also enormous. We are currently the second-largest producer of hydroelectricity in the world, producing more electricity from hydro power than any country other than China. More than 60 percent of Canada's electricity comes from hydro power, and that percentage will only increase as more sites are developed. By some estimates, Canada has the ability to bring 25,000 megawatts of new hydroelectricity generation onto the North American power grid over the next 50 years. The critical importance of Canadian hydro to the greening of the North American electricity system lies not only in the size of these new sites, but also in the fact that Canadian hydro, once it's connected to the North American grid, serves as a sort of North American balancing wheel or battery, offsetting the intermittency of other renewable sources such as wind and solar. Steven Chu, the Nobel Prize–winning physicist and former US energy secretary, and I discussed this fact as the best illustration of the need to harmonize our countries' energy systems.

Canada's other renewable opportunities include wind and solar power, geothermal energy, tidal energy and biomass. Canada's renewable energy opportunities rival those of any other country in the world. Renewable energy (mostly hydroelectricity) already accounts for 17 percent of Canada's total primary energy supply.

Wind power accounts for 1.6 percent of Canada's electricity generation, and biomass another 1.4 percent. Moreover, wind and solar photovoltaic energy are the fastest-growing sources of electricity in Canada, although, in the case of solar, starting from a modest base.

Put simply, no other country in the world sits on a comparable inventory of oil, natural gas, uranium, hydroelectric, wind, solar and tidal resources. Equally germane is that none of the world's other industrial democracies comes even close. We are unique in the potential and in the possibilities we possess.

Canada Excels in the Production of Energy

In addition to having an enormous resource base or potential, Canada also excels in developing these resources. We are the world's fourth-largest producer and exporter of oil, the fourth-largest producer and exporter of natural gas, the third-largest producer and the largest exporter of hydroelectric power. We are also the world's second-largest producer and exporter of uranium. While much is said of OPEC, Canada's own oil production exceeds that of every one of the 12 OPEC nations except Saudi Arabia.

Canada produces 4.3 million barrels of oil per day (bpd), which is more than any of Venezuela, Mexico, Nigeria, the United Arab Emirates, Kuwait, Iran or Iraq. This level of production represents big business in Canada: Oil and gas activity alone generated about $20 billion in taxes, royalties and other revenues for various governments across Canada in 2013. It represents more than 53 percent of Canada's total exports and almost 25 percent of the value of the Toronto Stock Exchange. The energy sector is the single-largest private sector investor in the country, investing about $74 billion in the Canadian economy in 2013. Capital spending by the oil and gas industry accounted for 20 percent of total private sector capital investment in Canada in 2013.[2]

I can attest to the degree to which the Canadian economy depends on the energy sector. Frankly, it was the energy sector that carried Canada, relatively unscathed, through the difficulties of the great recession that began in 2008 and which even today continues to weigh on global economic growth.

Some hold the view that Canada should not be in the energy business and that we should pursue a different future. But the truth is that Canada's standard of living is tied very closely to our success in the energy industries that dominate our labour and capital markets, our government revenues and our technological and productivity advancements. This close connection is not just in Alberta, but across the entire country. It is also true that if one looks ahead to the demographic, economic and productivity pressures that Canada will face in the coming years, they highlight the need for a strengthened Canadian presence in the energy sector and a need for higher productivity and a stronger export performance. Our failure to recognize this need will lead to a deterioration of both the creation of private wealth and the financing of the public goods provided by governments across Canada.

Energy Is a Canadian Story, Not an Alberta Story

An aspect of Canada's energy story that is poorly understood is the extent to which all of Canada depends on and participates in the energy economy. In one way or another, every Canadian province can be said to be in the energy business. I didn't fully understand how true this was until the fall of 2009.

Certainly, I knew that the impact of Canada's energy industry is evident in every corner of the country. For instance, in 2004, while campaigning in Prince Edward Island, I made a whistle stop at that province's largest steel fabrication plant and was astounded to see that every component being produced there was being shipped to western Canada for incorporation into oil sands and heavy-oil assets. I also recall being surprised by my many discussions with Atlantic Canadian premiers, all of whom pointed out that a large and material variance in their provincial revenue budgets arose from the income taxes paid by the massive Atlantic Canadian workforce that commuted to Alberta's oil sands. Later, when I arrived on Bay Street as a banker, I was astounded at the concentration of energy loans among the portfolios of Canada's big banks.

But the biggest surprise for me came in late 2009, as I prepared myself as the environment minister for Canada's attendance at the Copenhagen Climate Change Conference, the COP 15, being held in December. My office referred to that period as the "Road to Copenhagen."

Part of my journey involved meetings with all the Canadian premiers, together with many of the provincial ministers of energy, environment and climate change. I undertook that effort in an effort to minimize the federal–provincial wrangling that had characterized Canada's participation in the previous COP (Conference of the Parties) meetings in places such as Nairobi (Kenya), Bali (Indonesia) and Poznań (Poland). My efforts were not entirely successful on that front, but they gave me an opportunity to learn that the future of every Canadian province is tied inextricably to our future as an energy producer, refiner and exporter.

This is obviously true of Alberta, which today produces more than 3.5 million barrels of oil a day. It is, however, equally true of British Columbia, Saskatchewan and the Northwest Territories, each of which shares the prolific Western Canadian Sedimentary Basin with Alberta. Today, a number of Canada's most successful oil and gas companies operate exclusively in Saskatchewan. The Northwest Territories and Nunavut share the extraordinary but largely undeveloped oil and natural gas resources of the Mackenzie Valley. Nunavut has the added dimension of the future opportunities and challenges associated with the offshore resources in the Beaufort Sea.

Quebec, British Columbia and Manitoba are all also in the energy business. The future of these three provinces is inextricably connected to our ability to freely trade Canadian hydroelectricity into the North American grid. Manitoba is also a hydrocarbon producer. Then-premiers Jean Charest and Gary Doer were as concerned about Canada's energy future as was the premier of Alberta.

Even in 2009, British Columbia harboured aspirations to be a major force in the export of liquefied natural gas. Since that time, three of the world's largest LNG exporters, Shell, ExxonMobil and Petronas, have expended billions of dollars on proposals to build LNG facilities on BC's west coast. Indeed, over the past decade, the province has been deluged with more than 20 competing LNG proposals, all linked to the prolific natural gas basins— the Montney, Duvernay and Horn River—which are shared by Alberta and BC.

Quebec and New Brunswick are both in the refining business and, although most Canadians don't realize it, New Brunswick is the largest exporter of refined petroleum products such as gasoline and diesel fuel to the northeastern seaboard of the United

States. Refining is the dominant industry in the province. Both Nova Scotia and Newfoundland and Labrador are in the offshore oil and natural gas business. Labrador is home to one of North America's largest hydroelectricity facilities, the Upper Churchill generating station. A new hydroelectricity facility, Muskrat Falls on the Lower Churchill, will connect the island of Newfoundland to Nova Scotia via the Maritime Link, which is being underwritten by both provinces.

Then there is Ontario, which benefits directly from the overall Canadian energy economy. The province is home to refineries and petrochemical plants. It is, for example, where Suncor headquarters its Petro-Canada marketing operations. The lion's share of Canada's hard capital assets is also manufactured in Ontario. As an example, the General Electric turbines that are indispensable to hydro projects, pipelines and in situ oil sands steaming units are built in Peterborough. Most significantly, Canada's financial services industry is headquartered in Toronto, and every Canadian energy project is financed through debt and capital markets in that city. Finance is Ontario's largest industry and, for the past 20 years, the financing of new Canadian energy projects largely underpinned the success of Canada's banking and financial services industry.

So, not only is Canada in the energy business but, more to the point, we are *all* in the energy business. This was borne out in my meetings with each premier. In fact, in 2009, during those consultations, I was struck by the degree to which a consensus actually exists across Canada on energy and environmental issues. This seems like a surprising statement, but later in this book I will offer a few observations on what that consensus looks like and how we can capitalize on its going forward.

For the moment, I simply make the point that the energy story is not an Alberta story. Indeed, it is not even predominantly a Western Canadian story. It is a Canadian story, and the future of every Canadian province is tied to our ability to produce and trade in energy.

Canada Is the Largest Supplier of Energy to the United States

Canada is and has been for decades the largest supplier of all forms of energy to the United States. To the surprise of many, it is Canada—not Saudi Arabia—that serves as the largest oil exporter into the US marketplace. As a result of geography, proximity and history, the vast majority of Canada's international trade has been and still is with the United States.

In 2015, the United States imported 9.4 million barrels of crude oil and petroleum products a day, and more than 3.75 million barrels of that total—or 40 percent—came from Canada. Canadian oil exports into the US market are larger than all the OPEC countries combined (2.8 million barrels per day), and they dwarf the imports from every other country. For example, in 2015, Saudi Arabia's exports into the United States totalled 1.058 million bpd; Mexico's were 758,000 bpd and Venezuela's 830,000 bpd. No one else even figures in the calculations.

The Canadian and American natural gas markets are similarly linked on a continental basis. Canada continues to be the source of almost 90 percent of US natural gas imports. However, the continental trading balance has begun to dramatically shift as US shale gas production escalates, capturing both American and Canadian market share. The most recent US Energy Information Administration data illustrate these trends. By 2015, Canadian exports of natural gas into the United States declined to 2,625,000 million cubic feet (MMcf) per year, down almost 30 percent from the decade between 2000 and 2010. In contrast, American natural gas exports to Canada and Mexico have risen almost 20-fold since 2000, in the case of Canada nearing 700,647 MMcf in 2015. Eastern Canadian consumers are increasingly consuming American, rather than Canadian, natural gas.

Canadian hydroelectricity is also an important continental export. The North American electricity grid is a continental one, linked on a north–south rather than an east–west axis, and Canada exports 10 percent of its electricity production into the northern United States, representing some 1.6 percent of total American electricity consumption.[3] Those exports originate in Quebec, Newfoundland and Labrador, Manitoba and British Columbia, and they are an essential aspect of the North American electricity system.

The American marketplace will almost certainly remain Canada's most important energy export market. Opportunities exist for Canada to continue to increase its market share in oil, natural gas and electricity. However, the United States will *not* be the main driver of growth in demand for Canadian oil and natural gas going forward. This is true for two reasons. First, the United States has dramatically expanded its own domestic production of both oil and natural gas. It is not an exaggeration to observe that US production increases have been so massive and have happened so quickly that they have transformed global energy markets and affected global geopolitics. Canada has not been immune to this trend, as Americans shift to the consumption of their domestic resources. Second, on the demand side, overall American oil consumption has begun to flatten. Increasing American consumption is no longer the primary driver of global demand growth. Instead, it is now the emerging economies—especially those in the Asia Pacific Basin, where consumption is increasing markedly.

Our energy relationship with the United States has become more complicated as a result of those developments. Not only has the United States re-emerged as the largest oil producer in the world, it has also re-emerged as Canada's major competition. Increased US production is a direct consequence of a sustained period of higher oil prices, which encouraged improved technologies in two related areas—directional drilling and fracking—unlocking previously inaccessible hydrocarbon reserves. The results have been nothing short of revolutionary.

In the years between 2008 and 2015, US oil production increased by more than 90 percent, from five million barrels per day to 9.6 million barrels per day. Natural gas production followed a similar trajectory, increasing from 25.6 million cubic feet per day (MMcf/d) in 2008 to 31.9 MMcf/d in 2014, an increase of more than 25 percent in only four years, almost entirely owing to new shale gas production.[4] In less than a decade, the United States has transformed itself from an importer of LNG to an LNG exporter. It has emerged as a dominant force in world oil production, and American supplies of refined energy products have transformed global supply-and-demand balances. All this has squeezed the economics and market penetration of Canadian oil and, especially, natural gas. Canadian natural gas can be produced at competitive prices, but much of it is at the far end of the continental marketplace and disadvantaged by transportation infrastructure costs.

This remarkable transformation in US energy supply has been

accompanied by a flattening of US consumption. This trend has occurred gradually, driven in large part by a decade of high oil prices that have encouraged new technologies to reduce consumption. New fuel economy standards have improved the fuel consumption of motor vehicles, and an emphasis on more efficient urban transportation networks has reduced demand. The availability of cheap natural gas has driven efficiencies across the transportation network and accelerated change in the production of electricity. New technologies, improved appliance efficiencies and a new conservation ethic, in particular among younger consumers, have led to significant improvements in energy efficiency in residential and institutional consumption. In the result, US energy consumption is not increasing and has, in fact, been steadily declining, accelerating downward since the great recession of 2008–9.

This flattening of demand is not unique to the United States: A similar trend prevails in most other Western democracies. Current projections anticipate a flat projection of demand for oil in the OECD countries right through to 2040, even taking into account population and GDP growth.[5]

Canada's Competitive Advantage in the Growth of the Asia Pacific

Canada is, however, an Asian Pacific country, and we are particularly well positioned to maximize our market share in the continuing growth in global energy demand.

Canada is proximate to the emerging markets of the Asia Pacific, and our production can increase to satisfy their increased needs. We currently produce more than 4.3 million barrels per day of oil equivalent. But we are fully capable of producing more than 5.2 million barrels per day by 2030, and the market for that increased production resides in the countries of the Asia Pacific.

It is important to recognize that world demand for hydrocarbons continues to increase inexorably. While some popular media attempt to portray a different picture, suggesting that the world has now entered a new post-hydrocarbon era, nothing could be further from the truth. According to US Energy Information Agency (EIA) projections, total world consumption of energy will increase 56 percent by 2040, and the largest projected increase in demand will be from emerging economies—particularly in Asia. The world currently consumes 96 million barrels of oil per day, but consumption continues to increase, headed toward 98 million barrels per day in 2020 and 103.5 million barrels per day in 2040.

Whether oil remains the main source for transportation, heating and electricity-generating fuel for another century inspires much debate and even more emotion. Certainly, the Paris-based International Energy Agency (IEA), which is unbiased and respected, is of the view that hydrocarbons such as oil and natural gas will be the dominant sources of energy for at least another generation, until 2040 at the earliest.[6] The EIA holds the same opinion. This is because no other current form of energy is as "dense"—that is, provides so many joules of energy per unit—and allows for such ready transportation and distribution. It is why a direct correlation exists between the consumption of hydrocarbons on the one hand and standard of living on the other, and it is why the emerging economies of the world are so focused on their ability to secure and consume energy resources.

Implicit within this discussion is the reality that Canada must diversify its export markets. We must make greater efforts to increase our opportunities in Asia, which is where the growing demand for energy is and where it will be for the next 25 or more years. Consumption has flattened, peaked and even declined in many Western economies, but economic growth and the rise of the middle class in Asia will drive the global energy economy for the next 50 years.

Canada's energy potential is staggering in its scale. We are the *only* industrial democracy in the world that has the ability to be fully energy self-sufficient in oil, natural gas and electricity, and which has the capacity to export significant volumes of those energy sources into the continental and global marketplace. Our resource base in renewables is also massive, reflecting the size and geographic footprint of our country and allowing us, for example, to lead the world in the production of hydroelectricity.

Despite these many advantages, Canada has failed to emerge in the international energy marketplace as a global force. Instead, we find ourselves a captive supplier to a single customer, one that has ample supply alternatives and one that has itself emerged as a competitive supplier of natural gas and, to a limited extent, oil. For a country whose economy is disproportionately based on exporting energy, this is more than an inconvenience. It is a major vulnerability.

The key to the development of all these valuable resources will be access to markets. This is true of our continuing exports to the United States, and it is certainly true of our need to access broader global markets. Canada's most pressing strategic interest is, in fact, the need for global market access.

The United States will remain a critical market for Canada, likely sustaining the 3.75 million barrels of oil per day that we export to that country, but Asia and the emerging economies are the markets that Canada should strive to access for new growth. For too long, it has been easy for Canada to be a single-customer trading nation, prospering as a captive supplier to the US market. We have been blessed by fortune and by geography, possessing a wealth of natural resources and sharing the continent with the world's largest and most successful economy—an economy that, for the most part, has wanted and needed as much energy as we could produce. Our linkage to the United States has allowed us to jointly construct the largest integrated free-market energy system in the world, benefiting both our countries. But in the process, we have neglected the obvious need to diversify our customer base toward the growing economies of Asia.

CHAPTER 2

Canada as a Global Energy Power:
The Need for National Leadership

C anada is not a global energy power. We should be, but we are not. Instead, we languish far behind our competition, marginalized as one of the world's most parochial energy producers.

For most of modern history, countries with oil have acted strategically when it came to that endowment. Think of the United States, which dominated world oil production through the mid-20th century; or the OPEC countries, which have done so in the time since; or the Russians, who continue to exercise a pervasive influence on both Asian and European energy markets. Energy, especially oil, has always been treated as a geopolitical asset by those who have it and as a geopolitical necessity by those who don't.

Canada has been an exception to that rule, content to drift along, treating our vast oil and natural gas reserves as mere commodities no different from the other products we export, such as iron ore, zinc or molybdenum.

We have one of the world's largest asset bases of oil, natural gas, uranium, coal, hydroelectricity and renewable energy. We have strong capital markets, highly functioning labour markets, sound environmental regulations, solid democratic institutions and the social cohesion and stability that come from respect for the rule of law. We are also largely free of the social turmoil and religious conflicts that destabilize, to one degree or another, almost all the world's other major energy producers. And yet, Canada has not exercised the authority implied by this long list of competitive advantages.

We have global mining companies, global aerospace companies and global engineering firms, yet there are no successful global energy companies headquartered in Canada. The few Canadian companies that once had international capabilities, such as Petro-Canada and Talisman, have now been sold and their global assets dismantled. Our market reach isn't global, and we serve increasingly as a massive supplier of discounted resources to the United States, lacking the pipeline and port capacity and, until recently, even the desire to reach global markets. Remarkably, we haven't even built the pipelines to reach many of our own Canadian consumers.

Canada's failings lie in the absence of national leadership and in the failure of our country to assert itself globally. When it comes to our energy resources, we lack a national vision of who we are or where we are going. We have no strategy other than to leave the management of Canada's energy resources to corporations and to the provinces. Not surprisingly, the results have reflected provincial, rather than national, priorities. Frankly, Canada hasn't emerged as a global energy player because we haven't shown much interest in becoming one.

We have left the provinces to adjudicate the pace and scale of resource development, to govern their exports and to manage environmental standards and controversies. This they have done to satisfy local as opposed to national, or in the case of climate change, international, expectations. We have become the world's most insular of energy producers, constricted by infrastructure limitations and reputational challenges that are a direct consequence of diminished national ambition. When it comes to the development of new markets and the pipelines, ports and facilities needed to reach them, we have embarrassed ourselves, stumbling along, abandoning Canadian proponents and foreign investors alike to a morass of interprovincial jealousies and unresolved indigenous land claims that are well beyond the ability of the private sector to resolve. And our private sector energy corporations, while exceptional within their own competencies, have been embarrassingly parochial in their own ambitions. How could the world's most richly endowed industrial democracy not field a single international energy company? Corporate leaders, for their part, contend that the answer lies in the timidity of our capital markets, which will neither sponsor nor support international efforts by Canadian companies.

There are exceptions to these comments. Quebec, for example, has pursued a more visionary approach to the development of its hydro resources, attentive always to what is in the province's best interest. But in a sense this exception proves the point, because what is in Quebec's best interests has not always been what is in Canada's. The long-standing dispute between Quebec and Newfoundland and Labrador over the revenues from the Upper Churchill Hydro Project, one of the most corrosive arguments in the history of our country, illustrates that fact. Still, Quebec at least has had a plan. Canada has not.

Successive national governments have failed to view Canada's vast energy endowment as a strategic asset, or to consider the global geopolitical opportunities it confers on our country. As a result, we have been completely lacking in national vision when it comes to the development of Canada's energy resources. This is not a partisan observation; it isn't that Canada's policies or priorities have been Liberal when they should have been Conservative, or vice versa. The point is that there hasn't been any overarching federal strategy at all. Despite the obvious opportunities associated with the broadening of Canada's market footprint into the Atlantic and Asia Pacific basins, there has been no meaningful federal commitment to develop the institutional or physical infrastructure to reach either market. I was surprised to learn, when first elected to the House of Commons, that Canada has no energy ministry and that the federal Department of Natural Resources was a second-tier government department. Given the importance of energy and natural resources to the Canadian economy, the department should be one of Ottawa's most important.

It will upset some to frame it this way, but when it comes to the development of Canada's natural resources, especially our energy resources, Ottawa, as Prime Minister Pierre Trudeau once commented, acts as the "head waiter" to the provinces. The provinces, in turn, have often acted as the head waiter to industry, leaving no one to attend to the best interests of Canada. The best illustrations of where this short-sightedness has taken the country are our lack of global market access, our discordant climate change policies and our failure to successfully include Canada's indigenous peoples as economic partners in the development of our resources. Each of these issues is examined later in this book.

I appreciate that, under our Constitution, the provinces are responsible for the development and management of their own natural resources. No one disputes this fact. The important point, however, is that, when it comes to the export of those resources or the environmental consequences of developing them, it is the federal government that is paramount. So too is federal jurisdiction over interprovincial pipelines, ports and the protection of coastal waterways. And when it comes to Canada's unresolved indigenous land claims, including those in British Columbia, they too are the legacy and legal responsibility of Ottawa. I am not advocating that Canada's national government encroach on the constitutional authority of the provincial governments over their natural resources. Nor am I advocating that the private sector give up on its own obligation to practise responsible resource development. What I am advocating is that the federal government do its job and find the courage to act to advance the interests of the country on matters within its own jurisdiction.

Canada has the potential to redefine itself as a global force in the energy world. We are already a leading energy producer, but we need to link that productive capacity to the global marketplace, exporting beyond the United States and into the Atlantic and Asia Pacific basins. Canada will realize that dream only through new national leadership.

Canada must start with a new strategy surrounding our energy relationship with the United States. We need to work with the United States to advance our North American competitive advantage in energy and the environment, and Canada should do so as an equal partner and not as an economic supplicant. We can strengthen our energy and environmental partnership with the Americans, but it will be our national government that must lead those efforts. We can and will put the Keystone XL Pipeline debacle (detailed in Chapter 5) behind us, and we can deepen the continental market opportunities for Canadian energy, both renewable and non-renewable. But doing so will ultimately depend on two people: the president of the United States and the prime minister of Canada.

Canada also has an important role to play as a global exporter. We must exploit our comparative economic advantage by achieving broader export access into both the Atlantic Basin and the Asia Pacific Basin, and we must use the availability of those resources to advance our own geopolitical objectives: reciprocal free-trading relationships, foreign investment, the outbound penetration of Canadian technologies and the advancement of Canadian environmental objectives. All this will require leadership, especially from our national institutions.

Canada can build the pipeline and port facilities needed to export Canadian oil and natural gas into the Asia Pacific Basin, but our inability to do so has been a national failure, not a provincial one, and it will take federal leadership because all the areas of current disagreement fall within the legal and political authority of the federal government: the regulation of interprovincial pipelines and export facilities, the protection of coastal waterways, the resolution of indigenous land claims and the delineation of a national framework to include indigenous peoples in resource development.

Canada can also lead again when it comes to the environment and climate change, but it will take an assertive federal government to make that happen. Canada's national policies must be more than a mere inventory of the province's individual efforts. The federal government must find ways to enlist the efforts of the provinces to advance Canada's overall effort because our ability to trade with the world and open new energy markets will depend, at least in part, on the country's climate change credentials and its stature as an environmental leader.

Canada also has the capacity to be fully energy independent, something that is beyond the reach of any other industrial democracy. But to achieve this goal will require a federal government that is prepared to "perfect" the Canadian common market. Only Ottawa can resolve the impasse over the Energy East Pipeline, and frankly, if the common market that is at the heart of the Canadian experiment isn't working, it is surely the job of our national government to fix it. Realistically, neither Ontario nor Quebec can be counted on to do so.

In all these respects, we need national vision, national leadership and a strategic sense of where our geopolitical strengths and opportunities lie.

Our Strategic Interests—The United States

For the past 50 years the United States has been the primary market for Canada's energy resources, and it will undoubtedly continue to be Canada's primary energy market into the future. We should continue to value and nurture this important relationship. Our prosperity depends on it. We should, however, also understand why our energy relationship with the United States has changed so fundamentally over the past decade.

Canada and the United States have worked together to build the largest and most successful energy marketplace in the world. Sheltered beneath the umbrella of successive free trade agreements, our integrated energy systems have driven prosperity on both sides of the border. I have been an outspoken advocate of the benefits of that marketplace for most of my life, and I continue to believe that as long as Canada and the United States work together, we will enjoy a competitive advantage over the rest of the world in terms of energy security, industrial competitiveness and the quality of our environment. Indeed, we have an opportunity to strengthen those continental advantages.

The North American Free Trade Agreement has been enormously beneficial to Canada, affording us ready access to the world's largest and most affluent economy. Unfortunately, along the way, Canadians overlooked the fact that we need other customers as well. We also blithely assumed that, when it came to energy, Canada's interests and those of the United States would always be the same. As it turns out, they are not. In fact, in important ways, they are reciprocal.

Canada's interests and those of the United States will never be exactly the same because the United States is fundamentally a net energy consumer and an oil importer, and Canada is fundamentally an oil exporter—in fact one of the world's largest. The United States is a buyer. We are a seller. The current tension underlying our energy relationship with the Americans is attributable to this simple but important difference, and it is one to which we have been wilfully blind for a generation.

In January 2016, on my arrival at the Wilson Center in Washington, DC, I met US Energy Secretary Ernest Moniz, a respected physicist, a successful US Cabinet secretary and, by all accounts, one who likes and respects Canadians. On meeting me, and with the precision of the scientist that he is, Secretary Moniz instantly encapsulated the essence of our relationship as he smiled and observed, "Ah, yes, the Canadians, the producers."

For more than 50 years, Canada has indeed been one of the "producers," fulfilling the American government's need for "diversity of supply," a policy under which as many producers as possible service the American economy with abundant supplies of oil and natural gas. This has been a very wise policy from the American perspective, because supply diversity creates competitive pressure that in turn forces market prices downward. It also minimizes the risk of catastrophic supply disruptions such as the OPEC oil embargo of 1973, an experience that seared this imperative into the consciousness of the United States. Ever since, the Americans have been unwavering in their commitment to Winston Churchill's dictum: "diversity of supply."

Canada, by contrast, is a seller of energy, and we need access to as many markets as possible. In this sense, our interests and those of the United States are different. Daniel Yergin, the eminent American energy authority, said, "Oil-importing countries tend to think in terms of security of supply. Energy-exporting countries turn the question around. They talk of 'security of demand' for their oil and gas exports, on which they depend to generate economic growth and a very large share of government revenues."[1] It's just about that simple.

The current tensions in the Canada–US energy relationship trace back to this very dynamic. While we don't think of ourselves in these terms, Canada is now the third-largest exporter of energy in the world, surpassed by only Saudi Arabia and Russia. But unlike those countries, Canada has only one customer. This of course worked, until it didn't. Global prices and continental prices once tracked each other reasonably closely, but over the past decade, as supply increased, the market balance or leverage in the Canada–US energy relationship began to shift in favour of the

United States, imperceptibly at first, but then rapidly. Today, as a consequence of the energy supply revolution, the American marketplace is sometimes oversupplied, not because of imports but because of its own oil and natural gas production.

This shift happened first with natural gas, which for that reason sold for many years in North American markets at a huge discount to international prices. Oil prices have now followed suit. By the time of the great price collapse of 2015–16, Canadian oil enjoyed the sad distinction of being the lowest-priced oil in the world, selling for as little as $12.50 per barrel. We don't get global prices for our energy—we get continental prices, which are less, increasingly a lot less. Within the North American marketplace we have become a "price taker," forced to accept prices that are often well below global prices. To be clear, this is not because the Americans are taking advantage of us. American oil from remote places such as North Dakota suffers the same fate. This is simply how free markets work when they are oversupplied or when you don't have enough pipelines.

Canada's reliance on a single customer now costs our country billions of dollars. A recent report by the Canadian Chamber of Commerce, drawing on the work of the Canadian Energy Research Institute and the Canada West Foundation, illustrated that our lack of access to world markets costs us between $30 million and $70 million in forgone economic benefits *each day*. The Canadian Imperial Bank of Commerce pegged our losses at $50 million per day, or $18 billion a year, in forgone taxes and royalties to Canada. A 2012 report by the Canadian Energy Research Institute estimates that, if we fail to realize currently planned pipeline projects, it could cause Canada to forgo $1.3 trillion in GDP and $276 billion in taxes by 2035.[2]

I was one of the first elected Canadian public figures to warn Canadians that our energy interests and those of the United States were not the same. In the months that followed my comments in 2010, I was counselled by many Canadians to be cautious lest I upset the Americans and disrupt the Canada–US apple cart. After all, the commonly held view at that time was that Canada's energy relationship with the United States was subject to an unwritten and implied condition: exclusivity. Put simply, many Canadians assumed that, as long as we didn't afford the Chinese access to our oil, we would be at liberty to export as much of it as we wanted to the Americans. This is no longer the arrangement, if indeed it ever was. This understanding was clear to me because I participated in President Barack Obama's inaugural visit to Canada and saw that the interests of the United States and Canada would now be viewed differently, particularly as they related to energy.

By 2012, the balance of power in our energy relationship with the United States had shifted so dramatically that President Obama would have the luxury of doing something unthinkable to any other American president since Richard Nixon: He rejected the construction of a North American pipeline that would move new volumes of Canadian oil into the US marketplace. He chose to do so for reasons relating to climate change, but he was able to do so because the United States now has many alternatives to Canadian oil.

The important point is this: When it comes to energy, the United States is the world's largest consumer, and its policies, priorities and decision making are framed around a core principle—*diversity of supply*. This fact doesn't mean that we cannot work together; nor does it mean that, in many other respects, our policies are not fully congruent. They are, and they should be.

However, exclusivity for anyone, including Canada, isn't part of the offering. Frankly, it never was.

The question now is about the future. It is a future that is anything but certain and which will test the resolve of both Canada and the United States when it comes to the energy trade between our two countries. It would be a mistake for Canadians to assume that the future will be one of business as usual. The evidence of more complicated times can be found in the trade protectionism on display during the 2016 American presidential campaign, and in the increasing hostility and militancy of both environmental activists and Aboriginal Americans toward the pipelines and other infrastructure that are essential to Canadian energy exports. Canada has rarely been more dependent on, or more vulnerable to, unexpected political developments in the United States.

To date we have not shown the collective ambition or sophistication to break away from the continental trap even though it has cost us tens of billions of dollars in private and public revenue, and even though it has limited our global influence as one of the world's largest energy producers. Content to play checkers, leaving chess to others, we have declined to pursue a global presence in the energy world, even as the North American market has moved from beneath us and even as representatives of the new emerging Asian markets plead with us to partner with them.

Our Strategic Interests—Accessing World Markets

There is an alternative vision of Canada's future: as a country that exports its oil and natural gas to both the continental and global marketplace, and where Canadian hydroelectricity increases its

North American market share. It is a vision that will require political leadership. And, while it is one that will expose us to the gale-force winds of competition, the prize will be worth it. We need to be ready for the competition that this change entails because, whether we like it or not, Canada is engaged in a global foot race every day—competing for markets, technologies, skilled workers and foreign direct investment.

We have obvious competitors such as Australia, whose resource-based economy shares many similarities with our own, but in the fast-paced world of today, global competitors emerge quickly to contest export market share and foreign investment. A good example is the United States, which has moved in a few short years from being the prime consumer of Canadian natural gas in insatiable volumes and at high prices to becoming one of our major competitors in the liquefied natural gas (LNG) business. Australia's performance has been even more impressive, because in 10 years that country moved from being a middling gas producer to the world's largest LNG exporter. The pace of change has been dizzying.

Many assume that competition is the exclusive responsibility of the private sector, yet nothing could be further from the truth because governments create the policies and set the fiscal frameworks within which the private sector functions and competes. For example, government provides security and manages macroeconomic and monetary policy. Those businesses that wrestle daily with trade barriers, investment restrictions, pipeline approvals, export permits, fluctuating exchange rates and competition policy know exactly how important governments are.

The role of government is especially important in the energy marketplace, as international competitors lodge multi-billion-dollar investments with 40- to 50-year life cycles. Imperial Oil's Kearl oil sands mine and Suncor's Fort Hills project, both in northeastern Alberta, have 50-year investment horizons. The LNG facilities under discussion on Canada's west coast similarly entail long-term investment plans. These projects are among the largest industrial projects on the planet—and the companies that are lodging investments of this magnitude are, more than anything else, seeking the confidence that the "country risk" is within acceptable tolerances.

This is an environment within which Canada should flourish since we have excelled at being a great place to invest. Consider it this way: The world has a lot of natural gas—indeed, the world may be awash in natural gas—but what the world does *not* have is a surplus of stable countries able to fulfill their contractual obligations over a 50-year period unmarred by contractual, social or political instability. This factor is, or should be, one of Canada's greatest strengths.

There is little doubt that successive Canadian governments have done very good work in preparing Canada for this competition: We have sound macroeconomic and monetary policies, and our exchange rate policies follow the market. Our banking system is the envy of the world. We also respect the rule of law, and basic property rights are assured. We have pursued liberalized microeconomic policies, including competition policy, and we have removed trade barriers whenever possible. We encourage foreign direct investment. Importantly, we have a high degree of social cohesion reflecting governmental stability and a relatively equitable income distribution. All these factors are positive and form an excellent foundation on which Canada should be able to develop our abundant natural resources and become an independent, secure and prosperous global energy powerhouse. Yet, as of late, we have become complacent and even careless in the management of our status as one of the world's best places to invest.

Canada is globally well-positioned because flourishing economies need secure sources of readily transportable energy. The advancements in the standard of living now under way in developing economies, especially those in Asia, are linked to the availability and affordability of energy—specifically hydrocarbons. To be sure, renewable energies are important and consumer preferences are slowing the consumption of hydrocarbons in many Western democracies. However, according to every reliable forecasting source, the world will remain dependent on oil and natural gas for the foreseeable future—at least for the next 50 years. Canada is one of a small number of producing nations that satisfies that demand. A very small group of countries own and control the production of the world's hydrocarbons. In fact, 10 countries, including Canada, produce two-thirds of the world's oil. And even within that group, Canada's position is unique because we are a Western democracy and because our natural resource endowment is *not* restricted to oil or natural gas but includes hydroelectricity and uranium, which are also in demand.

How then do we step up our game and pursue a new destination as a successful global energy player?

Our Strategic Interests— The International Competition

Canadians don't think about international energy markets very much. This isn't surprising since we have never viewed Canada's energy resources, especially our oil, as strategic assets, and we therefore haven't paid much attention to those who do.

Our competitors, however, do think about Canada, and the Organization of Petroleum Exporting Countries (OPEC) in particular pays attention to what we are doing. The reason, of course, is OPEC's concern about Canada's oil sands, which have emerged over the past 20 years as its dominant competition in the US market and which, it understands, will be an equally formidable competitor in the Asia Pacific Basin once Canada has export pipelines.

It is impossible to understand Canada's strategic interests as an energy producer, or to assess Canada's future role in the global energy marketplace, without some attention to international energy markets and an appreciation of the important role that OPEC has played, and will undoubtedly continue to play, in global energy markets.

The cartel has been the most successful oligopoly in market history, exercising both geopolitical and geo-economic power that has continued to counterbalance Western-based market capitalism and globalization. It is a global force that survives and prospers after more than 55 years as the most successful state-run, anti-competitive force in the global marketplace. Today, OPEC has 12 member states—Algeria, Angola, Ecuador, Iran, Iraq, Kuwait, Libya, Nigeria, Qatar, Saudi Arabia, the United Arab Emirates and Venezuela. Ominously, over the course of 2016, Russia has emerged as a non-member "partner" in OPEC's efforts to influence global prices.

OPEC has controlled world oil prices in the ingenious way that all cartels do, by constraining overall output while simultaneously maintaining spare productive capacity which allows it to balance the market, sometimes favouring high prices, sometimes low prices. OPEC has exercised this influence on the price of oil, using cartel consensus, government interference and manipulation of production and markets to control the supply and, hence, the price of oil. The history of the cartel and the correlation between its conduct and oil prices is complex and well beyond the scope of this book, but few would disagree that the cartel was the dominant global influence in driving the price of oil precipitously downward in 1986 and maintaining prices at lower levels for the decade that followed; or that it was equally successful in driving prices upward to historic highs in the years between 2000 and 2014. In the time since 2014, OPEC directed its efforts to suppressing prices to drive competing supply sources such as US shale oil, deep-water oil and the Canadian oil sands out of the market, eventually contributing to a price collapse in the market. More recently, since 2016, OPEC and its allies—including Russia—have begun to assert themselves to stabilize production and prices.

Alberta's oil sands deposit is the only oil reservoir in the world that compares in size to the fields held by OPEC members such as Saudi Arabia and Venezuela. The statistics are telling: 17.9 percent of the world's proven oil reserves are found in Venezuela, 16.1 percent in Saudi Arabia, and 10.6 percent in Canada. No one else really compares, and the United States, in particular, is relatively oil deficient in that only 2 percent of the world's reserves are located there.

OPEC worries about Canada's oil sands because the resource is large enough to disrupt the cartel's ability to balance the market. In other words, it's not just that we are a competitor; it's that we have the potential to become a large enough competitor to undermine OPEC's business model. This is why OPEC freely concedes that part of its challenge has been to maintain its own oil production at levels that will keep oil prices below the cost of large-volume alternatives such as the Canadian oil sands or the United States' shale oil. Over the past decade, the two taken together have already proven to be completely disruptive to OPEC's ability to control prices.

Canada's strategic interests and those of OPEC are therefore quite different. We are one of OPEC's largest competitors, and the volumes of oil that we are capable of producing have real implications for its business model. This reality is illustrated by the fact that Canada, not OPEC, now dominates US oil imports. In 2015 the United States imported 9.4 million barrels per day (bpd) of

Figure 2.1: US Imports of Crude Oil and Products by Country of Origin, 1975–2015

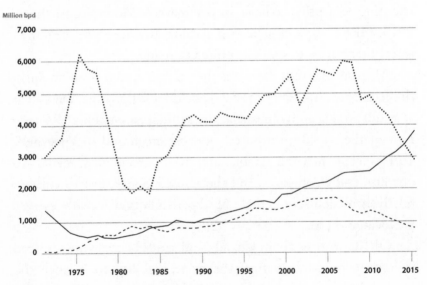

······ U.S. Imports from OPEC Countries of Crude Oil and Petroleum Products
—— U.S. Imports from Canada of Crude Oil and Petroleum Products
--- U.S. Imports from Mexico of Crude Oil and Petroleum Products

Source: U.S. Energy Information Administration (Aug. 2016)

Note: The U.S. Energy Information Administration defines "crude oil and products" as crude oil, natural gas liquids, liquefied refinery gases, and refined petroleum products such as gasoline, diesel and biofuels including ethanol and biodiesel. See eia.gov/dnav/pet/pet_move_impcus_a2_nus_ep00_im0_mbblpd_a.htm petroleum products. Figure 2.1 shows that Canada accounted for 3.75 million bpd, or 40 percent of those imports. All 12 OPEC countries together accounted for only 2.9 million bpd, or 30 percent of US imports. The figure also shows the rapid rise of Canadian exports to the United States as oil sands projects came online in the last decade, and the decline of OPEC's and Mexico's exports to the United States (although Mexico's case is different, being tied to the overall decline in production in that country).

Even more concerning to OPEC is the prospect that Canada might get its house in order and achieve pipeline access to either the Asia Pacific Basin or the Atlantic Basin. OPEC currently dominates both the European refinery markets and the emerging markets of Asia and would not welcome Canadian competition of one or two million barrels of oil per day in either basin. In light of all this, is there still any doubt that OPEC worries about Canada? You bet it does!

How then does Canada fit into a global oil market that is dominated by such an oligopoly? And what should we understand about OPEC's recent efforts to push back against its competitors, including Canada?

We need to recognize, first of all, that our economic interests are fundamentally different from OPEC's. OPEC is Canada's main international competitor in the oil business, and the ongoing development of the Canadian oil sands and the export of Canadian oil into the international market will force the cartel to defend its market share by pricing to meet Canadian competition. At some point, the full weight of the cartel will be pressed against us.

For the moment, we simply need to recognize that everyone in the energy world, including Canada, lives in the shadow of OPEC and that the cartel has every intention of defending its market share and continued dominance of global oil markets. There can be little doubt in the time following the price collapse of 2015 that the world—and the global oil and gas industry—continues to live with the consequences of OPEC's production and pricing choices. This is the unavoidable reality with which Canadian decision makers, whether in government or industry, must live. So, too, must everyone else.

Canada's strategic interests in all this are relatively clear: They lie in the support of free markets and in the promotion of investment stability, which in turn is predicated on price stability. In pursuit of those objectives, we find common cause with the United States and the world's other industrial democracies. Together we can aspire to lessen the impact of market instability caused by players such as OPEC and Russia.

In this context, Canada and the United States are important partners with shared objectives. As we have seen, increases in oil production in both Canada and the United States have reduced North America's dependency on "foreign" oil and afforded the two countries an opportunity for energy self-sufficiency that is the envy of the rest of the industrial world. Canada and the United States need to remember that this achievement is a North American accomplishment, not an American one or a Canadian one. We have achieved energy self-sufficiency by harnessing our collective resources within the framework of the world's largest and most successful integrated free energy market. We need to keep it that way.

The energy systems that Canada and the United States share must therefore become ever more integrated and eventually more integrated with those of Mexico. Moving forward, Canada will need to maintain its bilateral alliance with the United States. Our economies and energy infrastructure are completely integrated across our national borders, and we must maintain our collective focus on harmonizing our efforts and advancing what till now has been the most successful integrated free-market energy system in the world.

Canada must also maintain its emphasis on multilateralism. We have been historic supporters of the International Energy Agency, and that must continue. So, too, should our support of the International Energy Forum. Obviously we must also continue to provide leadership on energy and environmental issues among the G7 and the G20, and on initiatives such as the Major Economies Forum on Energy and Climate (MEF) that was created by President George W. Bush and officially launched by President Obama.

There is, however, a much broader global prize within reach. Canada and the United States now have the collective ability to weaken OPEC's control over international oil markets and oil pricing, and to limit the cartel's worldwide economic and political influence. North America's productive capacity for oil and natural gas now greatly exceeds our consumptive needs, and the availability of Canadian oil, together with Canadian and American natural gas exports, provides our two countries with the potential to shift the balance of power in the global energy marketplace. We can stabilize free markets through the delivery of competitive supply, at once undermining the world's most significant anti-competitive cartel while reducing the risk of Middle Eastern instability as a destabilizing influence on energy supplies.

This objective is important to both Canada and the United States. The United States, which has had a long-standing policy of promoting diversification of oil and gas supplies around the world, has aggressively pursued an agenda of promoting democracy and human rights. Broadly stated, Canada shares those objectives but in a more nuanced and typically reserved way. The tone may differ, but both countries benefit as the power of authoritarian governments in oil-producing states is weakened.

To accomplish all this Canada must, however, assert itself as a global presence in the energy world and learn to be a more strategic player.

CHAPTER 3

A Canadian Global Strategy:
What We Need to Do

I come from a line of professional hockey players, so competition comes naturally to me. My father, Eric Prentice, played briefly with the Toronto Maple Leafs in 1943, and he remains to this day the youngest Leaf in the team's history. He was barely 17 at the time, so his record seems likely to endure.

Dad played in the NHL for only a handful of games—a "cup of coffee," as he used to say. But his brother—my uncle Dean Prentice—played in the NHL for 22 seasons and was known as one of the "iron men" of the Original Six era. He broke in with the New York Rangers, was Andy Bathgate's left winger and once scored 32 goals in a season at a time when 50 was the threshold of superstardom. He also played for Boston and Detroit, and later Minnesota and Pittsburgh.

I played hockey too, and in fact I still do. I could skate pretty well and I was scouted at an early age. But, like my father, I was never heavy enough, and an ugly knee-on-knee check destroyed my left knee when I was 17. I still love the game, and I still think that it brings out the very best in Canadians, in particular our passion to compete and win. That's how I like to see Canada.

Countries as well as companies and sports teams compete and, whether we like it or not, Canada is in a global competition.

In August 2007, when I was Canada's industry minister, I was introduced to economist Richard Vietor's book *How Countries Compete: Strategy, Structure, and Government in the Global Economy*.[1] His thinking influenced much of the work that I carried out as industry minister. For example, it shaped the government's response to L.R. (Red) Wilson's 2008 report for the Competition Review Panel, *Compete to Win*, which provided recommendations on how we could improve Canada's global competitiveness. My subsequent international experiences as a government minister, as a banker and as the premier of Alberta only reinforced my belief that Canada is engaged in a global foot race every day, competing for markets, technologies, skilled workers and foreign direct investment.

Canadian leaders must realize that we are competing globally for markets and customers, and take the appropriate actions. To wit, Canada needs to develop a comprehensive strategy that focuses on our long-term national interests and the advancement of our potential as a global energy player. It is particularly important in this period of volatile energy prices that Canada develop clear-eyed policies that leverage our strengths and maximize our interests. A national interest–based strategy will allow us to maximize the value of our resources, succeed as a continental partner and exercise our geopolitical muscle as a powerful player in the energy world. That strategy must encompass our energy, climate change and environmental policies with a view of upping our game as a sophisticated and responsible global supplier.

Canada must become more strategic in its approaches to these issues. Our oil, natural gas, renewables and hydroelectricity are our most important resource endowments, and we should develop them in a manner that maximizes the interest of our country. This is less about having a national strategic plan, although that would itself be an improvement. It is more about having a philosophy about our sovereignty—about who we are, what we are doing and what we expect in return. Does any Canadian seriously advocate a future as a captive supplier of discounted resources to the United States? Does anyone in the United States seriously dispute that their country will benefit from having a stronger, worldlier ally at their side?

Energy and the environment are among Canada's most important comparative advantages in the coming century. The quality of our environment, coupled with the breadth and rich-ness of our resource base, sets us apart from the rest of the world. When it comes to energy, Canadians enjoy a triple advantage over the rest of the world. No one else enjoys the energy security we do; few possess the industrial cost advantage we do; and, most significantly, no one else has the environmental advantages we do. This is Canada's Triple Crown, and these will be among the defin-ing competitive advantages of Canada, and indeed North Amer-ica, during this century, a time that has already been darkened by conflict, mass human migration, overpopulation, resource limita-tions and environmental degradation.

The Components of a New Approach

What are Canada's strategic interests in such a time? The compo-nents of an interest-based strategy must include the following goals.

CAPITALIZING ON CANADA'S ENERGY ADVANTAGE

Canada's oil, natural gas and hydroelectricity comprise our most important resource endowments, and we should embrace and resolutely own our global position. We should develop and export those resources in a manner that maximizes the strategic advantages to Canada. We must develop our energy, climate change and environmental policies in concert. They need to be mutually reinforcing, and they must themselves be a source of competitive advantage to Canada.

We must strengthen our capacity to export into the United States and seek the full harmonization of our energy, climate change and environmental policies with the Americans. At the same time, we must exploit our comparative economic advantage by achieving broader export access into both the Atlantic Basin and the Asia Pacific Basin, and we must use the availability of those resources to secure reciprocal free-trading relationships where we want them. We must be attentive to our desire to foster foreign investment in Canada and to our need to advance the outbound penetration of Canadian technologies. Our exports, in particular our natural gas, can and should be used to advance the de-carbonization of the electricity systems in emerging markets by averting the use of coal. New sources of Canadian hydroelectricity can and should achieve the same objectives in North America.

Canada should also work bilaterally with the United States and multilaterally with our other allies to use Canadian exports, in concert with the exports of others, to broaden and strengthen international energy markets to improve energy security and price stability. Canada will be a stronger partner if it is a more diversified exporter and a stronger, more integrated presence in global energy supply chains. Canada's role as both a producer and an exporter of energy must always be balanced by our obligation to be a supportive presence in the work of our global allies in protecting the stability of the world's energy marketplace. In that context, we must continue to support international energy institutions such as the International Energy Agency and the International Energy Forum. We also have obligations to participate in multilateral efforts to respond to emergencies and to protect shipping routes. The Northwest Passage will need to be part of that discussion.

To carry out any of these endeavours, we need the federal government to assert leadership

BECOMING A GLOBAL EXPORTER

Canada's strategic policy framework must begin with the recognition that we are one of the world's largest energy exporters and that we need national policies that reflect the complexity and diversity of Canada's asset base and our diverse regional interests. This observation may seem obvious, but Canada's position is an intricate one with profound and sensitive regional differences across the country. Our economy is in equal parts built around the export of high-carbon products and low-carbon products. We are at once a major producer and exporter of oil, natural gas and refined petroleum products, as well as of uranium. We are also one of the world's most successful generators and exporters of hydroelectricity. We simultaneously possess the world's largest developable hydroelectric assets and the world's largest oil sands reserves. We also have environmental responsibilities and obligations to our indigenous peoples.

The point is that although every Canadian province is in the energy business, no two provinces are in the same energy business. It would be dangerous to ignore this reality. We need a national approach that reflects the wide geography and complexity of Canada's position and, importantly, it must be a framework to which every Canadian province subscribes.

LEADING ON CLIMATE CHANGE AND THE ENVIRONMENT

The world will always have high expectations of Canada when it comes to climate change, grounded in the fact that we are a respected democracy with a long tradition of multilateral leadership on global environmental issues. We must also recognize that our greatest resource endowment, the oil sands, also attracts concomitant environmental expectations. One can reasonably expect that, in a world increasingly concerned about carbon emissions, the issues surrounding fossil fuel production, market access and border adjustments will become ever more tightly wound and increasingly demanding. We have been slow to recognize that the reassertion of Canadian leadership on energy and the environment will be the only acceptable response.

Canada's energy and environmental policies must be integrated and must fully encompass our climate change objectives. We must also continue to focus on the harmonization of our environmental standards on a North American basis, maximizing positive environmental outcomes while protecting our competitiveness in trade-exposed industries. Our policies on the environment must also encompass a broader vision of the opportunities that exist for international co-operation, including the positive environmental benefits associated with the development of Canada's liquefied natural gas (LNG) industry and the export of cleaner-burning natural gas to reduce emissions in emerging economies.

FORMING ECONOMIC PARTNERSHIPS WITH CANADA'S INDIGENOUS PEOPLES

It is impossible even to think about a book on Canada's energy future without discussing the central role that the First Nations must play. We have failed in our attempts to secure the support of indigenous peoples for pipeline access to either the Atlantic or the Pacific coast. The support of Canada's indigenous peoples is critical to the emergence of Canada as a successful global energy player. More than that, Canada's indigenous peoples need to be economic partners in those developments.

Later in this book I put forward the proposition that the ports and pipelines that afford Canada access to the Asia Pacific Basin must be owned, at least in part, by the First Nations. I am confident that this is possible, but it will require leadership from both government and industry to make it happen. This objective requires renewed efforts, including the appointment of special negotiators carrying the authority of Canada's prime minister. Canada will need to address the environmental concerns of First Nations and must partner with them in the protection of Canada's coastal waterways and on the needed investments in marine infrastructure and training.

This goal should not be as difficult as we have made it. The energy and extractive resources sectors are the main areas of opportunity to work out partnerships among our Aboriginal peoples, industry and government. The economic prospects and jobs created by oil, natural gas, pipelines, LNG terminals, ports, wind farms and hydro facilities are proximate to the first peoples who live there, and in most cases they have a legal basis on which to negotiate some element of participation.

FINISHING THE JOB OF CONFEDERATION— COMPLETING THE INTERNAL COMMON MARKET

We produce vastly more oil and gas than we consume. Remarkably, however, Canada has not yet perfected its own domestic market and still imports 740,000 barrels per day, each and every day, of costlier Saudi Arabian and African crude oil, and now a lot from the United States, to supply our east coast refineries. Moreover, we generate much more hydroelectricity than we consume internally; yet about 12 percent of our electricity is still produced by coal. Canada should be energy secure, and our efforts to diversify our markets must begin at home and must include steps to open the entirety of the Canadian common market to our own oil, natural gas and, where possible, clean electricity. Ultimately, this goal will require investments in both pipeline infrastructure and extensions to electricity grids; for example, to move hydroelectricity eastward from British Columbia and westward from Manitoba into Saskatchewan.

MAINTAINING THE CONTINENTAL MARKETPLACE

Canada must continue to maintain the continental marketplace as a core strength but work to improve access for renewable electricity into the United States. We currently export 2.9 million barrels per day of crude oil into the American marketplace, and we need to preserve and build on that market share, primarily by increasing our throughput capacity to the Gulf coast. We must also pursue access to areas of the US marketplace where there is a market for larger volumes of Canadian renewable and non-renewable energy. In the context of hydroelectricity, Canada must similarly pursue deeper market access into the American marketplace, along the eastern seaboard and in the American Midwest.

FOCUSING ON THE STRATEGIC IMPORTANCE OF MARKET DIVERSIFICATION

For Canada, the guarantee of prosperity lies in market diversification, and we must resolutely pursue multiple markets. Diversification should include the emerging markets of the Asia Pacific Basin and those among our traditional allies in the Atlantic Basin. Our efforts need to focus on pipelines, but also on the relationships that we must cultivate and the institutional presence that we need to market ourselves internationally.

First, we need tidewater access to the Asia Pacific Basin. The energy growth markets of the world are in the emerging economies of Asia, including China, India, Malaysia, Indonesia, South Korea and, to a lesser extent, Japan. These are the burgeoning markets of tomorrow, and Canada must access them by way of its Pacific coast because that is where the country's competitive advantage lies. Canada will require new industry leadership to ensure that its west coast First Nations are essential partners in the development of these projects. The federal government, by definition, will need to support those efforts.

We also need tidewater access to the Atlantic Basin. Other

international markets are accessible via Canada's east coast and, although we do not enjoy the same competitive advantage in the Atlantic Basin that we do in the Asia Pacific Basin, it is important that Canada also secure tidewater access to the Atlantic coast. Canada enjoys strong historic and cultural linkages to Europe and is fully capable of developing important market relationships in the United Kingdom, France and other Western democracies. Access to the Atlantic Basin also provides access to the US Gulf coast and, while that routing is circuitous, we need to secure it as an important "fail-safe" for our North American marketplace.

IMPROVING OUR COMPETITIVENESS AND ABILITY TO ATTRACT FOREIGN INVESTMENT

Finally, Canada's energy and natural resource opportunities will always be tied to our industrial competitiveness, particularly our ability to attract inbound foreign capital. Put simply, our resource base and our ambitions exceed the capital that we have available in Canada, and we must maintain our stature as one of the world's most attractive places to invest. Canada has never had adequate domestic capital to finance its energy industries or other ambitions. We need to ensure that our foreign investment rules welcome inbound foreign investment. Moreover, our energy opportunities will always be tied to our industrial competitiveness. Canada is one of the world's most dependable energy producers, but we are also one of the world's highest-cost producers.

Canadian public policies must recognize this challenge and focus on improving our competitiveness by ensuring that our regulatory frameworks, royalty structures, taxation policies and labour markets advance our industrial competitiveness. We must also recognize that climate change policies cannot be determined in isolation from questions surrounding our trade competitiveness, especially with the United States. Canada must also lead in the development of science and in the application of that science to improvements in industrial processes. But above all, we should have clearer rules and be more welcoming of capital investors.

Canada's Strategic Interests

These are the components of a new approach—that of a confident energy supplier with a broad global market reach.

We have a tendency to undersell ourselves, but these opportunities are real. The game of power politics doesn't come naturally to Canada or to Canadians. The truth be known, we have never been particularly aggressive about our history or capabilities as an energy producer. We preferred the quiet comfort of our role as the invisible supplier of enormous quantities of oil and natural gas to the United States. It wasn't until the Keystone XL Pipeline controversy that most Canadians, and nearly everyone in the United States, had any idea that America's largest foreign supplier of petroleum was not Saudi Arabia, Kuwait, Iraq, Mexico or Venezuela.

Other countries, of course, are less modest. In the result, Canada has been outflanked by many of our global competitors who have aggressively sought out their own commercial interests well ahead of us—even though, in some cases, their resource base is not as large as Canada's. The Russians, Australians and Americans have all leaped ahead of us as LNG suppliers. So, too, understandably, has Qatar, given its enormous natural gas reserves. And in the case of oil, Canada remains the world's only large producer whose product is mostly landlocked and therefore realizes less than global prices and lags behind the entire field in our ability to sell to the world marketplace. Even the Americans, who prohibited the export of their own oil for the past 45 years, have now authorized exports. In the case of renewables other than hydroelectricity, we lag behind countries such as Denmark, Germany, China and the United States in terms of investment. We have, in sum, been anything but a global powerhouse.

Canada can and should be a powerful and progressive force in the energy world, but first we need to decide whether we have the courage that this role requires, and if so, what framework policies would be necessary to support such broader ambitions.

Whether we choose this future is up to us to decide. Whether we choose to remain a captive supplier to a heavily subscribed continental market, accepting the risks that are implied by such dependency, is our decision. And whether we choose to have our labour markets and capital markets driven by decisions made elsewhere is also our decision. Ultimately, we and we alone have the ability to redefine our role in the global energy economy. And if we decide to up our game on the international stage, we will also have to set aside our parochial attitudes and learn to play a new game with some highly sophisticated players.

PART TWO

Canada and the United States

CHAPTER 4

*The Continental Trap: How Canada Unwittingly
Lost Its Energy Sovereignty*

The day was January 4, 2014, and I was caught in my own personal continental trap—at Toronto's Pearson International Airport.

I was on my way to Houston to give a speech and to meet with Ryan Lance, the CEO of ConocoPhillips. My trip coincided with an Arctic front that swept southward across the continent, freezing all of eastern Canada and the northeastern United States. The news sources said it was the coldest weather in a generation, and someone came up with the imaginative idea to call it a polar vortex. Perhaps it was exactly that, but my father and grandfather would have just called it a cold snap.

In truth, it wasn't really all that cold—at least by Canadian standards. It was -20°C in Toronto, which is more or less a typical winter day in Winnipeg or Saskatoon and, frankly, a warm winter outing in Iqaluit or Yellowknife. However, Toronto's Pearson airport seems increasingly challenged by any weather other than sunshine, and so I spent seven frustrating hours there, only to have management summarily close the entire airport with the meek explanation that it was "too cold" to carry on. That timid surrender to winter didn't strike me as a very Canadian response, but there you have it. I did eventually get to Houston, although not in time for my speech, all because of the polar vortex and the closure of Canada's largest airport.

ConocoPhillips is the largest independent energy company in the world, with important assets everywhere that counts, including Canada. Ryan Lance is tough, plain-spoken and one of the most experienced executives in the North American energy industry. He was the first American oil executive to call on Congress to lift the US ban on oil exports, and I was going to Houston to talk with him about it. It was a controversial position at that time, and the US president opposed it, but Lance knew that American oil companies needed to escape the "continental trap"—the supply overhang and low prices that had come to characterize the North American energy market for certain kinds of lighter oil.

The Americans "trapped" their own oil on the continent in 1975, when they imposed a ban on US oil exports to preserve their domestic stocks in the aftermath of the OPEC oil embargo. For most of the 40 years that followed, it didn't matter much because the United States didn't have any oil to export anyway. In those years, both Canada and the United States were producing as much oil and natural gas as they could and, even with substantial imports, the Americans could barely keep up to escalating demand. No one really wanted to export oil from the United States because no one needed to.

The advent of the energy supply revolution of the 21st century changed all that and, as technological innovations unlocked

American shale oil, American production soared in the years between 2010 and 2015, virtually doubling from five million barrels per day (bpd) to over nine million bpd—leaving parts of the continent awash in lighter oil from places such as Texas and North Dakota. The United States is home to the largest refinery complex in the world, but most of those refineries are not configured to run on this sort of lighter American oil. Instead, they use heavier (and cheaper) oil from places such as Venezuela, Mexico and Canada. Therefore, as production of lighter American shale oil increased, prices for that product dropped, opening up a gap between the international benchmark Brent prices, which averaged \$53.96 per barrel in 2015, and West Texas Intermediate, which averaged \$49.53 in the same year.[1] (Brent Crude, produced in the North Sea, is the leading global price benchmark for Atlantic Basin light sweet crude oil. Other well-known classifications—or price benchmarks—include the OPEC Reference Basket, Dubai Crude and West Texas Intermediate [WTI]. In North America, Brent and WTI prices serve as comparators for eastern seaboard refineries, which have access to international crudes priced against Brent, versus refineries further inside the continent, which mostly have access to US and western Canadian crude oil slates priced against the WTI benchmark.) Americans, unlike Canadians, weren't prepared to stand for that.

Ryan Lance's views interested me because Canada has similarly segregated itself from the global marketplace, not by an embargo but because we have no pipelines to ports and therefore cannot actually reach global markets. We are restricted to a single geography or market, the United States, and we therefore cannot obtain global prices. It has been an expensive mistake, costing us tens of billions of dollars in lost royalties, profits and taxes, and it invites questions on how one of the most sophisticated industries, in one of the world's most sophisticated countries, could have made such an egregious error. But we did.

The economic impact on Canada has been extreme. As noted in Figure 4.1, Canadian crude oil doesn't sell at global prices because it isn't a global product. Instead, it sells at continental prices, which reflect a smaller universe of buyers and sellers. In a continental market that is periodically oversupplied, as ours is, the results can be devastating because continental purchasers often don't need our oil and can access cheaper supplies from other domestic or international sources.

Figure 4.1: Price Differential of Heavy Oils—Mexican Maya and Western Canada Select, January 2010–January 2016

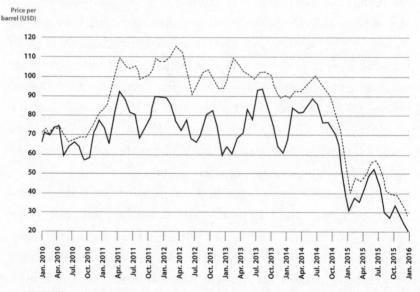

---- Mexican Maya
— Western Canada Select

Source: U.S. Energy Information Administration (Aug. 2016), "Spot Prices." See eia.gov/dnav/pet/PET_PRI_SPT_S1_M.htm

This continental pricing discount is known as the differential and, as shown in the chart, it can be steep. The Canadian heavy oil benchmark price is referred to as Western Canadian Select (WCS), which trades at a discount to light oil owing to the higher cost of refining it. The discount is referred to as a heavy oil differential. That said, Mexican Maya heavy oil is similar to WCS and both are easily refined on the US Gulf coast, but Maya trades at a higher price in large part because it has access to international markets. Differentials are complex and are driven by a number of factors since there are multiple classifications and grades of oil, but ultimately a large component of the discount reflects our lack of negotiating capacity and our status as a captive supplier. When continental prices falter, Canadian suppliers don't have access to alternative markets to search out higher prices. Canadian oil is especially disadvantaged in an oversupplied market because it comes from the far end of the continental supply chain and much of it has heavier physical properties and is harder to refine and store. We also face infrastructure limitations brought on by pipeline and rail deficiencies. All these factors can work against Canadian oil and, since 2010, they have done just that.

A typical day illustrates the point. On December 14, 2015, in the midst of the great oil price collapse of 2015 but even before prices reached their nadir in February 2016, international Brent prices dropped to $38 per barrel. West Texas Intermediate prices for American oil dropped to $35 per barrel. The crudes known as Venezuelan Basket, Iranian Forozan and Colombian Vasconia all transacted at $31 per barrel. Saudi Arabian Heavy and Ecuadorian Oriente both slipped to $30 per barrel. The lowly Indonesian Duri and the Mexican Mix dropped to a mere $28 per barrel. But the biggest loser of all was Canada's Western Canadian Select, which transacted at $22 per barrel—enjoying the dubious distinction of world's cheapest oil. A few weeks later, it crashed further and reached a low of $12 per barrel.

None of this is discriminatory or anti-Canadian or unfair. It is the law of supply and demand. It is the free market at its most brutal—the application of the same rules that apply at Walmart.

History and economics tell us that free markets work. Oil is valuable only if it can be transported to a market. It is more valuable if it can reach multiple markets. And it is most valuable of all if it can access global markets. Having somehow forgotten these timeless laws of supply and demand, we have watched as differentials widened in the years since 2010, reducing Canadians to making desperate arguments about "ethical oil" and being "best friends" with the Americans and so on. All that is, of course, irrelevant and more than a little demeaning. Markets are markets.

Eventually, of course, Congress and the US president did listen to Ryan Lance. The export ban was repealed in December 2015 and, within a month, ConocoPhillips was able to watch a tanker full of American light crude oil depart a Gulf coast port, headed for higher global prices. Canada, meanwhile, is still talking about oil exports. We are at least 10 years away from shipping our western Canadian oil to China, to India or, for that matter, to New Brunswick.

How did one of the world's most sophisticated countries get itself into this position? More importantly, how do we get out of it?

The Evolution of the Continental Energy Market

The Canadian and American oil and gas industries share a fascinating history and one that is, for the most part, continental.

The Canadian oil story began with a discovery in the 1850s near Sarnia, Ontario. In 1880, 16 refiners in southwestern Ontario were able to band together as the Imperial Oil Company, Limited— which still exists today.

Discoveries followed in the west, and the modern western Canadian petroleum industry began with the discovery of the Turner Valley oil field south of Calgary in 1914 by Bill Herron, a fearless Canadian entrepreneur. Herron had been a modestly successful railway contractor in Ontario but became an amateur geologist after a vacation to the oil fields of Pennsylvania early in life. He moved to Alberta in 1905 and settled on a ranch near Okotoks, south of Calgary. In 1911, he decided to investigate rumours of a local swamp gas nuisance adjacent to the nearby Sheep River. Using his amateur geological skills, he concluded that the gas was in fact petroleum gas seeping from an underlying anticline. Back then, Bill Herron was almost certainly the only rancher in Alberta who knew what an anticline was. In the years that followed, he aggressively acquired the mineral rights to what would become the most valuable acreage in the first Turner Valley oil boom.[2]

Herron created the Calgary Petroleum Products Company and secured all the land in the vicinity of the first Turner Valley find. That syndicate, founded in 1913, was at its inception a local Canadian enterprise, made up of prominent Calgarians such as lawyers James A. Lougheed and R.B. Bennett.[3] However, in a pattern that has continued to this day, it soon became obvious that the financial capital required to develop the Calgary Oil Field, as it was then known, exceeded western Canada's funding capabilities. This was true despite the tenacity of Herron and other early Canadian wildcatters. That early history is a fascinating story, as capital-starved Canadian entrepreneurs struggled in vain to attract the interest of eastern Canadian and British financiers in an effort to counter the growing influence of Standard Oil of New Jersey and its Canadian proxy, Imperial Oil Limited.[4]

By the mid-1940s, the Canadian oil and gas industry represented a healthy mixture of Canadian and American enterprises. To be sure, large and respected US companies such as Texaco and Mobil Oil, among many others—as well as Canadian companies controlled by American interests such as Imperial Oil—held dominant positions in the business. Still, the industry retained a character that was strongly entrepreneurial and independently Canadian.

Throughout the 1950s and 1960s, the capital base and managerial talent of the industry continued to evolve in a profoundly North American manner, quite unlike the pattern of industrial development elsewhere in Canada. Capital, drilling technology and people flowed relatively freely between Calgary, Oklahoma City, Houston and Dallas. Indeed, to this very day, Calgary remains the most American of all Canadian cities, and the impact of early expatriate Americans on the civic character of that city is today accepted and celebrated. Not surprisingly, therefore, when the Canada–United States free trade debate erupted in the mid-1980s, it was western Canadians generally, and Albertans specifically, who were among the most ardent supporters of continental integration.

Canada Goes It Alone—Pierre Trudeau's National Energy Program

The Canada–US energy relationship was never problem-free, however, and while the Canadian and US oil and gas industries share a common history, the two developed and prospered on parallel, rather than intersecting, tracks. The North American energy marketplace was not really "continental" in those early years and, although capital, technology and managerial talent flowed freely between the two countries, neither oil nor natural gas necessarily did. Governments on both sides of the border continued to pursue domestic energy policies that were intended to advance and protect their own industrial and security interests. This pattern reflected a long history. In fact, domestic tariffs over American coal and petroleum products formed part of Sir John A. Macdonald's National Policy as far back as 1879.

The late 1960s and the entirety of the 1970s were particularly problematic, especially after the OPEC oil embargo of 1973. Friction emerged as early as March 1969, when newly elected Republican President Richard Nixon hosted Prime Minister Pierre Trudeau in Washington. Although the two men appear to have despised each other from the outset, they discussed many issues in that first meeting and Nixon eventually tabled a proposal that the two countries move toward a continental oil policy. The reality even then was that rapid growth in America's oil consumption was exceeding its production, with Canada emerging as a significant and growing supplier to make up the difference. Between 1960 and 1975, total American oil and natural gas imports increased from 23 percent to 39 percent of US consumption. By 1967, Canadian oil imports into the United States exceeded those from the Middle East and had tripled to 18.7 percent of US demand.[5]

Trudeau was unenthusiastic about Nixon's request for a continental energy policy, and between 1970 and 1974 he went even further, promulgating a number of nationalistic measures with energy implications that seriously alarmed the US administration. In 1974, for example, the Canadian government created the

Foreign Investment Review Agency (FIRA) to screen proposed foreign direct investments in Canada, including those of American energy companies. The Trudeau government also created Petro-Canada, a publicly owned national energy company. And then, remarkably, immediately after the July 1974 federal election, Prime Minister Trudeau announced his government's intent to aggressively pursue Canada's own energy self-sufficiency by imposing an embargo on oil exports to the United States. The Trudeau government did eventually relent on the proposed embargo but imposed a federal tax increase on oil exports and a border price increase on natural gas exports to the United States. The Nixon administration weakly objected, but by then it was fully preoccupied by the Watergate scandal.

It is interesting to note, in light of the recent debacle surrounding the Keystone XL Pipeline, that as far back as 1969 the Nixon administration attached special importance to the Canadian oil sands as a secure and dependable source of energy for the United States. The advantages afforded by Canada were seen to be compelling: Canada was viewed as a politically stable ally, already deeply integrated economically with the United States and able to transport its oil into the American market through pipelines, which would be less vulnerable to attack or disruption. Nixon's national energy policy therefore assigned particular importance to Canadian oil. In a series of policy speeches leading up to the energy policy, increasing imports from Canada figured prominently.[6]

The tension between Canada and the United States over energy policy between 1969 and 1980 improved slightly during the first years of President Jimmy Carter's term. However, after the re-election of the Liberal government in 1980, Prime Minister Trudeau again moved aggressively, enacting his National Energy Program (NEP), which was anything but continental in its aspirations. To this day, the NEP remains highly divisive in Canada. It led to ongoing resentment of Canada's Liberal Party in western Canada and arguably contributed to an emerging crisis in Canadian national unity. It also severely strained Canada–US relations.

The NEP was a massively invasive intrusion into the Canadian energy sector. It disrupted the free market by legislating price differentials between domestic and international (American) prices. It drew distinctions between "old" and "new" oil, forcing suppressed market prices for the former. It imposed export taxes, production taxes and petroleum incentives that advantaged Canadian firms over their competitors. It restricted foreign energy companies from accessing frontier basins, and it forced foreign companies to allow Petro-Canada to back in to certain ownership rights. In its wake the new Crown corporation, Petro-Canada, itself moved aggressively to acquire Petrofina and BP Canada in 1981 and 1982.

All told, it would be hard to envision a suite of policy measures more offensive to western Canadians or, as it turned out, to the new Reagan administration in the United States. For the Americans, continental energy security remained a pre-eminent concern throughout the 1980s. Viewed through that lens, the measures put forward by the Trudeau government were worrisome indeed. The Reagan administration formally protested the NEP, and a deep chill settled in over Canada–US relations until the eventual election of the Progressive Conservative majority government of Prime Minister Brian Mulroney in 1984.

Continental Integration— The Free Trade Agreement

The negotiations that led to the Canada–United States Free Trade Agreement of 1988 were initiated by President Ronald Reagan and Prime Minister Brian Mulroney, and the idea appears to have been discussed as early as the so-called Shamrock Summit in Quebec City, on St. Patrick's Day, 1985. The communiqué from that summit committed both parties to exploring all possible ways to expand trade and investment; the agreement that was ultimately announced on October 5, 1987, reflected two-and-a-half years of intense effort and drew its inspiration from the positive personal chemistry between the two leaders.

The Canada–United States Free Trade Agreement (FTA) effectively achieved Nixon's ambitions of a continental oil policy. The energy industry on both sides of the border strongly supported the agreement. The FTA reflected a clear symmetry of continental interests. The Canadian energy industry was able to consolidate and expand its market access into the United States, and the United States was able to establish guaranteed access to Canadian oil and natural gas at market prices. Moreover, from a US perspective, the United States was able to secure an important concession from Canada, effectively ensuring that, in times of constrained supply, Canadian suppliers were compelled to maintain exports to the United States at a level that was proportionate to "Canadian total export shipments of that commodity in relation to total Canadian supply."[7] Concurrently, the egregious provisions of Canada's National Energy Program were repealed. What Canada obtained was full and unrestricted access to the world's largest energy marketplace, at a time when increasing US consumption and faltering American domestic supply required massive increases in American imports.

Canada and the United States had come a long way since President Nixon first tabled the notion of a continental energy policy in 1969. To be clear, the two countries had moved 180 degrees in the hundred years since Sir John A. Macdonald's National Policy. Since the coming into force of the Free Trade Agreement, Canadian exports of oil to the United States surged from about 600,000 barrels per day in 1987 to 3.17 million bpd in 2015—an increase of about 500 percent. The trajectory for natural gas was similar. Times were getting much better for energy exports into the United States.

The George W. Bush Years— Continued Continental Integration

The energy relationship between Canada and the United States continued to flourish until the end of the presidency of George W. Bush. I know that because I was there, at least for the last two years of that administration.

The Harper Conservative government was elected on January 23, 2006, and sworn in on February 6, 2006. I soon found myself at the centre of the development of Canada's energy and environmental policies. I was then the minister of Indian affairs and northern development and, at the prime minister's request, also chaired the government's powerful Operations Committee, as well as a special Cabinet committee on environment and energy security. I was also the "political" minister for Alberta and northern Canada and empowered to keep a watchful eye on Canada's pipeline files.

In retrospect, relations between Canada and the United States were pretty good back then and, while there certainly were irritants, none of them related to energy. In the years after the terrorist attacks of September 11, 2001, the Bush administration was largely preoccupied with border security, and that challenge, together with the intractable and bitter dispute over softwood lumber, dominated the agenda. When it came to energy, the principal concern of the US administration continued to be ensuring ready market access to as much Canadian oil and natural gas as possible. The seemingly insatiable American consumption of Canadian oil and natural gas continued to drive Canadian exports, capital investment and job growth. By 2008, according to Statistics Canada, energy accounted for more than $90 billion of Canada's trade with the United States, a full 20 percent of Canada's total exports.[8]

The United Nations Framework Convention on Climate Change (UNFCCC) had begun to gain momentum in those years, too, but the Copenhagen and Paris conferences were still a long way off. Canada, unlike the United States, was a signatory to the Kyoto Protocol, so the international negotiations on climate change were of continuing political concern on our side of the border. Still, they didn't really figure into our dialogue with Americans. In those years, the principal concern of both countries' administrations was our joint competitiveness and the continued build-out of the continental infrastructure called for under the Free Trade Agreement. It was unthinkable that, only a few years later, an American president would turn down a continental energy pipeline proposed by a Canadian company.

I made several trips to Washington in those years and met Vice-President Dick Cheney to discuss energy issues. Cheney was particularly hands-on when it came to energy matters, and he took a keen interest in the Mackenzie Valley Pipeline, which was then being put forward by Imperial Oil/ExxonMobil, Trans-Canada Pipelines and the Aboriginal Pipeline Group. Both governments were also concerned about the competing proposals under consideration to move Alaskan natural gas through Canada to the United States, and we discussed how best to coordinate our efforts. The Bush administration was concerned that it would be able to count on Canadian government support for both projects. Our government was an ardent proponent of all continental pipelines, and we wanted to ensure that position was well understood by the White House. To that end, we committed to strike a Canadian regulatory process that would move forward concurrently with the American process and be adequately funded and staffed to ensure an expeditious review.

I liked Vice-President Cheney. I found him to be well briefed, professional and extremely focused on outcomes. He was particularly interested in energy issues and also enjoyed good stories about Atlantic salmon fishing in Labrador, a passion of mine as well. One memorable exchange we had underscored the understanding that was then at the heart of the Canada–US energy relationship. I was going on at length about the merits of Canada's oil sands when the vice-president cut me off. "Listen," he said. "We want as much of Canada's oil as we can get."

The controversy over the Keystone pipeline and the Canadian oil sands would await the Obama presidency. We didn't need to wait long.

Canada and President Obama—
Ships Passing in the Night

President Barack Obama was elected on November 4, 2008, and sworn in as the 44th president of the United States in January 2009. His first foreign trip would be his visit to Canada one month later, on February 19, and I was one of three Canadian ministers who attended those first meetings between Prime Minister Harper and the new US president. It was clear from the outset that everything had changed.

President Obama's rise was, of course, meteoric. The night of his election victory in 2008, my daughter Kate, who was then a student at the School of the Art Institute of Chicago, called me from his victory celebration then under way at that city's Grant Park and said, "Listen to this, Dad. This guy is the new president of the United States," while holding up her cellphone so I could hear the crowd as Obama gave his victory speech.

I recounted that story to the president when we first met in Ottawa, and he was visibly touched. Later, as he was leaving, he crossed the room, grasped my arm and said, "Phone your daughter and tell her that the president of the United States says thank you for being at Grant Park that night. My own daughters were there, and it was a night we will never forget. Tell her I appreciate her being there, too." He meant every word of it. Only a gifted politician would have.

It was, however, immediately clear when we met in February 2009 that the new US administration's views on energy, oil, climate change and continental integration had changed irrevocably, as had the forward agenda for Canada–US relations. Working together as North American partners was of less interest to the

Obama administration than it had been to its predecessors, and it more narrowly focused on its domestic challenges with its climate change agenda. It was also clear that the new administration didn't see Canada as a helpful ally on climate change. This wasn't entirely a surprise. Barack Obama had campaigned on the issue of climate change and, just a few months before, in December 2008, I had met Senator John Kerry at the COP 14 meeting in Poznań, Poland, where we shared substantive views on energy, climate change and the oil sands. We knew what was coming.

My greatest frustration with the Obama administration wasn't its focus on the environment or its concerns about climate change, both of which I largely share. Rather, my frustration was over the lost opportunity of his presidency for Canada and the United States to work together on energy, the environment and climate change. While our two countries maintained a dialogue in the eight years that followed, the Obama administration was never really willing to seriously engage Canada to search out continental solutions on the important issues surrounding energy and the environment. How much of this unwillingness related to the challenges in the relationship between the president and the prime minister is unclear to me; only they can speak to that. Certainly, we made some progress in the time that I was Canada's environment minister—for example, on tailpipe emission standards. Sadly, however, for the most part the Obama administration was indifferent to, if not openly dismissive of, the continental environmental potential of our two countries.

My own interactions with the president and his advisers were always cordial and professional. I came to know and respect both US Energy Secretary Steven Chu and Michael Froman, the president's international climate change leader and later his US trade representative. I was able to work closely with Carol Browner, the president's domestic climate change leader, and I enjoyed a positive working relationship with Lisa Jackson, the administrator of the Environmental Protection Agency. But progress on joint initiatives, including the Clean Energy Dialogue, was incremental, and I know that after I left, the relationship continued to deteriorate.

I don't accept that the Harper government was "at fault" because our environmental policies were at variance with the expectations of the newly elected president. I acknowledge that Canada's climate change positioning was challenging between 2006 and 2008, but so, too, was America's; and our domestic policies were at least as far advanced as those of the United States. The United States also had its domestic challenges, as illustrated by the eventual defeat of the Waxman-Markey climate change legislation in Congress. This was a comprehensive bill, supported by President Obama, that would have established an economy-wide cap-and-trade system to limit American greenhouse gas (GHG) emissions. Although it passed the House of Representatives with the slimmest of margins, it never made it through the Senate. Thus, President Obama was unable to pass any of his landmark environmental legislation, even when the Democrats controlled the Senate.

The point is that, in 2009 and 2010, we repeatedly offered to work with the United States to arrive at new and different policies—provided they were continental policies. We did so during the Clean Energy Dialogue and throughout the Major Economies Forum process, which served as the president's climate change table. I represented Canada at both tables in 2009 and 2010, and I continually indicated our willingness to move toward continental standards and policies. I recall vividly the personal criticism that followed my statement that Canada would move to a cap-and-trade system if the United States did so by passing the Waxman-Markey bill. We enthusiastically committed to the harmonization of carbon standards across the transportation grid, beginning with motor vehicles. And the plan to phase out Canada's coal-burning electricity plants, which I negotiated, was years ahead of the United States' plan to phase out its plants. We repeatedly pushed for a more ambitious continental agenda with Energy Secretary Chu and with Carol Browner, and, as we readied ourselves for Copenhagen, I made the point in the Oval Office that Canada and the United States should show leadership through concerted continental action. Neither the Canadian oil industry nor the oil sands were off limits in those many discussions, and our position that we would work together with the United States on continental carbon pricing for industrial emissions was well known.

The historical context is important. Until the arrival of President Obama, every US president since Richard Nixon had advocated the incorporation of Canada's energy resources, including the Canadian oil sands, into North America's energy marketplace. Indeed, that was one of the main reasons our two countries signed the Canada–US Free Trade Agreement and, a few years later, the North American Free Trade Agreement (NAFTA). It should not be forgotten that the US negotiators had made energy and the oil sands a priority in the free trade negotiations in the 1980s.

In the case of Canada, we fought a national election over that free trade pact. The 1988 election was a turning point in modern Canadian history because Canadians made a choice that seems all the more remarkable today: We agreed to compromise our Canadian sovereignty by guaranteeing the availability of Canada's energy resources to the United States in the event of future shortages. And, in the 25 years that followed, companies on both sides of the border invested billions of dollars not only to develop the oil sands, but also to provision American Gulf coast refineries to process Canada's bitumen and heavy oils.

It was therefore completely unimaginable that a new US president would turn his back on that history, on our North American partnership and on the NAFTA energy relationship.

Trapped—The Risks of Having Only One Customer

Unfortunately, having all our eggs in that one basket makes Canada highly vulnerable in both an economic and a political sense. The first vulnerability is economic—oil is a global commodity, and having only one customer makes us a price-taker in a subset of that global marketplace. Today, a barrel of Canadian oil no longer transacts at its intrinsic value but sells, instead, at a lower price than it is really worth because it is selling into a smaller continental market—one that is characterized by flattening demand and extraordinary increases in supply.

However, that is only the beginning of the problem. Those lower prices, in turn, weaken the economics of Canadian companies relative to their global peers. Lower cash flows reduce profits and suppress Canadian rates of return and, ultimately, investment. This is one of the reasons that the market valuations of Canadian energy companies reflect a discount measured against their international competitors, commanding less capital, financing and investment than they should. In effect, we have "ring fenced" investment in the Canadian energy industry by cutting it off from international pricing.

Other consequences logically follow. For example, Canadian companies are disadvantaged relative to other global players because their cash flows and rates of return are diminished in comparison, which in turn calls into question why such companies would choose to remain fully invested in the Canadian marketplace. Put another way, an industry that cannot command global prices loses its ability to compete globally for inputs such as capital, labour and even technology. It doesn't happen overnight, but over time our competitiveness diminishes.

The second vulnerability is political and relates to a loss of our sovereignty or, at a minimum, a loss of our ability to exercise our sovereignty. Since we have only one customer, we have no escape from a range of policies and actions that—rightly or wrongly—seek to advance American interests while subordinating Canadian ones. This dynamic is not unique to the energy trade; the discrepancy in the economic girth of Canada and that of the United States—the old saw about the mouse sleeping with the elephant—has always exacerbated risk on the Canadian side of the relationship. What has happened, however, is that our major energy customer is now our major energy competitor; more accurately, our one and only energy customer is now our major energy competitor. As we now know, the United States will always do what is in its best interest. That is the very definition of vulnerability.

The rejection of the Keystone XL Pipeline isn't the only evidence of Canada's growing vulnerability to US domestic energy policies. For more than a decade, a number of public authorities within the United States have been pursuing policies, such as "low carbon fuel standards" and "renewable portfolio standards," that impede our ability to freely sell our energy products, including clean hydroelectricity, into American markets.

The Continental Trap

I value our friendship and partnership with the United States, and I have been an outspoken advocate of strengthening our joint competitiveness through deeper economic integration of our two countries. But I am also a proud Canadian, and I know that we must be more realistic and strategic in our thinking. We will never fulfill our promise as an energy producer unless we successfully expand our horizons beyond the North American continent and become a global energy supplier.

Both countries have now expanded their energy production beyond what we can consume in North America, and neither of our countries can afford to ignore that reality. The marketplace has been letting us know for some time and, ironically, the most compelling evidence of why Canada should extricate itself from the continental trap is the cold reality that the Americans saw the problem and have already removed themselves. Rest assured as well that American entrepreneurs already fully appreciate the opportunity to export Canadian crude oil and natural gas, whether in raw or refined form, from US—rather than Canadian—ports, driving American investment, jobs, profits and taxes.

I return to the important point that, when it comes to energy, the United States is both the world's largest producer and the world's largest consumer, and its policies, priorities and decision making will always be driven by its national interests.

Canada is a net exporter of energy, and our policies, priorities and decision making must be framed around *our* national interests. The North American marketplace will always be critical to Canada, but it can never again be our only market. It is in our national interest to secure access to as many markets as possible, in the process achieving the widest possible customer base, achieving the highest possible prices and minimizing the economic and political risks of the loss of any single customer, or of a disagreement with any single customer. I say all this as a Canadian nationalist.

CHAPTER 5

The Keystone XL Debacle:
Canada's Lesson in Realpolitik

O n November 6, 2015, President Barack Obama formally rejected the Keystone XL Pipeline, bringing to a close a seven-year controversy over the project that has demonstrated irrevocably that US and Canadian energy interests are often dramatically different. The episode undoubtedly changed Canada–US relations forever and, while it is not yet possible to know what the long-term implications will be, some things for sure will never be the same.

The president's decision was made by way of a ratification of the decision of Secretary of State John Kerry, agreeing with the secretary's conclusion that the pipeline would not serve the "national interest" of the United States and should be rejected. The thing feared most by Canada, a formal and negative National Interest Determination, accompanied the decision.

The Keystone XL Pipeline was designed to move increasing volumes of both Canadian and American oil to the US Gulf coast, and the president's decision marked the end of years of continuing uncertainty, frustration and intrigue that saw Canada, its relationship with the United States and the controversy surrounding the oil sands all thrust into the centre of partisan American politics. The comments made by the president and the secretary of state in the days that followed, acknowledging that the refusal was based not on the merits of the project but rather on perceptions and international climate change politics, stunned even the most seasoned observers of Canada–US relations.

Remarkably, the State Department's formal decision had acknowledged that the proposed project would not significantly affect the level of GHG emissions from Canada's oil sands or the demand for heavy crude at US refineries but pointed out that the United States must prioritize actions that were "not perceived as enabling GHG emissions globally." Secretary Kerry added that the "critical factor" in the decision was that the approval of the pipeline would have "undermine[d] our ability to continue to lead the world in combating climate change." President Obama added that, "frankly, approving this project would have undercut that global leadership . . . and that's the biggest risk that we face."[1] Put another way, the president needed to reject the Keystone XL Pipeline to enhance his standing at the climate change negotiations in Paris in December 2015.

The Keystone controversy was never really about the Keystone XL Pipeline, or about the company that proposed it. The underlying issue was always climate change and Canada's oil sands. But why?

To begin with, from an American perspective, the oil sands are Canadian, not American, and the jobs that hung in the balance seemed to be Canadian, not American. The reality is, of course, much more complex, but that didn't matter. The oil sands are also visually dirty, in a *National Geographic* photography sort of way. And the fact that the oil produced from the Canadian oil sands is subject to tougher environmental rules—including those relating to carbon emissions—than the oil produced anywhere else in the world, including the United States, didn't matter; nor did the fact that America's coal-burning electricity plants produce 50 times more carbon emissions than the whole of Canada's oil sands complex. None of this mattered. The Keystone XL Pipeline had become an environmental symbol, and battles over symbols never turn on the facts—they turn on "perceptions," which, remarkably, is exactly what the secretary of state conceded was the basis of the decision.

This chapter does not purport to be the definitive history of the Keystone XL debacle. I was there at the beginning and at the end. I can speak to what I observed while I worked with the Obama administration and also share my views on what the entire unfortunate experience should teach us about our relationship with the United States and our relative strategic interests. For Canada, it has been a harsh lesson in both *realpolitik* and the vulnerabilities of the continental trap.

About the Keystone XL

The Keystone XL Pipeline was designed to satisfy the demand for heavier Canadian crudes at US Gulf coast refineries and to keep those refineries operating at optimal efficiency by provisioning them with the kind of crude oil they were designed to process. In fact, the Keystone XL project was merely an enhancement of an existing pipeline doing just that. TransCanada already owned and operated 2,639 miles of interconnected oil pipelines that traversed the United States on a north–south axis. That network, described as the Keystone Pipeline, already ran from Alberta to the US Gulf coast. It consisted of four interconnections:

1. the Keystone I Pipeline, which ran from Hardisty, Alberta, to Steele City, Nebraska (opened in 2010);
2. the Cushing Extension Pipeline, which ran from Steele City to Cushing, Oklahoma (opened in 2011);
3. the Gulf Coast Pipeline, which ran from Cushing to Nederland, Texas (opened in 2014); and
4. the Houston Lateral, which ran from Nederland to Harry County, near Houston, Texas (opened in 2016).

Construction of the Keystone I Pipeline began in 2005. By 2011 the pipeline was fully operational, carrying Canadian crude oil to Cushing, Oklahoma.

The Keystone XL Pipeline was designed to expand Trans-Canada's system capacity by some 830,000 barrels per day and to improve the operation and profitability of the existing system. So, on September 19, 2008, TransCanada submitted its application to the US State Department for a presidential permit. The State Department would review TransCanada's Keystone XL application for the next seven years, coordinating the overall review of 10 other federal agencies and multiple state agencies.

The Arrival of the Obama Administration

I was Canada's minister of the environment when Barack Obama was elected president of the United States, and my interaction with the Obama administration began with Senator John Kerry.

A few weeks after the November 2008 election that carried Barack Obama into the White House, I had the opportunity to meet then-senator John Kerry (Democrat, Massachusetts) at the Conference of the Parties (COP 14) meeting in the medieval city of Poznań, Poland. The senator had been the Democratic Party nominee in the US presidential election of 2004, losing to George W. Bush, and our expectation at the time was that Senator Kerry, as much as the new president, would drive the US agenda on climate change and the environment. So John Kerry was key to Canada's interests.

To be clear, the purpose of the meeting had nothing to do with the Keystone XL Pipeline. I was meeting Senator Kerry to get a better understanding of the intentions of the incoming administration relative to Canada, energy and climate change. At that early stage, no one could have predicted that continental pipelines would become the essential political nexus between climate change activism and Canada's oil sands.

Senator Kerry was skeptical about meeting with us. Canada's reputation on climate change had by then reached its low ebb, and I was trying to change that. We knew Kerry to be a passionate advocate on climate change, and I had made a point of reading his book *This Moment on Earth* on the flight to Europe. Senator Kerry didn't disappoint us, and the first part of our meeting was taken up by a detailed discussion about the science of climate change.

We were well prepared for the meeting, and I engaged Senator Kerry on how Canada and the United States might work together. I summarized Canada's vision of a possible continental agreement on climate change as an early win for the new president. The suggestion seemed to surprise him, and he made it clear that he planned to meet with President Obama on his return to the

United States. I outlined the arguments that we had developed in advance with Derek Burney, the former Canadian ambassador to the United States, describing how Canada and the United States might work together to demonstrate leadership in advance of the Copenhagen Climate Change Conference in 2009.

We discussed the importance of expanding and upgrading the North American electricity grid and agreed that the most compelling way to reduce North American carbon emissions would be to close coal-burning electricity plants. The senator questioned me about Canada's capacity for renewables such as geothermal, solar, wind and tidal. He seemed especially interested in the Bay of Fundy.

We discussed Canada's oil sands in some detail, and Senator Kerry repeatedly returned to the necessity of reducing emissions and adopting targets that were even tougher than those being proposed by incoming President Obama. Our discussions about the importance of continental action were very frank: I pointed out that the close integration of our economies meant that the absolute level of Canadian and US targets mattered less than their *relative* level. In other words, Canada could live with targets that were high or targets that were low, *provided they were the same in both Canada and the United States*. At that time, Canada was well ahead of the United States in some of the analytical work on the trade and competitiveness implications of various climate change policies. I chaired the Cabinet committee on that subject and pointed out that we had limitations on how much further Canada could go in regulating industrial emissions without a better understanding of where the Obama administration was headed. Senator Kerry agreed but offered no comment on the timing or direction of the administration.

As the meeting progressed, the senator became more engaged. I heard later that he had inundated his staff with questions about the "Canadian proposal," observing that we had "really done [our] homework." It was evident from my meeting that he had not thought much about Canada, or how we might work together. This would be a continuing frustration at our end.

President Obama Comes to Canada

Just two months later, after his swearing-in as the 44th president of the United States, President Obama undertook his first foreign trip, visiting Ottawa on February 19, 2009. I was one of three Canadian ministers engaged by Prime Minister Harper in that early summit. That morning, as the prime minister met with the president, Ministers Jim Flaherty (Finance), Lawrence Cannon (Foreign Affairs) and I met with our respective counterparts; in my case, Carol Browner, the president's environment and climate change adviser. Following those meetings, Prime Minister Harper hosted a lengthy luncheon in the historic office of the Speaker of the Senate. The prime minister and the president attended, as did Minister Cannon, Minister Flaherty and I.

I have on many occasions read and reread my notes from that first encounter with President Obama and his key advisers—the obvious question being whether those early meetings foreshadowed Canada's eventual problems with the president. In retrospect, my discussions with Carol Browner provided some insight on what would follow.

Ms. Browner was well known in the United States as a partisan environmental activist, described by some as hyper-partisan, but our meetings were very constructive—at least within the bounds of what she was authorized to do. We spoke in depth about climate change and more specifically on how Canada and the United States might work together in the year leading up to the Copenhagen COP meeting. We discussed a number of avenues for early progress, and I emphasized our desire to proceed quickly with the harmonization of fuel efficiency standards across the transportation grid, starting with passenger vehicles. Eventually, she and I would achieve that objective. It is ironic, looking back, that the most successful initiative that Canada and the United States would undertake to reduce carbon emissions over the next decade would be agreed on in the first 15 minutes of that very first meeting.

We also discussed the oil sands. Ms. Browner was surprisingly circumspect in her observations about the oil sands, and the full measure of the Obama administration's eventual hostility toward them wasn't really evident at that early time. She did refer to the oil sands as the "tar sands," but she was for the most part simply curious about the technologies and environmental performance standards that we thought achievable. She was also curious about the early-stage technologies surrounding carbon capture and storage, and we specifically discussed the commercial prospects of the Weyburn project in Saskatchewan, where American carbon was being sequestered in a Canadian reservoir and used to enhance the recovery of oil.

We did discuss the growing importance of Canada's oil sands to the US economy, and I emphasized that Canada represented a reliable and secure source of supply for the United States, especially when compared with alternatives such as Venezuela and the Middle East. Not unexpectedly, she seemed indifferent to the North American supply–demand balance for oil and neither agreed nor disagreed with my position.

We had agreed in advance that the president and then the prime minister would announce the creation of a "Clean Energy Dialogue" that afternoon, and I pressed her to expand that dialogue into a broader agreement to harmonize North American energy and environmental standards. We had been pushing the Americans for several weeks to expand the ambitions of the proposed dialogue, but they had been steadfast in their intent to confine the dialogue, to joint efforts on energy research. I disagreed with this narrow focus and told Ms. Browner exactly that. She explained that the president was unwilling to expand it beyond "research" initiatives, and she observed that the dialogue would likely be overseen by the US Energy Department, rather than the White House or the Environmental Protection Agency (EPA). Sensing my frustration, she emphasized that the Clean Energy Dialogue represented an opportunity to work together on areas of common interest.

We discussed cap-and-trade, the prime minister and I having agreed in advance that we would try to get a better understanding of where the new president was heading. Neither the prime minister nor I believed that Congress would ever adopt a cap-and-trade regime. Ms. Browner was, however, enthused about the prospects and indicated that the United States was looking closely at the European Union's proposal to adopt "global caps" in relation to specific industries. I indicated that we were open to examining how we might work together on such an initiative but emphasized again that I felt there were opportunities for more immediate and successful continental action, since we shared air sheds and watersheds. She indicated a desire to collaborate on some other North

American environmental initiatives and stated that Lisa Jackson, the newly announced head of the EPA, would likely be interested in discussing continental improvements to improving our regulations on mercury, NOx (nitrogen oxide), SOx (sulphur oxide) and particulate-matter emissions.

At the outset of the private luncheon, the president asked Carol Browner and me to recap the essence of our discussion. This we did, and the president and the prime minister confirmed their intent to announce the Clean Energy Dialogue later that afternoon. Much of the rest of the luncheon was devoted to the serious economic circumstances then facing the world, and the need for coordinated government "stimulus" as a solution to what is now known as the great recession of 2008–9.

During that first meeting with the president, we also discussed the Canadian pipeline projects then under review by the US administration. I understood the prime minister had referenced them during his private meeting with the president, and Keystone XL was certainly referenced during our luncheon. Frankly, however, these projects did not attract much discussion, at least at the luncheon, because intercontinental pipelines were then the least controversial aspect of Canada–US relations. Trans-Canada had already obtained a presidential permit for the Keystone I project (March 14, 2008), and Enbridge's application for the permit for the Alberta Clipper Pipeline was then well under way and would, in fact, be obtained from President Obama himself in August 2009. Both those projects would carry escalating volumes of Canadian oil into the heart of the US industrial economy. TransCanada had only just filed its application for a presidential permit for the Keystone XL Pipeline. We knew that it was to be the largest of all the North American interconnections, and we referenced it during our luncheon. We viewed the requirement for a presidential permit as something of a formality since no US president had ever rejected a continental interconnection, and our interaction with the George W. Bush administration, as described in the previous chapter, was focused on securing as many continental connections as possible.

It was also hard to imagine in the face of the effort Canada was then mounting alongside the United States in Afghanistan that the United States would not welcome Keystone XL's additional 830,000 barrels per day, on top of the (then) 2.2 million barrels per day of Alberta crude already making its way into the American marketplace. The two issues were never linked as a quid pro quo, but it seemed hard to believe then that the United States would not want to continue to work with its closest ally to strengthen the continental energy grid in the face of the uncertainty and confusion present in the Middle East and elsewhere.

The meeting with Carol Browner and the luncheon with the president reflected the excitement of a new beginning in terms of how Canada and the United States might work together. The Canadian public, in particular, was giddy with excitement about the visit. Privately, however, my concern based on my meeting with Ms. Browner was that, for the most part, she was completely indifferent to the historic—and in our view, special—relationship that Canada shared with the United States. The intent of the Obama administration, as stated repeatedly, politely and firmly, was to confine its work with Canada on energy and climate change to those areas where our respective research investments would benefit each other. In the two years that followed, the administration would repeatedly reject our invitation, on multiple fronts and in multiple ways, to expand the relationship between our two countries on energy and the environment.

It wasn't so much that we disagreed on fundamental objectives, although there was some of that, too. It was more that we disagreed on the importance of continental action. We were interested; the United States wasn't. The Clean Energy Dialogue would prove to be a frustration. It achieved only incremental progress and, over the next 18 months, my ongoing efforts to engage Energy Secretary Steven Chu to expand the work of the dialogue would be continually rebuffed. My chief of staff, Steve Kelly, would eventually take to acerbically calling it the Clean Energy Monologue. It was obvious from the outset that our two countries were moving in different directions.

The Keystone XL Saga—Process, and More Process

The Keystone XL application was then in progress, and things did move quickly at first. Enbridge had obtained its presidential permit for the Alberta Clipper project in August 2009, and the approval process for Keystone XL seemed to be moving along in a similarly expeditious manner. In April 2010, for example, the US State Department issued a Draft Environmental Impact Statement which concluded, among other things, that the incremental GHG emissions from the project would be "minor." In October of that year, then–secretary of state Hillary Clinton publicly stated that the State Department was "inclined" to provide a presidential permit.

Those were, of course, the opening days in the Keystone XL saga, and we expected the president would want to run a fair process that would withstand judicial scrutiny. But we also expected him eventually to approve the project, provided it reflected world class engineering and environmental standards. While the approval of the pipeline did not dominate my early work with the Obama administration, I was the Canadian minister responsible for pipelines, and I raised the importance of Keystone XL at every meeting with Energy Secretary Chu and EPA Administrator Jackson. The prevailing view, not unreasonably, in 2009 and 2010, was that President Obama would eventually come to the "right" conclusion and we should avoid embarrassing him or his government and allow them the time they needed to pursue their regulatory approvals in their own way. Quiet diplomacy was seen as our preferred strategy.

Unfortunately, the broader political environment began to shift dramatically in late 2010. That summer, Americans witnessed the explosion of the *Deepwater Horizon* oil rig in the Gulf of Mexico, together with Enbridge's Line 6B spill of 900,000 barrels of diluted bitumen into the Kalamazoo River in Michigan. The two incidents, taken together with TransCanada's difficult landowner negotiations in Nebraska, elevated public opposition to energy projects across the United States.

Moreover, by late 2010, the climate change picture had also begun to change for the US president. The Copenhagen Climate Conference in December of 2009 had been seen as a failure, with the president suffering the embarrassment of pursuing the Chinese president through the backrooms of the Bella Centre. The president's ambitious plans for a domestic cap-and-trade regime had been blocked by the US Senate, and the Democrats were to lose control of the House of Representatives in the November 2010 midterm elections. President Obama had learned the painful lesson that Congress did not share his climate change agenda and that he would have to abandon legislative levers, which he could not control, and focus on executive levers, which he could. And so he turned, with increasing authority, to his executive powers, the use of moral suasion and bilateral and international climate change negotiations—all of which placed Canada, and the Keystone XL Pipeline, in the very crosshairs of US domestic politics.

In November 2010, I retired from federal politics and returned to the private sector. As I look back, it was always difficult to ascertain where the president and his administration were headed when it came to Keystone XL. We weren't alone in that sense. I don't recall any discussions with anyone close to the president who was willing to express an opinion about the Keystone XL project or elaborate on the president's intent—I don't think anyone knew what he intended to do. Every discussion ended with the same reluctance to express an opinion, other than the obvious fact that the president would himself decide the matter. It was, after all, a presidential permit. For example, throughout 2009 and early 2010, I sensed in my discussions with Lisa Jackson and Steven Chu that they felt it likely that the president would ultimately approve the project. The energy secretary said as much to me before I left office. It seemed more about the choices the president needed to make to manage his domestic midterm politics along the way.

As Canadians, we sought comfort in the smallest of positive signs, such as Secretary of State Hillary Clinton's comments to the Commonwealth Club of San Francisco in October 2010 that the State Department was "inclined" to approve the project. But, for the most part, clarity was impossible to find.

By April 2011, the storm clouds had begun to mass, and the president would offer the following startling comments at a Pennsylvania town hall meeting: "These tar sands, there are some environmental questions about how destructive they are, potentially, what are the dangers there, and we've got to examine all those questions."[2]

The State Department's work actually seemed to answer the

president's inquiry. The department released a Supplemental Draft Environmental Assessment in April 2011, which again concluded that the project would have only minor effects on GHG emissions. Its Final Environmental Impact Statement (FEIS) followed on August 26, 2011, and concluded for a third time that the pipeline would not materially increase GHG emissions.

Still, everything that could go wrong with the politics of the Keystone XL project did. The prime minister's description to an American reporter while in New York on September 21, 2011, that the decision was a "no brainer" seemed to harden President Obama's resolve, and his intentions became all the more opaque. At a joint press conference with Prime Minister Harper in December, Mr. Obama expressed the view that he was keeping an "open mind" on the project. Would he or wouldn't he?

For a period, it seemed as though he would approve the project once the regulatory process had ground its way through to a satisfactory conclusion, thereby mollifying the environmental activists close to the Democratic Party. After all, the State Department's own 2011 analysis seemed to point in that direction, opining that Canada's oil sands would continue to develop with or without the Keystone project. There were, of course, those who thought the opposite and felt that the regulatory process would provide the president with the climate change rationale that he required to say no. Then, for a time, it seemed as though the approval was inevitable—delayed, however, until after the president's re-election the following year. The relationship between Canada and the United States was, after all, far too important to allow a pipeline to come between us. Wasn't it?

TransCanada and the Canadian government were surprised and stunned, however, in November 2011, when the State Department announced it was delaying its decision on the presidential permit application in order to allow additional time to gather information on alternative routing in Nebraska around the ecologically sensitive Sandhills area. By then local, regional and national US politics had reached a fevered pitch.

In December 2011, Congress weighed in, passing a legislative provision intended to force the president's hand, which required him to either approve the project or report his reasons to Congress within 60 days. The president refused to be boxed in and said so on January 18, 2012, when he denied the presidential permit while making it clear he would expect and consider a renewed permit application. The president himself seemed uncertain about Keystone XL in 2012, and he added to the confusion surrounding the project when he made a campaign stop in Cushing, Oklahoma, in March 2012. "Now, right now, a company called TransCanada has applied to build a new pipeline to speed more oil from Cushing to state-of-the-art refineries down on the Gulf Coast," he said. "And today, I'm directing my administration to cut through the red tape, break through the bureaucratic hurdles, and make this project a priority, to go ahead and get it done."[3]

* * *

In the time after President Obama's re-election in 2012, the politics of the Keystone XL Pipeline began to assume an importance vastly disproportionate to the pipeline itself, increasingly straining the relationship between the Obama and Harper administrations. To confuse matters further, in his second inaugural address, on January 21, 2013, President Obama warned that "we will respond to the threat of climate change" and that "America cannot resist this transition, we must lead it."

It is doubtful that Canada had ever mounted a more intense

diplomatic lobby on anything. The Governments of Canada, Alberta and Saskatchewan all pushed hard in Washington, employing diplomats, ministers, oil executives, lobbyists and even advertising in the DC metro—the city's subway system. Sadly, it all missed the mark.

Gary Doer was an incredible force for Canada in Washington. His appointment as Canada's ambassador to the United States was a stroke of genius on the part of the prime minister, arguably the best foreign posting appointment our Conservative government ever made. He brought the skills of a seasoned politician to Washington, building on relationships he already had, and he took the American capital by storm. Barely a year after his appointment, he was selected by his peers as the "most effective" foreign diplomat in Washington. Sadly, his tenure was marred by the ongoing weight of the Keystone controversy and by the strains the project had introduced to every facet of Canada–US relations. It permeated everything Mr. Doer did, and it coloured every relationship that Canada had in Washington.

Back home in Canada, confusion reigned. Prime Minister Harper, stung by criticism that he had failed to build a constructive personal relationship with the US president, turned his attention to China and the possibility of the Asia Pacific Basin as an alternative market for Canadian oil. Harper's earlier trip to China in 2012, while useful, seemed to mark an about-face in his views on Canada's relationship with that country. The threat only hardened American opposition to Keystone XL, and its detractors seized on the fact that Canada had no port or pipeline egress to China and was having problems with its own domestic pipelines.

About the same time, Minister of Natural Resources Joe Oliver linked opposition to the Northern Gateway Pipeline to foreign "radical" environmentalist groups and, in the process, galvanized all of British Columbia's First Nations into a united and well-financed opposition to that project. Eventually, Canada's inability to build the Northern Gateway project would become a compelling argument available to America's opponents of Keystone XL. After all, if Canadians themselves were opposed to a bitumen pipeline across Canada, why would Americans support a similar pipeline across the United States?

Meanwhile, the process to study the pipeline ground forward.

In January 2014, the US State Department concluded for the fifth time, in its Final Supplemental Environmental Impact Statement, that the project would not materially increase GHG emissions, significantly expand the rate of extraction in the Canadian oil sands or increase heavy oil refinery demand on the Gulf coast.

By then, of course, the partisan American politics surrounding Keystone XL had reached a fevered pitch. On five separate occasions between 2011 and 2014, the House of Representatives passed bills authorizing the construction of the Keystone XL Pipeline. In 2014, the US Senate voted on whether to proceed to vote on a measure to authorize construction of the project, securing the support of 59 senators, one less than the 60 needed to advance the bill.

In January 2015, when the 114th Congress convened, the Senate passed the *Keystone Pipeline Approval Act*, which authorized the construction of the Keystone XL Pipeline, without any further action, or inaction, by the president. The bill cleared the Senate on January 29, 2015, and the House of Representatives on February 11, 2015. Congress promptly enrolled the bill and sent it to the president, who promptly vetoed it on February 24, 2015.

By then, the whole issue had become so politicized that only one thing was absolutely clear: The approval or rejection of Keystone would turn solely on US domestic politics and solely on the decision of one man—the president. In the meantime, its primary importance in the US political system would be as a fundraising vehicle for both the Democratic and Republican parties.

The Premier of Alberta Goes to Washington

By the time I became Alberta's premier in September 2014, the die had already been cast on the Keystone XL Pipeline. I recognized this immediately from two interventions. The first involved a trip to Washington in January 2015 and the second, surprisingly, involved Michael Bloomberg, the former mayor of New York City. It was clear from both efforts that the fate of the Keystone XL project had already been decided.

I went to Washington in January of 2015 for reasons well beyond the Keystone XL Pipeline. The economic ties between the United States and Alberta are much larger than any single pipeline, and our relationship needed to survive whatever happened on Keystone XL. Alberta's annual exports to the United States were $103 billion in 2014, primarily because Alberta is the single-largest supplier of petroleum to the United States. In addition, there is all the other two-way trade that goes on between the United States and Alberta—natural gas, petrochemicals, lumber, beef, and machinery and other manufactured goods. Alberta is completely dependent on the American economy, and if the province were a US state, its economy would rank 15th in the United States.

So the trip in early 2015 was important to our province, and it was important to my objectives as its new premier. We had begun the climate change rebranding of Alberta and would need to fight that battle on three fronts: here in Canada; in the United States; and globally, starting in Paris at the COP 21 meeting in December 2015. To do so, we were prepared to be innovative and to change Alberta's fiscal and regulatory policies. We were also prepared to change our approach to climate change and to strengthen our environmental regime, and we were prepared to lead and demand more from industry. We were, however, insistent on reciprocity of effort by our American neighbours on carbon pricing. We were prepared to lead, but we weren't prepared to be naive.

It was clear from the moment we arrived in Washington that the Keystone debate had fully polarized thinking about Canada and, especially, about Alberta. Part of the challenge that Alberta, and indeed, Canada faces in Washington is that, while the province's environmental record is at least as good as that of any state, decision makers in the capital have a largely superficial and negative perception about what we are doing. In fact, their view is almost cartoonish.

This is the very reason that Canada must always maintain the intensity of our diplomacy and advocacy efforts in Washington. At one point in a conversation, one of the participants—perhaps sensing my frustration—pointed out that we shouldn't be surprised by the depth of misunderstanding about Canada in Washington because there are well over one thousand registered lobbyists working for environmental groups in the capital and, by comparison, only one Gary Doer. I responded that, given a choice, I would pick Gary Doer in that equation. The point had been made, however. We may not be outgunned in Washington, but we are definitely outnumbered.

As an illustration of the overall problem, a luncheon discussion at the embassy turned to the question of whether Alberta and Canada would be able to keep pace with President Obama's intent first to phase out coal, and second to reduce the venting and flaring of methane in the petroleum industry. I almost exploded on the spot but instead politely pointed out that the coal policy President Obama was "discussing" in 2015 was modelled on the Canadian policy, which we had developed six years before and had been the law in Canada since 2012. Moreover, when it comes to the venting and flaring of methane, the jurisdiction in the world that everyone was trying to catch up to was, in fact, Alberta. At the time, the World Bank considered Alberta its partner of choice when it came to reducing methane emissions. In other words, in the two environmental fields that the US president was then trumpeting as partial solutions to climate change, Alberta and Canada were already acknowledged world leaders—a decade ahead of the United States on both fronts. I left the luncheon reminded, yet again, that Canada's problem isn't what we were doing, but rather the perception about what we weren't doing.

My second intervention on the Keystone XL Pipeline followed an editorial that Michael Bloomberg, the former mayor of New York, had penned on February 25, 2015.[4] In it, Bloomberg suggested that President Obama should use Canada's strong desire to see the Keystone XL Pipeline built as leverage to negotiate a climate deal in return, so that everyone could find a win. I called Mr. Bloomberg, spoke to him and engaged the help of Ambassador Doer to contact both the Prime Minister's Office and the White House to try to facilitate a last attempt to bridge our differences. I suggested that we employ Michael Bloomberg or Marvin Odum, the CEO of Shell in the Americas, as an intermediary because the president reportedly respected both men. I made it perfectly clear that Alberta was in the process of revising its climate change policies and was prepared to consider all reasonable solutions to resolve the impasse. We offered to put everything on the table. The back-and-forth carried on with Ambassador Doer for days, but he was never able to get any traction with our offer.

To this day, I don't know whether it was the Prime Minister's Office or the White House that wasn't prepared to make that last attempt. Perhaps it was both. All I really knew was that the Keystone XL project was dead. The president's confirmation came eight months later, on November 6, 2015.

Lessons Learned

What lessons can we draw from the Keystone XL debacle? The first and most obvious one is that the strategic interests of the United States and the strategic interests of Canada are not always the same. They can in fact be quite different, even when it comes to something as obvious as our trade in energy.

Knowing this to be the case, Canada will need to keep a clearer eye on its strategic interests when it comes to trade. The Canada–US relationship will undoubtedly survive the Keystone XL debacle, and trade—including energy trade—will continue. But Canadians will never again be as inattentive to their relative strategic importance to the United States. President Obama showed Canadians that they can never sleep comfortably if they have only one customer, and the rejection of Keystone XL has, more than any other factor, fuelled Canada's global energy ambitions.

Other important lessons emerged. We had always assumed

that the North American Free Trade Agreement (NAFTA) relationship was sacrosanct—at least when it came to the relationship between Canada and the United States. Unfortunately, President Obama's decision flew in the face of everything Canadians thought they understood about our free trade agreement with the Americans. The denial of such a presidential permit is unprecedented in Canada–US history, and TransCanada has now, in fact, initiated legal proceedings, contending that President Obama exceeded his lawful authority, acted arbitrarily and violated the express provisions of both NAFTA and the Canada–US Free Trade Agreement that preceded it. One of the key principles of NAFTA is that the "Parties recognize that it is desirable to strengthen the important role that trade in energy and basic petrochemical goods plays in the free trade area *and to enhance this role through sustained and gradual liberalization* [emphasis mine]."[5] Whatever else may be said of the Keystone XL saga, it certainly did not represent trade liberalization.

None of this should be cause for despair. Instead, Canadians need to stand up for ourselves and protect our interests. When it comes to energy in particular, the world has changed. The United States is now richly endowed with competing energy supplies, including domestic supplies, and American political players are now free to pursue other national interests, which in the case of President Obama included his own international climate change agenda. In the aftermath of the divisive 2016 US election, President Donald Trump will be similarly free to pursue other evolving American preoccupations, including trade protectionism. But President Obama's rejection of Keystone XL would have been unimaginable in any of the previous five decades because, frankly, the Americans needed that incremental Canadian oil supply back then. Today they don't.

To illustrate how dramatically things have changed, consider the evolution, between 2008 and 2015, in the State Department's definition of the US "national interest." In 2008, the Department of State issued a presidential permit for the first Keystone I Pipeline. It did so because the project served America's national interest for four stated reasons:

1. It increased the diversity of available supply among the United States' worldwide crude oil sources.
2. It increased those crude oil supplies from a stable and reliable trading partner.
3. Because the transport by pipeline avoided the environmental and security risks of transport by high seas and railway.
4. Canadian supply made up for the continued decline in imports from several other major US suppliers.[6]

Remarkably, eight short years later, the strategic interests of the United States had shifted so completely that a similar project would be refused on the basis that it would "undercut America's global leadership" and reduce the leverage of the American president at the December 2015 climate change negotiations. The continental energy relationship was viewed as an afterthought in the decision, and the secretary of state acknowledged in passing that the decision might lead to a cooling of US–Canada relations and might affect Canadian co-operation on hemispheric issues and international security. The unstated qualifier was, "But, so what!"

Canada's own strategic interests have similarly changed, even if we have been slow to recognize it, and they obviously lie in developing new, ancillary markets elsewhere in the world. And we had better get on with it because, as the protectionist rhetoric surrounding the 2016 US presidential election cycle illustrated, the denial of a presidential permit for a new pipeline is far from the worst thing that could happen to Canada.

CHAPTER 6

Hydroelectricity and the North American Electricity Grid:
Canada's Defining Advantage

Hydroelectricity will undoubtedly be one of Canada's defining competitive advantages in tomorrow's energy world. We are already well known as global leaders in the development of hydro-electricity and are additionally blessed with an immense undeveloped resource base, much of which could be brought on stream in partnership with our American neighbours to green the North American electricity grid and accelerate the transition to a lower carbon economy.

Canada's major hydroelectric installations are among the most impressive infrastructure investments in our country. In 2010, I visited one of the best known of those installations, the Churchill Falls project in Labrador, with then-premier Danny Williams of Newfoundland and Labrador. He and I inspected the Churchill Falls Generating Station, known as the Upper Churchill, and also visited Muskrat Falls and Gull Island, which together comprise the Lower Churchill project that the Government of Newfoundland

and Labrador was then considering and which is under construction today.

The scale of the Upper Churchill hydro facility is difficult to convey. The power station itself is one of the very largest in the world, generating 5,428 megawatts (MW) of electricity when all its turbines are running. Remarkably, the Robert-Bourassa Generating Facility in northern Quebec is even larger. The control centre of the Churchill Falls station, which consists of a long underground chamber that has been carved out of the granite of the Canadian Shield, literally vibrates with raw energy as thousands of tonnes of water course downward almost 15 storeys, onto a long bank of turbines. Imagine that this single facility produces enough electricity to light more than five million homes, and it does so with a negligible carbon footprint.

Canadian hydroelectricity is also an important continental advantage. It already accounts for 38 percent of the electricity sold in Vermont, 18 percent in Maine and 6 percent in New York State. We also sell hydroelectricity into the Upper Midwest: 12 percent of Minnesota's and North Dakota's and 6 percent of Michigan's electricity comes from Canada. Most important, as the United States moves to decarbonize its electricity system, Canadian hydro stands as a ready solution.

Canadian Hydroelectricity Today

Over the past 10 years, I have spent a lot of time with Canada's environmental critics and have always delighted in pointing out that our country is one of the world's leaders in the production of carbon-free hydroelectricity. In fact, more than 80 percent of

Canada's electricity supply does *not* emit carbon. This is a remarkable achievement that never fails to shift the equities in any discussion, even with our most vocal international critics.

Canada's most outspoken climate change critics are from countries with much "dirtier" electricity infrastructure than ours. In fact, most of the industrialized world depends largely on burning coal. To be fair, other countries, such as France and Norway, have electricity systems that are not hydrocarbon-based. But for the most part, the world's industrial democracies and emerging economies burn a lot of coal. And while it is well and good to drive a Tesla, if the electricity used to charge that electric car comes from a coal-burning thermal electricity plant, then the vehicle is, in fact, as "dirty" as any other.

Hydroelectricity is a solution to that problem. Today, hydropower plants provide more than 16.5 percent of the world's electricity production, and Canada is the second-largest producer of hydroelectricity in the world, ranking only behind China. In 2014, our country produced 387 terawatts (trillion watts) of hydroelectricity, accounting for more than 10 percent of the world's production. The majority of that Canadian production originates in Quebec (200 terawatts), but British Columbia (54 terawatts), Newfoundland and Labrador (38 terawatts) and Manitoba (34 terawatts) are all important producers of hydroelectricity.

Hydroelectricity is complex and expensive to develop. It represents a multi-generational investment, and the Canadian provinces that have made the difficult decisions to develop their resource base deserve applause for their tenacity and vision. Quebec, Manitoba and British Columbia are all now accruing the benefits of massive hydroelectric projects. Eventually, Newfoundland and Labrador will as well. Most hydro projects were controversial in their day, and all were economically challenging when the investment decisions were made. Over the longer term, hydroelectricity has proven to be a shrewd investment. As an illustration, the major cities in North America with the cheapest electricity are Montreal, Vancouver and Winnipeg, each of which benefits from hydroelectric supply sources that have been paid for and amortized over successive generations. This investment takes vision and commitment, as the history of hydroelectricity demonstrates.

The Legacy of Canadian Hydroelectricity

The story of Canada's hydroelectricity industry is a remarkable one that most Canadians don't know. It all began with the Ottawa Electric Light Company at Chaudière Falls in 1881, a relatively small-scale operation that generated power for municipal and local industry use.[1] Only four years later, Quebec's first hydro-powered electricity generation began with the commissioning of the Sault Montmorency power station, which was used to power street lamps in Quebec City.[2] The output of these water-powered facilities was limited by the capacity of small-scale generating facilities, which depended on demand and the largely unpredictable flow of water.

Hydro-power development expanded throughout Canada, though not uniformly in scale. In 1888, the first hydro plant in British Columbia was opened by the Nanaimo Electric Light, Power and Heating Co.[3] Water was first diverted from Niagara Falls for electricity purposes in 1893; two 1,000 horsepower units generated 2,200 kilowatts to power the Queenston-Chippawa electric railway.[4] Niagara is now, of course, a major hub for national and international hydro-power production.

A major development in hydro power in Canada came with the first long-distance transmission of hydroelectricity, in 1897. Noted as the first transmission of its kind in the entire British Empire, power was successfully transmitted from Saint-Narcisse to Trois-Rivières along the Batiscan River in Quebec, a distance of 35 kilometres.[5] Just two years later, DeCew Falls 1 in St. Catharines, Ontario, delivered power at 22,500 volts over double that distance.[6] These developments in transmission line engineering led to more remote site build-outs and a proliferation of long-distance transmission lines.

By the early 1900s, all provinces except Prince Edward Island and Saskatchewan had established significant hydroelectric generation capacity. By 1950, hydroelectric power stations supplied more than 90 percent of the country's electricity generation— driven by skyrocketing demand for electricity as the country urbanized, industrialized and modernized. In the time since the 1960s, hydroelectricity's share of Canada's total generating capacity has declined, falling to about 60 percent in 1976, where it still is today. This decline can be attributed to rising transmission prices due to increasingly large distances between hydro stations and major population centres, as well as to the cost advantage of fossil fuel–fired thermal electric generation.

Interestingly, Canada does not have a national electricity grid. The development of our electricity system has instead tracked the geography and demography of the US and Canada and consists of four distinct regional grids, each aligned on a north–south, as opposed to an east–west, axis. Not surprisingly, the development of Canada's hydroelectric resources was accompanied by almost constant debate between the provincial and federal governments over whether Canada would have a national power grid, who would regulate it and where the surplus power would go.

Quebec and Ottawa stood on opposite sides of that debate, and the province was successful in its opposition to Prime Minister John Diefenbaker's plan to create a national power grid. In a letter explaining his refusal to participate in Diefenbaker's gathering of industry and provincial stakeholders to discuss the feasibility of a national grid, Quebec premier Jean Lesage made his province's position expressly known. The premier recognized the importance of discussing such a grid but refused to participate "under the tutelage of the federal government."[7]

The Liberal government of Prime Minister Lester Pearson took a decidedly more North American approach to the development of Canadian hydroelectricity. The pursuit of a national power policy was set aside in 1963, in favour of higher integration with US networks.[8] The continental opportunities that this presented fuelled the construction of some of the largest hydro plants in Canada, especially in the province of Quebec.

The Hydro-Québec Story

Hydro-Québec is one of Canada's most remarkable Crown corporations. The corporation was created in 1944, when the Quebec government established the Québec Hydro-Electric Commission, now known as Hydro-Québec, by expropriating the Montreal Light, Heat & Power (MLH&P) Company. Realizing it needed much more than the 600 megawatts produced by the MLH&P generating facility, Hydro-Québec began a significant period of growth. It expanded the Beauharnois facility in 1948, then built the Bersimis-1 and Bersimis-2 generating stations in the 1950s, followed by the Carillon generating station (1959–64).

Quebec's Quiet Revolution began in 1960 with Jean Lesage's Liberal government. Lesage named one of his new "Dream Team" members of the National Assembly to Cabinet, the 38-year-old René Lévesque, making him minister of hydroelectric resources and public works, then minister of natural resources. It was during his tenure in the Lesage government that Hydro-Québec greatly expanded. In the 1962 election campaign, the Liberals' slogan was *maîtres chez nous*—masters in our own house. One of the key planks was to nationalize the remaining 11 private or municipal electric companies, which were seen as being controlled by outside interests that were gouging consumers. Only a few weeks after the re-election of the Lesage government, Hydro-Québec purchased the remaining electricity operators—some might say it was a hostile takeover, but at least they were bought for slightly above their market value. This is how Hydro-Québec "nationalized" the electricity-generation system in Quebec.

In the years that followed, Hydro-Québec expanded dramatically, building massive new hydro projects along Quebec's North Shore—the Manicouagan-Outardes complex of seven generating stations—which included building the largest dam in the world: the 1,314-metre-wide (4,311 feet) Daniel-Johnson Dam. The corporation also led the way in the design and construction of long-distance transmission lines, building the first 735-kilovolt lines in 1965 to transmit power over very long distances.

René Lévesque eventually left the Liberal Party and founded the Parti Québécois in 1968, but the Liberals under Robert Bourassa continued to expand Quebec's hydro potential. In 1971, Bourassa announced the construction of a 10,000-megawatt hydroelectric complex in the James Bay area, on the La Grande River, which would have four generating stations: LG-1, LG-2, LG-3 and LG-4. The LG-2 generating station, inaugurated in 1979 and producing 5,616 megawatts, is the most powerful in the world.

A pause in new developments in the 1990s resulted from environmental and First Nation issues. But after the province signed *La Paix des Braves* with the Quebec Cree Nation in 2002, projects in the James Bay area resumed. More recently, La Romaine on the north coast of the St. Lawrence, near Havre-Saint-Pierre, was started in 2009; the project will add more than 1,500 megawatts of clean power.

Hydro-Québec is a public corporation that reported $13.6 billion in revenues and a net profit of $3.4 billion in 2014. Remarkably, 99 percent of all the electricity produced by the corporation—almost every single one of the 165 TWh of power it sold to customers—comes from renewable sources. The corporation has trained and developed world class engineers, built the fourth-largest hydroelectricity generation capacity in the world and exported clean energy into the United States. It is another great story of our country's industrial development—and also about our energy and environmental future.

The Lower Churchill Story

Newfoundland and Labrador is also pursuing a future as a North American powerhouse in hydroelectricity.

The Churchill Falls generating station in Labrador is also one of the world's largest. It was commissioned in 1967, following an acrimonious commercial dispute between Newfoundland on the one hand and Quebec on the other. The boundary between Labrador and Quebec has long been disputed. However, the commercial disagreement between the two provinces over the Churchill Falls project finds its origin in the bitter negotiations to save the project from bankruptcy in the late 1960s.

Those negotiations saw Hydro-Québec, which had been a minor partner in the development, skilfully out-negotiate the project developer Brinco, as the project teetered on the edge of bankruptcy. Brinco maintained majority ownership of the Upper Churchill facility. However, its corporate successor, Nalcor (in effect, the Province of Newfoundland and Labrador), was saddled with long-term operational agreements that severely disadvantaged it and favoured Hydro-Québec. Newfoundlanders consider those contracts unconscionable, but the agreements do not expire until 2041, running 65 years. Despite years of unsuccessful court proceedings and political wrangling, the contracts remain in force, effectively unchanged since they were negotiated.

I don't intend to get into the merits of this commercial dispute. It is almost certainly the most bitter and corrosive provincial disagreement in our confederation and will be resolved only when the existing contracts expire in 2041, at which point Newfoundland and Labrador will assume full control of a sizable portion of North America's cleanest and cheapest hydroelectricity. Newfoundland and Labrador, once our poorest province, will in due course be one of our richest.

Newfoundland and Labrador is also now in the midst of the construction of the Lower Churchill project at Muskrat Falls. It consists of both a hydroelectric project and the associated transmission infrastructure linking Atlantic Canada's electricity grid and ultimately affording access to the northeastern American marketplace. The Lower Churchill, arguably the best undeveloped hydroelectric source in North America, consists of two phases. Muskrat Falls, which is now under construction, will be an 824-megawatt generating facility; and Gull Island, which will be constructed as a second phase, will add an additional 2,250 megawatts of generating capacity. The first phase of construction also includes the so-called Labrador Island Link that will transmit power from Newfoundland and Labrador to Nova Scotia. Nalcor is responsible for the construction of the Muskrat Falls dam and generating facility, as well as the Labrador Island Link. The Maritime Link will be constructed by Emera Inc., Nova Scotia's publicly controlled electricity provider.

The entire project represents a courageous step forward by the Governments of Newfoundland and Labrador and Nova Scotia, and complex commercial off-take arrangements between the two provinces underpin the project. The green credentials of the project speak for themselves: The Maritime Link will bring more than 3,000 megawatts of carbon-free electricity onto the North American grid—the equivalent of taking 3.2 million cars off the road each year. It will ensure that Atlantic Canada has one of the greenest electricity systems in the world.

The linkage into the North American grid has added significantly to the cost of the project. Both the Labrador Island Link and the Maritime Link are challenging and expensive. They do, however, solve the essential problem that Newfoundland and Labrador has struggled with since the 1970s—namely its inability to reach an agreement with Hydro-Québec to export power from the Lower Churchill across Quebec. The two Atlantic links resolve that stalemate and free Newfoundland and Labrador to pursue its own commercial opportunities in the Canadian and American marketplace. Moreover, the presence of those connections will substantially improve the negotiating position of Newfoundland and Labrador with Quebec as the off-take agreements on the Upper Churchill wind down through to their expiry in 2041.

A $7 billion federal loan guarantee underpins the entire Lower Churchill project. The project was readily financed by Nalcor, accessing international debt markets through Canadian banks. And although the project may well have been financeable at a higher cost without the loan guarantee, the attractiveness of a Canadian "sovereign assurance" was compelling to the markets. Prime Minister Harper's decision to make a federal loan guarantee available to advance the Lower Churchill will stand the test of time as one of the most significant decisions of his administration.

British Columbia and Manitoba

Having described some of the history and more recent projects in eastern provinces of Canada, I would be remiss if I skipped the two western provinces leading in the generation of electricity from hydro power.

Manitoba Hydro today operates 15 hydroelectric facilities on the Saskatchewan, Winnipeg, Burntwood, Laurie and Nelson rivers as well as two thermal and four diesel generating stations together producing more than 33.2 TWh of electricity. The early power companies were private entities. The Winnipeg Gas Company was incorporated in 1873 to provide gas lighting to the streets of that city.[9] A few years later, in 1880, the Manitoba Electric & Gas Light Company was incorporated by the Province of

Manitoba to "supply light and heat in Manitoba by gas, electricity or other means."[10]

The first hydroelectric generating station in Manitoba was built in 1900 on the Little Saskatchewan River by the Brandon Electric Light Company to service the town of Brandon. Private interests led many other projects such as this one. The use of electricity expanded and smaller communities wanted to be serviced, but private firms had little incentive to deploy that kind of capital for little profit and so the province began taking over this new "public good." In 1916, Manitoba established the Manitoba Power Commission (MPC) to bring electricity to communities outside of Winnipeg; during the 1920s, more than 30 towns and villages were electrified.

By 1955 only three utilities remained in the province, and in 1961 Manitoba Hydro was created with the purpose of providing electricity to Manitobans. Manitoba Hydro employs 6,500 people in its 21 facilities plus headquarters; it exports $500 million worth of electricity to the United States, mainly into Minnesota and Wisconsin.

British Columbia also created a Crown corporation to generate, purchase, distribute and sell electricity in 1961—the same year as Manitoba did. The British Columbia Hydro and Power Authority—or simply BC Hydro—operates 31 hydroelectric generating stations and three natural gas–fuelled thermal power plants. About 92 percent of BC's electricity is produced by hydroelectric generating stations for the most part situated on the Columbia and Peace rivers. British Columbia also has two other utilities. The City of New Westminster runs its own electric utility, and the Kootenay region is served by Fortis, BC.

The first hydroelectricity was produced by the Buntzen Powerhouse at Buntzen Lake, just north of Coquitlam, in 1904. Most facilities were built between the 1940s and 60s, with the Revelstoke Dam in 1984 being the newest (until BC Hydro completes the "Site C Clean Energy Project" (Site C) on the Peace River in northeast BC, in 2024).

Many independent power producers in British Columbia have smaller-scale projects with which BC Hydro has 105 Electricity Purchase Agreements (EPAs)—everything from "run of river" generation or non-storage hydro, to biomass, biogas, municipal solid waste and gas thermal. Together, these projects represent 18,902 gigawatt hours of annual supply, which is about 25 percent of British Columbia's domestic supply.

All this adds up to some impressive statistics: Canada is the second-largest producer of hydroelectricity in the world, and that clean, zero-emission form of energy accounts for 60 percent of this country's electricity. We have the potential to build a lot more hydroelectric capacity that could be harnessed to our energy and environmental advantage, particularly with our southern neighbour (which still produces 33 percent of its electricity from coal, 33 percent from natural gas, and only 6 percent from hydro power).

The 2015 US Quadrennial Energy Review

In January 2014, President Barack Obama issued a Presidential Memorandum directing his entire administration to participate in a Quadrennial Energy Review (QER). This followed the President's Climate Action Plan of 2013, also in response to a recommendation by the President's Council of Advisors on Science and Technology, to conduct an administration-wide QER that would enable the federal government to translate policy goals into a set of evidence-based executive actions, legislative proposals and budget items for federal investments. The exercise was jointly coordinated by the White House's Domestic Policy Council and the Office of Science and Technology Policy, with support from the Department of Energy.

What transpires from this QER is the recognition that the United States should do more to co-operate with Canada and Mexico in ensuring its energy security objectives, as well as enhancing the reliability of the complex US energy system.

How Canada Fits into a North American Electricity Policy

Canada's capacity to generate hydroelectricity is a defining North American advantage. We have excelled at the delivery of hydro-electricity into the American marketplace, and new continental opportunities will continue to unfold as the United States seeks to wean itself from the rampant burning of coal. The North American electricity network is the world's largest and safest system of production, transmission and distribution, with more than 340,000 kilometres of high-voltage transmission lines traversing the continent.

The system is structured around four synchronized interconnections, which are oriented, at least from a Canadian perspective, on a north–south axis, facilitating the delivery of large volumes of Canadian hydroelectricity into the US marketplace. Thus, Quebec achieves ready access to the northeastern seaboard of the United States; similarly, British Columbia and Manitoba are able to access western and Midwestern American markets, respectively.

Canada does not have a national electricity grid and is unlikely to develop one in the foreseeable future because electrons follow demand and population, so a national grid crossing the largely uninhabited expanse of the Canadian Shield would be of doubtful merit. Having said that, continued regional integration of the North American system is a highly desirable outcome—and that includes the Canadian side of the border. The Governments of Quebec and Ontario, under the leadership of Premiers Kathleen Wynne and Philippe Couillard, are to be commended for their 2015 initiative to move clean Quebec hydroelectricity into the Ontario marketplace. Alberta and Saskatchewan, which both have limited hydro potential, would similarly benefit from the movement of cleaner electrons into their provinces from British Columbia and Manitoba.

What is truly exciting, however, is the untapped potential lying before us. Canada has the capacity to bring more than 25,000 megawatts of hydroelectricity onto the North American grid over the next 20 years, significantly greening the continent's electricity grid. The $7 billion Lower Churchill project represents the first such expansion, but it is by no means the only one. BC Hydro is now aggressively pursuing the construction of the 1,100-megawatt Site C project. Manitoba Hydro has the ability to pursue the 1,485-megawatt Conawapa project, depending primarily on its ability to access markets in the American Midwest and in Alberta and Saskatchewan. In Alberta, private sector proponents are pursuing that province's only truly significant hydro possibility, the Slave River project, which has the potential to deliver 1,200 megawatts of "run of the river" hydroelectricity into the oil sands region. And Quebec, not to be left behind, has the potential to develop the Mécatina project, following on its development of the

Romaine-2 and Eastmain 1-A projects. All told, these megaprojects (which I referred to as "nation-building infrastructure" in several speeches) represent the largest potential for cleaner, greener electricity on the North American continent. We should be pursuing them more aggressively as a matter of national vision.

In the short-to-intermediate time frame, however, the economics of these projects are challenged by the market dynamic of low natural gas prices. It is less expensive today to construct new power plants that burn natural gas rather than coal, and this is exactly what has happened in the United States. Generators have begun to reduce their dependency on coal by converting existing facilities to natural gas, moving away from the historic role of natural gas as a peaking fuel. Paradoxically, the opposite has happened in Europe, where natural gas prices are much higher—causing generators to expand the use of coal quite markedly.

For Canada (and all of North America), however, it is the longer-term potential that is important, and Canadian hydro represents a profound continental advantage. Natural gas is cleaner than coal to be sure, but hydro emits no carbon whatsoever. Moreover, among the range of alternative renewables, hydro has the advantage of dependability and storability. This is a matter that I discussed on several occasions with Steven Chu, the US energy secretary and Nobel Prize–winning physicist. If you view the North American electricity system as a continental whole and analyze our collective resource endowment as a collective opportunity, then Canadian hydro is indeed compelling. Not only does it afford cleaner electricity but, when coupled with on-stream storage capacity, it also provides predictability and dependability. In effect, a significant portion of North America's electricity needs can be satisfied by Canadian water, which can be stored and drawn on when required for baseload consumption. Natural gas remains available for peaking purposes and to augment solar- and wind-power generation. It is important to note that this is not the stuff of abstract science. Indeed, the very shrewd and immensely lucrative business model of Hydro-Québec has been based on recognition of this reality for several generations and it is, in effect, where Newfoundland and Labrador is now also headed.

There are real environmental costs associated with large-scale hydro projects. We must ensure that the costs and benefits of hydro projects are carefully weighed through a sound regulatory process. Our decisions must be based on science, and we need to be mindful of the overall ecological consequences of damming rivers and flooding valleys. But we must also accept that, if we forgo certain choices, there are consequences to economic progress and to the advancement of civilization. If the reduction of carbon emission is to be an imperative, as it must be, then we must make progress where we can. Those in the environmental movement who advocate that we shut down existing coal plants, avoid the consumption of hydrocarbons such as oil and natural gas, and eschew nuclear and hydro because of the attendant environmental risks are completely unrealistic. Amid the array of available alternatives, large-scale Canadian hydro must be part of the solution.

With that in mind, imagine a customized Canadian hydro plan that would serve the best interests of regional hydro producers in this country, as well as serve consumers throughout North America. With 63 percent of our electricity being generated from hydro, it is well within our grasp to become a world leader in clean energy—Quebec already is—producing 96 percent of its electricity from hydro power. Given also that more than half of Canada's hydroelectricity is generated in Quebec and that the province has considerable expertise in executing and financing complex energy projects, it is certainly a leading voice in the national conversation we need to have about our approach to changing energy markets. Quebec is also particularly well-positioned to take advantage of the changes in the continental game.

In 2012, Canada passed legislation that will see the use of coal phased out as older power plants are retired over time. But south of the border, one-third of GHG (greenhouse gas) emissions are from coal-fired power generators. The high-demand, high-population region of New England is a prime example of the huge potential for Canada that still exists in the continental electricity market. Today, more than half of New England's electricity comes from burning fossil fuels, with just about 15 percent coming from hydro and renewables. The grid for distributing that power also needs to be upgraded. If the Canadian provinces that produce the lion's share of hydroelectricity—British Columbia, Manitoba, Ontario, Quebec, and Newfoundland and Labrador—develop a co-operative strategy, this is precisely the sort of opportunity from which they could all benefit. It would be all the more beneficial if they could as well find a way to agree on a long-term pricing structure for their customers. Factoring in the jobs that would be created by infrastructure related to pipelines and oil sands, we're talking about a real economic renaissance for this country.

The evidence of that is powerful. Research conducted by the Canadian Imperial Bank of Commerce and published in a report entitled *Energizing Infrastructure* quantifies the economic ripple effect from the billions of dollars earmarked for capital investment in Canada's hydroelectricity sector over the next 20 years. Including the $50 billion in projects by the end of this decade, current expansion plans for capacity, transmission and distribution in Canada ring in at close to $295 billion. CIBC economists calculate that for every $1 billion investment in the sector, 1,100 jobs are created. If you do the math, we're talking about 320,000 jobs building electricity infrastructure over the next two decades. It's hard to imagine a more compelling case for working together—especially when the current unemployment rate is stuck at about 7 percent nationally and at over 10 percent in Calgary as I write this.

Quebec's export of hydroelectricity already brings in well over a billion dollars a year, and plans to develop the sector's potential could increase that figure significantly over the next few years. The Quebec government's vision of Le Plan Nord will see an additional 3,500 megawatts (MW) added to the province's already-astounding 35,000 MW of existing hydro-generating capacity. By way of context, total electricity generation from all sources—including coal—among the six-state New England region is 32,000 MW. It means Hydro-Québec alone has more hydro capacity than New England's total electricity generation from all sources combined. That represents tremendous economic potential—all the more if you factor in the jobs that are created as a result of this growth.

But whether it is oil, gas, hydro power—or any other commodity for that matter—market access remains the key issue. And in both eastern and western Canada, that reality is complicated by the fact that we have just a single market. Almost 99 percent of our energy exports are sold into the United States.

For example, despite NAFTA, Canada's access to the power market in the northeastern United States has become increasingly complicated by the implementation of renewable portfolio standards. These standards are intended to proactively nurture the development of homegrown green energy options—which is certainly a commendable objective. But the standards also have the effect of limiting imports of lower-cost, clean power from Canada, which drives up long-term prices for American consumers at the same time as it curtails the development of the export infrastructure that would transport it.

There are also more traditional territorial issues, such as the ongoing dispute in New Hampshire over the proposed 290 kilometre Northern Pass power line, a line that would allow an additional 1,200 MW of hydro to move from the Quebec border to Deerfield, Massachusetts. New Hampshire, despite its public commitment to reduce its reliance on coal-fired electricity, isn't all that keen to help out with its neighbour's energy agenda.

In the face of all this, Canadians must work together to build new energy-trading relationships and look at existing ones with a fresh, innovative eye. We must develop the discipline to see beyond short-term markets when assessing long-term opportunities—something that doesn't come naturally to a country of commodity traders and interprovincial challenges. On top of all that, we also need a healthier sense of urgency. The reconfiguration of the continental energy market on which Canada has relied so completely for so long is happening fast.

As abundant, affordable, clean and reliable hydroelectricity becomes an increasingly dominant source of supply, it will in turn foster the competitive advantage of lower operating costs for a range of businesses. That drives further growth, further demand, and markets robust and broad enough to support both shared and individual plans. Furthermore, Canada benefits to no small extent from the increased export of hydroelectricity on a strictly environmental basis. Given that airborne pollutants don't stop at the border, reducing the use of coal and reducing GHG emissions would improve North American air quality.

Few countries are within reach of such immense economic or environmental opportunity. If we recognize this fact, if we're smart about it, we can build our country, create new jobs and sustain a long-term economic stimulus that will help ensure prosperity for future generations. That's not to say that projects on the scale required are without setbacks or risk. That's all the more true at a time when international markets create unforeseeable variables and volatility. To be successful, Canada needs to control what it can. That means domestic agreement on a common purpose, and commitment to a shared vision of what this country can be.

Quebeckers already understand this process. In the early 1970s, the Government of Quebec and business leaders identified the massive potential of the untapped energy resources in the north of the province—and they took a bet on their ability to develop it. James Bay is a testament to the fact that vision and determination can prevail. The hard work done on that project served as a template for future development and helped to frame the negotiations required to get resource development in northern Quebec off the ground. Canada is exceptionally well-equipped to face the challenges—and capitalize on the opportunities—that lie ahead. One of the resources we sometimes forget to value fully is the ingenuity and determination of Canadians.

A North American "Grand Bargain" on Hydroelectricity

Canada's interests and those of our American neighbours intersect when it comes to large-scale Canadian hydro. One of the best solutions to the carbon reduction challenges we face is Canadian hydro, and we should be working together with the United States to develop renewable portfolio standards and transmission infrastructure that will achieve exactly that. Time will tell whether we are visionary enough to do so.

The US–Canada electricity grid is already highly integrated as we export about 60 terawatt hours (TWh) of electricity per year to the United States and import about 12 TWh, according to the latest data from Canada's National Energy Board.[11] What is needed is political will at the most senior level to push the file forward.

The Canadian Electricity Association was asked to provide comments to the US Department of Energy as it prepared the groundwork for the *Quadrennial Energy Review*. It made six recommendations:

1. As a fundamental principle of policy, recognize the interdependency of the U.S. and Canadian segments of the larger North American grid;
2. Avoid erecting barriers that may inhibit inter-jurisdictional electricity trade;
3. Update and enhance the efficiency of the U.S. permitting process for cross-border electricity infrastructure and trade;
4. Affirm and support the existing framework in place for the development of mandatory electric reliability standards for the North American grid;
5. Recommend actions to enhance public–private sector, as well as government-to-government coordination and sharing of timely and actionable threat information; and
6. Expand existing U.S.–Canada programs to support research, development and/or demonstration of innovative grid modernization technologies.[12]

The 2015 QER does recognize that the Canada–US energy relationship is "highly intertwined" generally and that "the electricity systems of the United States and Canada are fully interconnected" and benefit from a "seamless border"[13]—essentially adopting the CEA's first recommendation. The policy recommendations emanating from the 2015 QER also support the CEA's recommendations 5 and 6. The opportunities lie in enhancing inter-jurisdictional electricity trade, permitting more vital infrastructure projects and ensuring common reliability standards.

I would add another recommendation to those proposed by the CEA: because President Obama's Clean Power Plan explicitly permits states and utilities to import Canadian electricity in order to meet the United States' new emission targets, the six cross-border electricity transmission projects currently awaiting the presidential approval process should be authorized.

I believe that the Canadian government would be willing to entertain these recommendations. We will have to wait and see how President Trump might approach them, but I can assure you that these ideas are being discussed in Washington, DC, today. The groundwork is prepared. Now decisions must follow.

PART THREE

The Environment as Canada's Global Competitive Advantage

CHAPTER 7

*Canada's Bumpy Road from Kyoto to Paris: The Dangers of
Signing International Treaties We Cannot Live Up To*

I decided to write this book while I was in Copenhagen, Denmark, in December 2009, representing Canada at the United Nations Climate Change Conference—the so-called Copenhagen COP 15. I was Canada's minister of the environment and, while I proudly represented Canada at Copenhagen, I was also fully aware that few Canadians had represented our country abroad under more adverse circumstances. That reality had been clear to me since October 2008, when Prime Minister Stephen Harper informed me at the PM's residence at Harrington Lake that I was to become Canada's new environment minister.

Copenhagen marked an international watershed because it marked the effective end of the 1997 Kyoto Protocol and the absence of any binding global consensus to replace it. In a sense, Copenhagen signalled the painful, although essential, break from the Kyoto Protocol to a more enduring agreement, which the 2015 Paris Agreement hopefully represents. Viewed through that prism, Canada's own struggles with the complicated economic and public policy issues surrounding climate change no longer seemed unique. But for Canada, the Kyoto Protocol and the onerous targets that we agreed to a decade previously were a particular blunder—one that would have disastrous implications, both domestically and internationally.

It was, however, at Copenhagen that I first saw an opportunity for Canada to move beyond the Kyoto Protocol. I recognized that Canada would need environment and climate policies that matched the breadth and ambition of our objectives as an energy producer. In the days after Copenhagen, I began to articulate the notion that, if Canada was to have a future in the energy business, we would also need to excel in the business of the environment—they are flip sides of the same coin. As far as the rest of the world was concerned, Canada's stature as a major industrial democracy and our status as a major energy producer attracted concomitant responsibilities toward the environment and the planet. Copenhagen demonstrated that it would be folly to attempt the one without the other.

COP 15 also illustrated that most of the rest of the world had been challenged to get their domestic houses in order, with the result that Canada would be given a second chance to do so. Subsequent events, including market developments here in North America, have borne out that view.

The Hypocrisy of Kyoto

The Kyoto Protocol was signed by Canada in 1997 and subsequently ratified in Parliament in 2002. The agreement was ambitious, but it was flawed because the only parties that were required to reduce their emissions were a handful of affluent nations, known as the Annex II countries. The United States may as well not have been part of that annex because it had refused to ratify the protocol or take on greenhouse gas (GHG) reduction obligations under it. In the result, countries such as Canada accepted onerous responsibilities to reduce their emissions, even though the world's largest carbon emitters, including the United States, China and India, had no such obligations.

Canada compounded its problem under the Kyoto Protocol by agreeing to a reduction commitment that was arguably the most onerous of any signatory. Under the treaty, Canada agreed to reduce its GHG emissions by 2012, by a full 6 percent below its 1990 level of 461 megatonnes. In actual fact, in the time between the base year of 1990 and 2008, Canada's emissions actually grew by some 24 percent, meaning that, by the time of the Copenhagen meeting, Canada would need to reduce its carbon emissions by a full 30 percent to meet the Kyoto target. By 2009 then, as the gulf between Canada's actual emissions and our Kyoto target widened absurdly, Canada's position at the climate change table became exceedingly difficult.

Canada's position as a signatory to the Kyoto Protocol was always untenable because we had agreed to reduction targets that were completely unachievable. I use the term "unachievable" knowing that there are those who differ in that opinion. But the passage of time has made it clear that Canada's Kyoto targets reflected a level of ambition and cost that was well beyond what Canadians or their government (either Liberal or Conservative) were prepared to accept. In fact, we know now that the Canadian Liberal government of the day knew that the Kyoto commitment was unachievable when it signed it.[1]

In some ways, Jean Chrétien was on the right track in wanting to build on Canada's environmental credentials. In the 1980s and 90s, the strength of Canada's brand reflected our environmental leadership both domestically and internationally, and the commitment of Canadians to sound environmental stewardship, responsible regulation, conservation and the protection of natural spaces was well known and almost universally respected. Canadians, led by Maurice Strong, served as the driving force behind the original Earth Summit, in Rio de Janeiro in 1992, and were seen as leaders in identifying global environmental risks and in helping forge collective responses.

There are good reasons why it was impossible for Canada to achieve the reductions in GHG emissions contemplated under Kyoto. For starters, our country is vast and sparsely populated, with a harsh northern climate, an energy-intensive economy and a relatively new industrial structure. Our economic growth rates and immigration rates were also quite robust during the time between 1990 and 2012, especially so when compared with many other Western democracies. Most important, at the very moment Canada signed the Kyoto Protocol, the production of oil from Canada's oil sands began its inexorable climb from 527,000 barrels per day to its current level of 2.4 million barrels per day. Achieving carbon reductions of 6 percent below a 1990 base year, in such circumstances, was impossible. Frankly, taking on a binding international obligation to do that would only risk Canada's environmental reputation. In the years that followed, that is exactly what happened as Canada's status diminished steadily from that of an environmental leader to that of a laggard and, even worse, a country that could not be taken at its word.

Canada's decision to bind itself internationally to an emission target that was unattainable, economically or politically, would prove a serious diplomatic mistake, ultimately damaging our international stature. Sadly, it would also drive deep wedges into Canadian society, pitting Canadians against one another over the environment. By October 2008, when I became the environment minister, Canada's reputation as a dogged recalcitrant under the Kyoto Protocol accompanied us to every climate change discussion anywhere in the world. In fact, by 2008 even the Americans, who had shrewdly declined to ratify Kyoto and were the world's largest greenhouse gas emitter, were guarded about their association with Canada.

The equally impossible task of extracting Canada from those obligations, even as the international consensus surrounding the protocol crumbled, fell to the Harper government. In 2006, then–environment minister Rona Ambrose was forced to advise the international community at COP 12 in Nairobi that Canada could not fulfill its Kyoto targets. A year later, at COP 13 in Bali, the next environment minister, John Baird, unapologetically disclosed that Canada's own domestic targets would remain modest and that the government would not adhere to another Kyoto construct by purchasing "hot air credits" to feign compliance. Canada's role as the reluctant democracy at the climate change table was by then fully vested.

Poznań 2008

By the time I arrived at COP 14 in Poznań, Poland, in December 2008, Canada had isolated itself internationally as the only respected democracy that had voluntarily agreed to a Kyoto target, subsequently renounced it, and refused to adhere to the sanctioned method of achieving compliance, namely the purchase of credits. We had, in all but name, withdrawn from the Kyoto Protocol. The unenviable task of actually withdrawing would be left to the hapless environment minister, Peter Kent, in Durban in 2011. It was a step that I refused to countenance during my time as minister.

When I arrived in Poznań, the Kyoto Protocol, and Canada's performance under that agreement, had become the most divisive and politically damaging issue facing the Harper government. Poznań proved therefore to be a challenge, especially for someone who was an avid conservationist and proud of the country's record of environmental accomplishment.

Poznań represented a beginning in our attempts to reassert Canada's place at the climate change table. My movements through the maw of 12,000 attendees were carefully managed, and we avoided most of the public humiliation associated with spectacles like the "Fossil Awards." We held back the withering media of previous COP meetings and were able to initiate a dialogue with the many young Canadians and Canadian environmental non-governmental organizations that were present in Poznań. And we began the process of advancing Canada's position in bilateral meetings with the United States, New Zealand, Italy, Mexico, Denmark and South Africa. I forged a good relationship with Senator John Kerry, then the incoming chair of the American Senate Foreign Relations Committee, and I also experienced for the first time the intractable negotiating style of China's climate change negotiator, Xie Zhenhua.

In the year following Poznań, we prepared ourselves as best we were able for the onslaught of Copenhagen. Negotiating sessions, either of the United Nations Framework Convention on Climate Change (UNFCCC) itself or of the newly formed Major Economies Forum (MEF) struck by President Barack Obama in March 2009, were held somewhere in the world more or less weekly. We sought to engage at every level and at every opportunity, struggling to build relationships as we articulated Canada's position by providing context to explain that the country's demography, climate and industrial structure, coupled with the expansion of our energy industry, all meant that our carbon dioxide emission profile was unlike that of any other Western democracy and certainly unlike any other Kyoto Annex II signatory. In actual fact, Australia, Japan, Russia and Norway faced similar issues, but Australia and Norway had wisely insulated themselves from international criticism by their shrewd climate advocacy and diplomacy, begun years earlier. Canada, despite our best efforts, remained deeply isolated.

To be sure, we did make some progress. We adopted a constructive tone at the UNFCCC table and brought in an extremely able new Canadian negotiator, Michael Martin, to effect that change. We worked hard at building relationships with the new Obama administration, the MEF countries,[2] and the so-called Umbrella Group countries.[3] At the climate change working tables, we were respected for our technical competence and our diplomatic skills. In fact, by the time the Copenhagen Conference convened in December 2009, the chief UNFCCC official, Yvo de Boer, publicly rejected accusations that Canada was a divisive force at the table and described us as a "constructive partner."

We also worked hard to rebuild working relationships with Canada's provincial and territorial governments. Throughout the summer of 2009, I criss-crossed the country and met every premier and most of the environment and energy ministers to ensure we had good relationships in place. Those sessions also informed some of the content of this book. We encouraged provincial participation in Copenhagen and included the provinces in federal briefing sessions and even hosted them at the residence of Canada's ambassador to Denmark, Peter Lundy. A group of respected Canadians accompanied us to Copenhagen to provide advice. Our communications team was the best, and the officials from Environment Canada who accompanied us and staffed our war room in Denmark were the brightest young minds from the department. But it wasn't enough. In retrospect, nothing would have been enough.

Copenhagen 2009

When December 13, 2009, arrived, more than 33,000 conference participants, 40,000 activists and 126 heads of state and government crowded into the Bella Centre in Copenhagen. By then, the international consensus surrounding the Kyoto Protocol had corroded to the point where the very mention of Kyoto engendered bitterness. Moreover, in the week following our arrival, the Copenhagen process had itself ground to a halt and all but collapsed beneath its own weight—destroyed by the sheer magnitude of the demands, complexities and unrealistic expectations that it had attracted. The discord between developing countries and the developed world was palpable in every corridor.

The Copenhagen COP 15 conference did offer drama and great political theatre. To be clear, Canada was never the focus at Copenhagen—far too much else was going on, with 193 countries struggling to find consensus. There were, to be sure, moments of unique Canadian pathos, and the rancour surrounding Canada's performance under Kyoto was never far beneath the surface.

Canada was awarded several Fossil Awards—a mock "award" given daily by the Climate Action Network, an umbrella group of environmental organizations active on the issue of climate change, to countries it deems to be climate change laggards. Ontario's environment minister, John Gerretsen, chose Denmark as the setting to pit his province against the federal government and, more significantly, against Canada's energy industry. The premier of Quebec, my old friend Jean Charest, upped the climate change ante by raising Quebec's philosophical disagreement with the federal government and the constitutional question of whether Ottawa had the requisite authority to bind the Canadian provinces. And, not to be outdone, Toronto's mayor, David Miller, took it upon himself to accept a Fossil Award on Canada's behalf and, in so doing, staged a display of his own personal angst, declaring himself an "embarrassed Canadian."

Matters reached a crescendo midweek, when an unknown party released a fake press release ostensibly from the Government of Canada, announcing aggressive new emission reduction targets. A second hoax press release followed, as did staged media interviews, which were then posted on social media channels. At home, the CBC obtained leaked Cabinet documents outlining the government's draft working positions on emissions targets and reported on them nightly.

Just when it seemed that things could not get any worse, they did. On December 18, I was called out of the plenary session amid a furor resulting from an altercation that had erupted between the prime minister's press secretary, Dimitri Soudas, and Steven Guilbeault of the Quebec-based environmental organization Équiterre, over the hoax press releases. Their pushing match was, of course, captured on film and shared with Canadians back home—much like a good hockey fight highlight.

I managed through all this maintaining a sense of humour, knowing full well that it was just another day at the office if you are Canada's environment minister attending an international conference.

Prime Minister Harper had arrived for the leaders' session on December 17, and he and I spent the better part of a day-and-a-half as witnesses to the largest and arguably most disorganized grouping of leaders in world history. For much of December 18 we waited, engulfed in speculation and turmoil—as did most of the world—as the representatives of the world's two giant carbon emitters, President Obama and Chinese Premier Wen Jiabao, came to terms. Ultimately, an accord was produced and while it attracted much international opprobrium, it was almost certainly the most that could have been achieved given the rising frustration and ensuing discord among everyone in attendance.

Conclusion—Canada's Kyoto Lesson

Canada was never the focus of COP 15. We were a secondary player in the maelstrom of Copenhagen and the failure of the Kyoto Protocol, ensnared like everyone else in the politics, the dissent and the bitterness surrounding the failure of Kyoto and the collapse of expectations surrounding what would replace it.

The lessons for Canada are clear, but in the aftermath of the Paris COP 21 conference we are at risk of repeating the mistake of Kyoto. It will be impossible for Canada to reduce its

GHG emissions by the amount committed to in Paris—a 30 percent reduction of our 2005 GHG emissions by 2030. To put this number in perspective, the entire Canadian transportation sector—all the cars, trucks, airplanes, 18-wheelers, locomotives and marine vessels—account for 23 percent of Canadian GHG emissions. All the oil sands in Alberta represent less than 8 percent of GHG emissions in Canada.

In effect, we have again signed on to targets that cannot be met without extreme consequences for our economy, and the Government of Canada has set itself up for failure at future COP meetings and, therefore, more finger-pointing and rancour at Canada's "betrayal" of the planet. In five years—when it will become even more obvious that the Paris commitments won't be met—it follows that Canada will be forced to rely on the "internationally transferred mitigation measures" contained in Article VI of the Paris Agreement on Climate, to claim that it is helping to reduce GHG reductions in foreign countries. Put simply, being unable to meet our Paris targets, we will be forced to pay for climate change measures in developing countries to feign compliance.

Going forward we need to be smarter and more strategic than we were when we signed the Kyoto Protocol and the Paris climate agreement. We need to ensure that we can live up to the obligations that we take on and that we can excel as a global leader and a continental partner in showing actual progress, which is to say reducing GHG emissions. I am not arguing that Canada should ignore its climate change responsibilities, but I know from experience that the international community measures COP promises against actual performance, not rhetoric, and we need to measure the commitments that we take on against what is achievable.

Perhaps it isn't surprising, but the most respected countries at the international climate change table are not the ones that take on the highest targets. Instead, they are the countries that are thoughtful and deliver on their commitments, meeting their targets while also demonstrating diplomacy coupled with scientific and technical excellence in areas that advance the agenda of reducing emissions. Ironically, these are all areas in which we excel. Having now bound ourselves to a target that will ultimately prove impossible to meet, we had better step up those other efforts—dramatically. Canada needs the most skilled diplomats and trade negotiators at the table when we consummate those commitments. We need to protect our interests, because every other serious player at the international climate change table is doing exactly that.

The bottom line is that Canada is held to a higher standard when it comes to environmental performance, whether by the international community or by Canadians themselves. If the United States or China or Indonesia doesn't meet its international climate change obligations, these countries somehow get away with it. Canada does not have that luxury.

CHAPTER 8

A Strategic Approach to the Environment: How to Be
a Global Environmental Leader

O ne of the most spectacular places I have ever been to in
Canada is the Cirque of the Unclimbables in the Nahanni
National Park Reserve in the Northwest Territories. It was 2009,
and I remember wishing that my father could have seen it with me.
My father, to whom I attribute my love for the outdoors, had died
of amyotrophic lateral sclerosis (Lou Gehrig's Disease) in 2003,
before I became the minister responsible for Canada's national
parks or was even elected to the House of Commons. Some of my
earliest childhood memories are of camping trips with him into
the heart of the Canadian Shield in northern Ontario.

For many Canadians, a first camping trip with a parent or
grandparent marks the beginning of a special connection with the
outdoors. This is certainly true in my case and in the case of my
own children. Canadian childhood memories are formed around
open campfires in provincial parks, at summer cottages, and on
hikes and canoe and ski trips into the great outdoors that define
this beautiful country.

My first trip with my father was to Night Hawk Lake, east of South Porcupine, near Timmins in northern Ontario. We camped near the lake in a musty old canvas tent. I remember the smoke of burning logs around the campfire and my father introducing me to "bush tea." I recall darkness descending. It was a clear, starlit night and I can still sense the wonderment of being alone in the outdoors with my father: the humidity of the summer air; the stillness of the lake; and the impenetrable silence, broken periodically by the cry of a loon. I remember worrying about bears—and my father reassuring me that there were none. Thirty years later I would provide those same assurances to my daughters, not really knowing whether there were bears or not. But my own father did know, because, of course . . . he was my father.

Those memories, and similar ones held close by other Canadians, are part of who we are. We occupy the most rugged and beautiful landscape in the world. We are the stewards of it, and I have always refused to speak about Canada and our commitment to the environment as an apologist.

The Environment as a Canadian Competitive Advantage

In my view, the wonder of Canada's natural environment and how we manage it will be one of our country's defining competitive advantages in the 21st century. Unfortunately, we aren't there now. We need to do a great deal to reassert who we are and to re-establish a position of both national and global environmental leadership. Some will find my comments harsh, but Canada's current circumstances demand a strong voice.

Canada is an environmental leader in many ways. We are recognized as one of the most advanced countries when it comes to conservation and the preservation of important ecological spaces. We are a world leader in sustainable forest management practices. We are, in fact, conservationists on a scale not seen since the era of Theodore Roosevelt, the great American president.

We are strongly committed to science and have applied our commitment vigorously—for example, in the protection of the Arctic. As another illustration, our science-based approach to the control and regulation of dangerous chemicals attracts international acclaim. Our Chemicals Management Plan (CMP), created in 2006, has made Canada a world leader in assessing and managing risks associated with some 4,300 different chemicals used in industrial processes.

And we have distinguished ourselves by our bilateral and multilateral efforts to make the world a cleaner place. Canada and the United States have shown the world how nation states can work together to protect common air sheds and watersheds, through initiatives such as the Acid Rain Treaty and successive Great Lakes Water Quality agreements. Many have forgotten, too, that Canada has been a committed partner in the international climate change process since it began in 1992.

Unfortunately, much of our good work is overshadowed by the criticism we have sustained at home and abroad on account of the perceptions surrounding our approach to climate change.

I use the term "perception" because Canada's climate change efforts have been more robust than we have been credited with. In fact, as a consequence of provincial policies in Quebec, Ontario, Alberta and British Columbia, 87 percent of Canada's gross domestic product, comprising 85 percent of the population, is now subject to some form of carbon pricing. The comparable figure in the United States is less than 25 percent. The truth is that, with the exception of California, very few American states have shown the same high level of ambition as British Columbia, Ontario, Quebec and even Alberta when it comes to climate change mitigation measures. I know that in the corridors of power in such places as Washington, DC, the recognition is slowly dawning that Canada is leading, rather than lagging, on climate change policies.

But Canada's greatest current concern is the fact that our critics increasingly include those who have a say over investment decisions and over our ability to export and trade with the international community. Canada is one of the world's most trade-dependent countries, and our ability to continue to access capital markets and export markets depends, in part, on the willingness of others to do business with us.

Focusing on environmental policy isn't therefore exclusively a question of morality. Increasingly, it is an economic imperative. The wave of concern over climate change crested around the time of the global financial crisis of 2008–9, but those who are paying attention can see that the next wave is building. International efforts resulting from the Paris Agreement will begin to focus on the hard metrics of carbon emissions and the heavy lifting of carbon reductions. The next wave will come, and it will be highest when it crests on our shores. Canada needs to be ready for it.

There are many who question the necessity or the wisdom of Canada seriously pursuing climate change policies. There are those who quite rightly question the efficacy of what others have done. There are also those who doubt the science—although among them increasingly few younger Canadians. And there are, of course, those who want to avoid the costs associated with any measurable policy steps.

In response, I would suggest that we consider the economic cost of doing nothing. I am not speaking of the economic cost of climate change adaptation itself, although those costs are real. Rather, I am speaking to the economic reprisals that Canada increasingly risks from our trading partners—especially in energy trade.

If you do not believe me, consider the facts. The most significant expansion of Canada's energy export capacity into the United States marketplace, the Keystone XL Pipeline, was blocked because the president of the United States did not want to be associated with our climate change policies. The Northern Gateway Pipeline project, the most significant proposed expansion of Canada's export capacity into the Asia Pacific Basin, has been blocked by First Nations because of concerns over Canada's environment and climate change policies. The Kinder Morgan Trans Mountain project was also challenged on environmental grounds, not only by Aboriginal communities, but also by affected municipalities in British Columbia's Lower Mainland. And the country's most significant eastward pipeline expansion, affording access to the Atlantic Basin—the Energy East Pipeline—is also being challenged by First Nations and by municipal and provincial governments, again on environmental grounds. These are facts, not opinions.

Moreover, environmental activists, buoyed by their success on Keystone, have now shifted their attention from "proposed" Canadian pipelines to existing, operating Canadian pipelines and calling into question our ability to maintain our existing exports without further battles. One cannot assume these problems away.

Canada needs to respond on the very issue our critics are using to attack our continued prosperity—the environment.

We also face other obstructions. For a decade, Canada fought a running battle across the United States over American low carbon fuel standards and across Europe over the Fuel Quality Directive, both of which amounted to a direct challenge to our environmental policies.

Global investors, including large pension funds, insurance companies and sovereign wealth funds, are under increasing pressure to avoid corporate investments in countries that cannot demonstrate forward-looking climate change policies, including those in Canada's energy sector. And a number of national energy companies, including Statoil, Total and Shell, are in the process of divesting themselves of oil sands assets, in part because of the associated environmental criticism. Reductions in capital flows into Canada are now measurable. Can anyone seriously contend, in the face of all this, that Canada should do nothing?

Clearly it is time for a change of approach and for national leadership.

I do not suggest that it will be easy for Canada to reassert its position as a global leader on the environment, and I also acknowledge that it is going to take many years to get to where we want to be. Paris was an important first step and, while I am concerned about our ability to meet our Paris target, I do commend the federal government for regaining Canada's international footing.

However, if I learned nothing else during my two years at the international climate change table, it is that climate change activism operates at two very separate levels. The first is the aspirational or philosophical level, where agreement is always possible; the second is the practical level of detailed reductions of carbon emissions, which is extraordinarily difficult—and frankly impossible—without real societal cost. Paris marked an important aspirational agreement—the world came together and reached a consensus that we want to materially reduce emissions. Now the hard part: the back-breaking detail of how, by whom and at what cost!

The Challenge of Canada's GHG Emissions

Canada's position on climate change is inherently challenging. We are one of the world's most successful industrial democracies, but our economy is still largely resource-based, with an emission profile that bears striking similarities to that of some of the emerging economies. This is not because we are bad people. It is because we have enjoyed higher economic growth rates than most of the developed world and because we are, in part, dependent on primary-resource industries that are heavy consumers of energy. Much of our industrial base is also new and reasonably efficient, and does not include obvious candidates for carbon reductions.

As noted in previous chapters, we are not just an energy producer—we are the world's largest energy exporter when you consider oil, natural gas, hydroelectricity and uranium in the aggregate. And our exports have been increasing—in the case of oil, dramatically. How could our emissions not increase in such a circumstance? Our oil and gas industries are very large and, while we are not unique in that respect, the Canadian oil sands are unique and in their infancy in terms of extraction technologies. On top of all that, Canada is an impossibly large country and it is very cold for most of the year. As I used to say when I was in politics, "We are a country of ten months of winter and two months of poor skating."

This is not to make excuses, but merely to point out that there are good reasons why Canada's industrial, transportation and household emissions are among the highest in the world per capita. There is little utility in comparing our national circumstances to small European states with fully developed post-industrial economies and concentrated populations. You can bike across Denmark in a day; Canada, by contrast, occupies a huge part of the world's land mass. Our circumstances aren't comparable.

Certainly we can reduce our emissions and we should, but the challenge is to do so without undercutting our standard of living. Often lost in the climate change debate is the simple reality that greenhouse gas (GHG) emissions are a measure of energy consumption, and energy consumption is a direct measure of one's standard of living. In his 2014 book, *The Moral Case for Fossil Fuels*, Alex Epstein underscores the quantum increases in basic human health, security and happiness that are derived from energy consumption. He documents, for example, infant mortality rates in parts of Africa where children die because hospitals lack electricity to run incubators or operating rooms, and he poses the ethical questions that follow.

It is also true that the ethical questions surrounding carbon emissions ultimately involve personal choices. It has become popular to attack energy companies because they personify the hydrocarbon economy, conveniently overlooking another "inconvenient truth," namely, that most carbon emissions result from our personal consumption of energy. Oil is a particular target, yet more than three-quarters of the emissions associated with oil occur when we consume it: drive our vehicles and heat our homes. According to Jacobs Consultancy, one of the world's leading technical consulting firms, crude oil extraction creates about 8 percent of the GHG emissions associated with a barrel of oil used for transportation; refining generates 13 percent; transporting the crude from the well to the refinery and from the refinery to the retail station is less than 2 percent; and the remaining 77 percent of GHG emissions from a barrel of oil is generated "tank to wheels"—when you drive your car or fly in an airplane.[1]

Our personal carbon footprints are attributable to the consumption of both public goods, such as hospitals and government buildings, and private goods, since large households have higher GHG emissions than small ones. Two vehicles emit more carbon than one; large flat-screen TVs use more electricity and have higher emissions than old ones; and having four televisions in one's house quadruples emissions. Vacations, cottages and airplane flights are luxuries not only in terms of lifestyle but also in terms of GHG emissions. You get the point.

I return then to the question: What does Canada need to do to reassert its position as an environmental leader?

The Need for National Leadership and a National Vision

It is now time for strong national leadership in energy and environment policy. It is time for an overarching national policy, driven by the national government as the arbiter of the national interest. The "environment" is an area of concurrent jurisdiction under Canada's Constitution, and so the federal government has the authority and the responsibility to act, but not unilaterally. Our Constitution accords the provincial governments a concurrent environmental authority for good reasons, and the federal government will need to recognize that fact as we strive to achieve a national consensus.

It is also clear that any national discussion on the subject of energy and the environment has the potential to quickly boil into a divisive national disagreement. Our prime minister, Justin Trudeau, has now recognized this problem as a consequence of his inaugural First Ministers Meeting on Climate Change, which did not achieve the accord he hoped for. Good intentions are one thing; the heavy lifting of raising taxes to cover climate change policies is something else entirely, and more difficult. Canada's premiers have demonstrated this difference time and time again, including during their discussions on the so-called Canadian Energy Strategy championed by the former premier of Alberta, Alison Redford. The interests of each of the provinces are sufficiently different from one another's that arriving at a consensual definition of the country's best interests isn't easy. I maintain, however, that accord is possible and it is undoubtedly necessary.

The bottom line is that Canada needs to undertake a new national effort to agree on and stake out the environment as a matter of strategic importance to the country. We need to reassert that the protection of the environment and global environmental leadership are shared Canadian values, and we need to define a national policy framework that will enable co-operative and complementary provincial action.

We should see the opportunity that this goal presents. Canada, after all, is not the only federal state to face these challenges. The subject of climate change has been at least as divisive in the United States as it has in Canada. President Barack Obama and Congress have been at loggerheads over climate change policy since Obama's election in 2008, forcing him to abandon the ambitious legislative agenda he had pursued during his first term in favour of unilateral executive action in the second. Progress there has also been halting, and the courts have even now stayed the president's Clean Power Plan, pending a ruling on its constitutionality.

The United States is dramatically divided on climate change. Republicans and Democrats obviously disagree. So, too, do the states; there aren't many environmental issues, for instance, where Texans and Californians agree. Of late, as the costs of action of climate change become obvious, Californians even disagree with one another. Across the United States, governments have pursued a smorgasbord of differing, sometimes conflicting, sub-national climate change policies. Canada is the same. Most of those policies are well intentioned, but they have done little to reduce carbon emissions and have instead wasted taxpayers' dollars on subsidies, compromised economic efficiency and restricted free trade.

Australia also has struggled with environmental issues. That country's climate change policies have swung madly back and forth, and the very leadership of the country has hung in the balance.

So Canada isn't unique on this account. We are, however, presented with a unique opportunity, and I return to the premise that every region of Canada benefits from the energy business—striking an appropriate balance between energy and the environment is of vital interest to every province and territory. One advantage that Canada's parliamentary system has always had over our republican neighbours to the south is that we can move both quickly and assertively when a national government chooses to.

What we require is the leadership and patience to define that national vision. Perhaps we can do this similarly to the initiative championed by Prime Minister John Diefenbaker in October 1961, at the Resources for Tomorrow conference held in Montreal.

Eight hundred people gathered for three days to discuss how Canada's resources could be best used to meet the increasing needs of Canadians, and ensure the welfare of future generations—what we might call today "sustainable development." We need to draw the national government and the provinces together and define a new way forward.

Anything less than a national framework on energy and the environment will be insufficient because every province has been struggling on its own for nearly two decades. The provinces have tried to do the right thing and attempted to move the country forward. Some have made real progress, while others have made virtually none. Some are pursuing regulatory solutions; others rely on carbon taxes. Some are focused on reducing industrial emissions while ignoring consumer emissions. Others have done the opposite. Some are subsidizing good behaviour, and some are penalizing bad behaviour. Some are pursuing cap-and-trade, while others eschew it. The important point is that the sum of those efforts does not amount to a national policy, and the buffet table of provincial policies has not satisfied our critics, either domestically or internationally.

Canada needs to repair its international stature as a committed partner in the reduction of GHG emissions. I know from experience that Canada's provinces, even the largest ones, gain little traction at international environmental events because the international community judges us on the basis of our national policies and national actions. Among our international critics, matters have reached the point where it is Canada's national interests that are at risk. Only a national response will satisfy our trading partners and the international community.

Some argue that it will be impossible for our federal and provincial governments to reach a national vision on these issues, but

I disagree. I believe there is greater consensus among the premiers on these issues than is commonly understood. During my time as a federal Cabinet minister and briefly as premier of Alberta, I was struck by the extent to which a desire to protect the environment was a strongly held value among all Canadian premiers. I was also struck by the maturity they displayed in recognizing that we require a national vision and national policies—but ones that recognize the differing circumstances of each province, including basic economic realities. This was evident in all my discussions with Quebec Premier Philippe Couillard and Ontario Premier Kathleen Wynne, and in my working partnership with Premiers Brad Wall of Saskatchewan and Christy Clark of British Columbia.

Frankly, the discussion we need to have among the prime minister and the premiers bears similarities to the very discussions taking place internationally. What we need is an agreed-on and strongly articulated national vision, coupled with the recognition of "common but differentiated" responsibilities. If others can achieve this goal, why can't Canadians?

The Elements of a National Vision

What then are the elements of a national vision surrounding energy and the environment? It is important to start from first principles. I say this, first, because principles can guide us and will ensure that we don't lose our bearings in times of ongoing change and volatility. I say this, second, because we are a respected democracy and the rest of the world holds us to a standard of transparency. We need to make our beliefs clear. Those beliefs need to be principle based, and we need to be seen to be taking action to achieve them. Transparency is also important in the commercial world. We live in a competitive world, where countries as well as companies compete, and those with whom we trade and do business must know where we stand.

These are the principles that should guide our environmental policies:

1. Canada as leader in the environment;
2. Canada as a global partner;
3. Canada as a continental partner;
4. a commitment to science and technology;
5. a commitment to world class regulations;
6. a commitment to flexibility and provincial equivalency;
7. the importance of consumers and free markets;
8. the importance of partnering with Canada's indigenous peoples; and
9. conservation as a Canadian value.

CANADA AS A LEADER IN THE ENVIRONMENT

First and foremost, Canadians must make it clear that we intend to be a global environmental leader, reasserting a value that we have been known for internationally. Put simply, if Canada is going to continue in the energy and resource business, then we must recognize that we are also in the environment business and we must excel at both. In the 21st century, any distinction between the two is a false dichotomy.

There are those who portray resource development and environmental protection as irreconcilable interests. The more complex and nuanced truth is that we can pursue both and we can achieve both. Indeed, the purpose of a modern, science-based regulatory regime that protects the rights of all citizens is to ensure that we strike the right balance and develop our natural resources while excelling in the protection and preservation of our natural environment. To be sure there are trade-offs, and occasionally difficult choices need to be made. But we can lead in both areas. Canada always has done that, which is why other jurisdictions study and emulate our regulatory frameworks and environmental legislation.[2]

The related reality is that we are committed to the continued development of our natural resources, provided we do so in a responsible way. Canada is in the business of extracting and exporting our natural resources, where possible in an upgraded form, and our economy and standard of living depend heavily on forestry, mining and energy. Our emissions profile reflects this reality.

I recently heard John Manley, the president and CEO of the Canadian Council of Chief Executives, describe resource extraction as Canada's "family business." This is an important point: We are not debating whether Canada will develop its resources. We are debating how Canada will develop those resources—and how it can be done in a more responsible and sustainable manner.

CANADA AS A GLOBAL PARTNER

Canada must aggressively re-engage as a partner in the global environmental and climate change process. We need allies and, as a matter of strategic importance, must build domestic and international partnerships and alliances and constructively engage with the rest of the world in pursuing environmental solutions and progress on climate change. If we are serious about being a major global energy producer, then we need to be a major global environmental leader. We need to be willing to work in good faith and in a spirit of co-operation. As someone who represented Canada at the Copenhagen summit, I can say from hard experience that we can't ever again allow ourselves to be off-footed and placed in a position where we are following rather than leading.

Prime Minister Trudeau has achieved some early success in this regard. The international community has thus far embraced the prime minister's energy in pursuing climate change policies in accordance with the Paris Agreement. Increased efforts have also been made by the government to address environmental concerns through stronger partnerships with our neighbours, the United States and Mexico. Time will tell how Canada's greater engagement will lead to an improved reputation. I remain hopeful and cautiously optimistic.

Part of our challenge is to establish substantive areas where we excel and where we can lead and assert a position of global leadership. We have lacked a strategic direction and, even though we lead the world in multiple fields, we have failed to signal those as areas of Canadian excellence, and we have failed to build the scientific and diplomatic muscle to lead among our global partners. Both carbon capture and sequestration and methane emission reductions illustrate this problem. Frankly, we have been lousy at international climate diplomacy and, while we are respected at a technical level, we have lacked the intellectual heft or federal–provincial coordination to showcase Canada's accomplishments.

We have allowed ourselves to be portrayed as a recalcitrant party at the climate change table even though some of our accomplishments in reducing emissions, when considered with our multilateral financial investments, exceed the contributions of many others. Countries such as Australia and Norway, whose records in reducing carbon emissions are no better than our own, have been enormously successful at the diplomacy surrounding climate change. We have not, and that needs to change.

CANADA AS A CONTINENTAL PARTNER

We must also commit to continental leadership and continental solutions. Air sheds and watersheds do not respect jurisdictional boundaries, and the cleanliness of our North American environment is a defining competitive advantage for both Canada and the United States. We sometimes miss the obvious. North America isn't perfect, but it is vastly superior to many of the other jurisdictions with whom we compete. By comparison, take Beijing, which I travelled to often as a banker. On most of my trips there, the smog was so thick that you could barely make out buildings only a block away. The air quality is so bad that North American and European staff will not move there to take up employment. Those already in Beijing often won't allow their children outside because of the particulate levels in the air. This is a stark reminder of the dramatic advantage that we have as Canadians and as North Americans—and of the fact that our environmental standards help us stand out in a competitive marketplace for commerce, investment and talent.

With that in mind, we must view the protection of the environment as a North American issue, and we must pursue continental solutions. Although there are important differences between Canada and the United States, there are also areas such as transportation, where our vehicular, rail and aviation infrastructures are identical, which should be subject to common standards. Similarly, appliance standards, building codes and construction requirements are common on both sides of the border. I know from my experience with motor vehicle GHG standards that Canada and the United States can harmonize standards and avoid the "tyranny of small differences."

We share a continental economy with the United States and, as a matter of principle, both our countries should avoid the economic dislocation arising from vastly different environmental standards on one side of the border or the other. We should not damage our industrial competitiveness by imposing costs, including environmental costs, on the Canadian side of the border that the Americans are not prepared to accept on the US side. Nor should the reverse occur. This has been a contentious point, and I acknowledge that we must guard against it being used as an excuse by those who want to do nothing. My observation would be that international climate negotiations are as much about trade competitiveness as they are about emissions reductions, which is why some of the most successful nations at these tables also bring their most respected and successful trade negotiators, New Zealand being a case in point.

My own views on this matter were formed while I was the chair of the federal Cabinet Committee on Environment and Energy Security. I became convinced from the economic analysis we undertook that seemingly small differences on the industrial price of carbon, imposed on one side or the other of the Canada–US border, would significantly skew capital investment decisions, unfairly penalizing either country. Carbon pricing is a significant consideration in the positioning of facilities in the petrochemical, cement, fertilizer and heavy-manufacturing industries, and neither country should be disadvantaged, particularly when the negative burden of pollution is borne on both sides of the border. If we work together with the United States, we can achieve a greater advantage by further harmonizing our environmental standards to make our continent an even more potent competitive force.

A COMMITMENT TO SCIENCE AND TECHNOLOGY

We must also accept that science and technology are our greatest allies in the protection of the environment and that we must at every level foster investments and improvements in the technologies by which we increase energy efficiency and reduce emissions. Obvious illustrations of this fourth point include the rapid improvements we have seen in the efficiency of batteries for electric cars, or the gradual enhancements to the cost effectiveness of solar panels. We have seen dramatic enhancements in appliance efficiency. Closer to home, on the industrial front, improvements in technology hold the key to quantum reductions in the GHG emissions arising from the production of heavy oils. Once again it will be free markets, encouraged by government regulatory standards, that drive those technological changes.

We must also, as a matter of principle, enlist science as our ally in responsible development. Our regulatory system must be science based and, indeed, good science must be the intellectual underpinning of everything we do on the environmental file. It is worth remembering that we would not today be enjoying the economic benefits of such a strong energy industry were it not for the assiduous application of science. The oil sands, in particular, are one of Canada's great scientific successes. We need to embrace science and technology to understand the ongoing and emerging challenges to our environment. We also need to embrace them as integral components of a potential solution.

A COMMITMENT TO WORLD CLASS REGULATIONS

As a matter of principle, Canada must insist on world class regulatory and monitoring standards. I remember speaking to officials at Environment Canada when I first arrived as their minister, telling them that the department needed to view itself as a world class regulator, and being surprised to learn that no one had ever challenged them in that way. It changed the morale in the department overnight. Frankly, a country's environmental ambition will be only as good as the regulations—and regulators—that support it. We must therefore work toward environmental protection standards that are national in scope, including those that apply to the GHGs. High standards must not be confused with delay and indecisiveness, and our regulatory system must adhere to the imperative of investor certainty and the need to conduct reviews in a thorough yet timely fashion.

We must also have proper enforcement and encourage responsibility by adhering to the principle of "polluter pay." And we must apply serious and meaningful sanctions against those who damage the environment with criminal neglect. During my time as environment minister, 1,600 ducks perished in a tailings pond in the oil sands. The company was judged responsible and the resulting sanction, which I supported, was the largest fine in Canadian history for an environmental offence. Our regulations must be smart, sound and forward looking. They must also have teeth.

A COMMITMENT TO FLEXIBILITY AND
PROVINCIAL EQUIVALENCY

Canada will require national flexibility in crafting workable policies. Ultimately, there are three ways to force reductions in carbon emissions. First, you can pay people to stop emitting—effectively subsidizing them to do something less destructive. Second, you can tax people who emit, accepting that increased carbon taxes will dissuade some but not all emitters. And third, you can force reductions by changing the legal or regulatory standards that govern the emissions.

There is a fourth approach, cap-and-trade, but it is really a market-based hybrid of the other three. Under a cap-and-trade system, the state imposes regulatory limits that "cap" emissions at certain levels and rewards good performance by granting positive credits to the poor performers that exceed the required standards. The good performers are allowed to "trade" their credits to firms that have been unable to meet the necessary standards. It is, in effect, a regulatory approach that uses market incentives to reward good behaviour and punish bad behaviour.

The approach is conceptually appealing, particularly to those who favour free markets, but the sheer complexities of the ensuing trades can lead to bizarre and unintended consequences, profiting traders and speculators, without any corresponding emission reductions. When I was the chair of the Cabinet Committee on the Environment and Energy Security, we modelled how a cap-and-trade system might work for Canada's electricity industry but rejected this approach because of those complexities as well as the unfortunate European experiences surrounding similar efforts. We opted instead for a pure regulatory approach, requiring industry to achieve certain standards or close down.

175

All four approaches can work and have different costs and benefits. I was never an ideological politician, and my own view is that the best way forward is to sensibly marry differing approaches. Depending on the emission target, each approach has its own political consequences. Flexibility is important because our provinces have pursued vastly different approaches or combinations of approaches—the concept of provincial equivalency is therefore key. Under a national policy, provinces should be expected to undertake equivalent efforts, while being allowed the flexibility to adopt mechanisms that suit their circumstances.

We should never discount the success of regulations that are carefully targeted to reduce emissions. Some individuals doubt the efficacy of a regulatory approach, but I disagree. A regulatory approach works most successfully in the reduction of large source emissions. Developing regulations that provide industry with the required time to change, innovate and adapt has proven the most successful way to reduce industrial emissions. I base this belief on my own experience in the regulation of both the automotive industry and Canada's coal-burning electricity plants.

Most telling, as an illustration, are the carbon reductions achieved through North American fuel economy standards for passenger vehicles based on levels we introduced in 2009. In the ensuing years, we have achieved quantum reductions in GHG emissions. Those regulations stand out as the most effective climate change steps taken by the Obama administration and Canada.

I confess that I am not a fan of subsidized environmentalism—the kinds of government-funded programs that funnel public money into schemes, whether green or otherwise. To be kind, such initiatives have a dubious record of success. During the early years of this century, Canada poured billions into eco-subsidies without seeing any meaningful improvement in environmental outcomes. A similar approach to public subsidies has challenged the competitiveness of Ontario's electricity system. The Americans had a similar experience in subsidizing the ethanol industry. The Europeans, especially the Germans, have spent billions subsidizing renewable energy projects that have also served to damage their industrial competitiveness and, as for the environment, they are now busily burning US coal, which is the dirtiest of all choices.

Consider by contrast Canada's thermal coal policy, which we will come to in more detail shortly. In keeping with that policy, the federal government has changed its regulations to require the phase-out of coal plants as they reach their end of life, at which time they must be replaced by a cleaner form of electricity generation, likely natural gas. The regulations are clear and consistent in their application. There are no public subsidies being paid to those who were clever enough to get to the front of the "renewable" line. There is no intricate ladder of caps and trades to profit investment bankers. Instead, we have regulations that compel a certain performance standard, failing which the facilities must be closed at a prescribed end of life. There are costs to be sure, but they are manageable if tied to the natural phase-out or "turnover" of the electricity-producing assets.

The important point, however, which I heard loudly and clearly during my meetings with other Canadian premiers and energy and environment ministers, is that each province will require some flexibility in advancing its policy framework, so long as the concept of equivalency prevails.

THE IMPORTANCE OF CONSUMERS
AND FREE MARKETS

As a matter of principle, I also believe that we should trust in the power of free markets and the power of consumers, especially when it comes to individual consumption and behaviour. People, rather than governments, can change the world. It is increasingly obvious that younger consumers in particular are more environmentally responsible and, when armed with full information, prepared to make greener choices and accept the personal cost of doing so.

THE IMPORTANCE OF PARTNERING WITH
CANADA'S INDIGENOUS PEOPLES

Here at home, we must work more closely with our indigenous peoples to build economic partnerships, founded on sound environmental principles. It should surprise no one that Canada's indigenous peoples, who have been here the longest and are connected more closely to the natural environment, have strong views on these issues. We need to listen to their perspective. I devote three chapters of this book to developing those ideas.

CONSERVATION AS A CANADIAN VALUE

It is also important that we continue to lead the world in conservation, the management of our public lands and the protection of natural space.

We are good at this work. We apply internationally recognized sustainable management principles across all publicly owned forests (approximately 94 percent of Canada's forests). We also have the world's largest area of forests independently certified as sustainably managed. This achievement is not solely borne by the government. The Canadian Boreal Forest Agreement, signed in 2010, is the world's largest conservation initiative. It provides a plan for stakeholders to balance boreal forest conservation with forest sector competitiveness. I was for a time the minister responsible for Canada's national parks. Generations of sound stewardship have ensured that Canada enjoys the world's most extraordinary tapestry of national parks and protected areas. With the active support of Prime Minister Harper, we expanded Canada's national parks system by almost a third—including new parks in the Torngat and Mealy Mountains of Labrador; a five-fold expansion of the Nahanni Park Reserve in the Northwest Territories; the addition of the Sable Island National Park Reserve in Nova Scotia; and the creation of the Gwaii Haanas National Marine Conservation Area in British Columbia. The expansion of the Nahanni was recognized as the most significant conservation achievement on the planet in a generation.

* * *

These are the nine principles that should guide us as we move forward. I refuse to accept that Canada is not a leader in the protection and advancement of the environment. No one in the world has been more successful than Canada in protecting the environment, and we need to return to the first principles underlying that success. We need to lead again. We need to apply those principles to the challenge of reducing our carbon emissions and greening our energy systems. It is to that subject that I now turn.

CHAPTER 9

*Climate Change: An Action Plan That
Will Reassert Canadian Leadership*

The fight against climate change is the defining environmental battle of our generation. It is a challenge rife with complexity, made all the more difficult by the disagreements that surround the topic and by the rhetoric and political opportunism that punctuate the debate. The challenge at the heart of it all affects every one of us. How do we materially reduce greenhouse gas (GHG) emissions while simultaneously maintaining our own living standard and raising that of billions of citizens across the developing world? It isn't about energy *or* the environment. It's about energy *and* the environment, which is why I have always refused to separate the two issues. They are flip sides of the same coin.

The availability of energy is fundamental to the quality of life of every world citizen. This is true whether that energy is derived from renewable or non-renewable sources; whether it originates in the burning of dung or hydrocarbons, in the implosion of nuclear atoms or from solar, wind or water. It is also true that the availability of plentiful and reliable energy correlates directly with one's standard of living. If you doubt that, spend some time in the developing world with people who don't have access to electricity. The related truth is that humankind has not yet devised an energy source that is less expensive, more transportable or more dependable than the burning of hydrocarbons, especially oil. It would be nice if we had, but we haven't. Therein lies the challenge: How can we solve the dual problem of advancing global living standards by expanding the availability of energy while saving the planet from the worst consequences of increasing carbon emissions?

I decided long ago that I was ill equipped to debate the science surrounding climate change. Anyone looking for an examination of that topic will need to find another book. Of course the science is fascinating, but the truth is that no one really knows what effect anthropogenic carbon emissions will have on the planet, or when, or whether those effects are avoidable or reversible at this point. However, that doesn't mean we should do nothing.

In the face of those uncertainties, I have always tried to approach climate change as a realist and a conservationist. The challenge for all of us is to surely "leave the campsite cleaner than we found it," and the reduction of GHG emissions is undeniably a good thing, in the same sense that reducing chlorofluorocarbons or acid rain was a good thing; or the elimination of effluent pollution into the Great Lakes was a good thing; or, for that matter, that the recycling of our own domestic refuse is a good thing. The real question is how to do it sensibly and affordably.

Prosperity and improvements to the quality of our environment are inextricably linked. To use a metaphor, they are travelling companions—perhaps headed in the same direction for different reasons, but headed there together nonetheless.

The challenge for Canada is that we are a respected world citizen that has simultaneously excelled in the protection of the environment and the production of both renewable and non-renewable energies. For us, the art of success lies in illustrating that it is possible to create smart policies that reduce GHG emissions without undermining our economy, reducing investment, destroying jobs and infuriating the very citizens whose political support is required to make the long-term societal changes that we need. None of this has been easy and it never will be, but the key to our success lies in doing our homework and getting the policy choices right.

Certainly, however, we shouldn't flinch or retreat in the face of the challenge. Canada has always led the world in the advancement of environmental causes and the striking of a sensible balance between economic progress and environmental stewardship. It is time for us to lead again.

Returning then to first principles, Canada needs a way forward on the specifics of climate change. Philosophical targets are necessary, but they are not sufficient. Prime Minister Trudeau deserves credit for his efforts to reassert Canadian environmental leadership in Paris at the Conference of the Parties (COP 21), but the focus will inevitably shift to the specifics of what Canada intends to do. The debate over Canada's climate change policies has now shifted from the philosophical level to the detailed grind of identifying emission reductions. Climate change policy is one area where the devil is truly in the details. What emissions are going to be reduced? When? And at whose cost?

Part of the challenge is to identify areas where we can excel not only in reducing our own emissions, but also in providing continental and international leadership in our work with our partners.

We must focus on areas where we have demonstrated our competence and where we can bring Canadian science and technology to assist others in reducing their emissions. And remembering that Canada is a federal state, we need to be mindful that, while all Canadians are in the energy business, we are not all in the same energy business—and perspectives vary widely from one end of Canada to the other. Canada's indigenous peoples also need to be part of Canada's approach to climate change.

In my view, the Canadian government should be directing itself to a series of sensible policies that will achieve emission reductions and establish a basis for Canadian leadership—both continentally and elsewhere. We need to identify those areas where Canada actually has the ability to reduce emissions and we need to focus on those areas as core strengths, using them to assert Canadian leadership at the international climate change table. Frankly, we have every opportunity to do this and to do it in areas that have been identified by others as critical to international progress.

A surprising degree of consensus surrounds the specific policies that governments around the world should be directing themselves toward if we are to limit the long-term rise in average global temperature to 2°C. For example, the 2013 report of the International Energy Agency (IEA), *Redrawing the Energy-Climate Map*,[1] notes that energy is at the heart of the challenge, since the energy sector accounts for two-thirds of global greenhouse gas emissions in that more than 80 percent of global energy consumption is based on fossil fuels. We can see that Canada is doing well in all four of the imperatives identified by the IEA, namely (1) the elimination of coal-burning electricity plants; (2) the control of methane emissions; (3) the adoption of energy-efficiency measures; and (4) the elimination of fossil fuel subsidies.

Canada's Emissions: The Facts

Facts are important when it comes to a discussion about something as complex as climate change and carbon emissions. This may seem self-evident, but I am struck by the superficiality of most opinion pieces on the subject. If you don't understand the origin of Canada's emissions, our so-called emissions profile, then you will be hard pressed to come up with solutions that are realistic or workable. The best and most reliable source of information on Canada's GHG emissions is Environment Canada's *National Inventory Report*, and a number of points are important.

First of all, Canada represents a very small percentage of the world's emissions—less than 2 percent of global emissions originate here. It is also true that we are one of the world's highest per capita emitters, reflective of our geography, size, weather and industrial structure. In 2013, Canada's emissions were 20.7 tonnes of GHGs per capita. That number has declined markedly since 2008 and appears to have stabilized at this level, but Canada's per capita emissions, along with those of Australia and the United States, are among the highest in the world.

Second, Canada's total emissions of 732 megatonnes of carbon dioxide equivalent reflect the composition of our national economy. Not surprisingly, the mining and oil and gas industries account for 25 percent of our emissions.[2] Industries that are emissions intensive, including smelting, refining, cement, and paper manufacturing, account for an additional 11 percent of our emissions. Agriculture accounts for 10 percent. Taken together, industrial activity represents approximately 50 percent of our emissions. Transportation accounts for 23 percent of Canada's emissions, mostly from automobiles and transport trucks. This last figure is roughly comparable to other industrial democracies such as the United States, and the number continues to increase even though significant improvements are being made to vehicular fuel efficiency.

Third, Canada's mining and oil and gas industries are significant sources of emissions, and they increase in direct proportion to increases in production. Since 1990, the emissions from Canada's oil and gas industry have risen markedly, reflecting the fact that Canada's production of bitumen and synthetic crude oil has risen by more than two million barrels per day. The emissions intensity of the oil sands operations themselves has remained fairly static since 2004, but the per barrel GHG emissions from oil and gas production overall have risen, reflecting the fact that an increasing amount of Canada's and indeed the world's oil production is non-conventional oil and has a more energy intensive production profile.

The oil sands comprise less than one-tenth of Canada's 2 percent share of the world's carbon emissions. In other words, the Canadian oil sands, which produce more than 2.4 million barrels of oil per day, represent less than 0.2 percent of global emissions. This figure is not insignificant, but neither is it a threat to the planet on its own.

Fourth, Canada's electricity-generating sector warrants comment since it produces only 12 percent of Canada's emissions, and that figure has been declining as a consequence of the closure of Canada's existing coal fleet, starting with plants in Ontario. In this respect Canada is strikingly different from most other industrial democracies, whose carbon footprints from electricity production are much higher. The figure in the United States, for example, is about 30 percent.

Finally, it is noteworthy that Canada's emissions vary significantly by province. Alberta has become the country's largest emitter in absolute terms, and Alberta and Saskatchewan are the largest per capita emitters by a significant margin. This statistic is accounted for in large part because of oil and gas to be sure, but the electricity generation in each of these two provinces comes mostly from coal-fired plants, and both Alberta and Saskatchewan have significantly large agriculture sectors. Those provinces that generate their power from hydro, most notably Quebec, have the lower emissions profiles.

The question now is what can we do specifically to lower GHG emissions and fight climate change while not hobbling our economy and reducing our standard of living?

An Action Plan on Climate Change

The Paris Agreement of December 2015 and the Vancouver Declaration on Clean Growth and Climate Change of March 2016 are important places to start when looking at what Canada needs to do to reduce its emissions. The Paris Agreement calls for significant reductions in global emissions to limit global warming to less than 2°C above pre-industrial levels, and if possible to limit such warming to 1.5°C above pre-industrial levels. The Paris Agreement is ambitious but not prescriptive and grants wide flexibility to each nation in determining how to achieve this objective. In Canada's case, the Vancouver Declaration reflects a specific agreement between our federal and provincial governments to adopt mitigation policies that will allow Canada to meet its 2030 target of reducing our emissions by 30 percent below 2005 levels.

That target for Canada is extremely challenging, and the heavy lifting surrounding how to achieve it has now begun at the level of the federal–provincial working groups. Canada's efforts will need to focus on five areas:

1. a national carbon price, applied on an economy-wide basis, that increases in stringency in a predictable way over time and which is designed in a way to address competitiveness concerns, especially as it relates to our continental trading partners, the United States and Mexico;
2. a continued focus on the decarbonization of Canada's electricity system;
3. the stabilization and gradual reduction of emissions from Alberta's oil sands;
4. a continued focus on energy-efficiency improvements to reduce emissions in the transportation sector and to improve the efficiency of buildings and appliances; and
5. a reduction of methane (CH_4) emissions.

Canada will also need to focus on obtaining credit for our measures to enhance forest sinks and to participate in and benefit from the "internationally transferred mitigation measures" discussed in Chapter 7. (These measures will require Canada to financially support climate change mitigation measures in developing countries.) The good news is that Canada is well positioned to lead in all these areas.

APPLYING A NATIONAL CARBON PRICE

In 2009, I warned Prime Minister Harper in Copenhagen that it would be impossible for Canada to meet its Copenhagen 2020 target of reducing Canada's emissions by 17 percent below 2005 levels without an economy-wide carbon-pricing mechanism. Canada's current target of reducing its GHG emissions by 30 percent below 2005 levels by 2030 is even more ambitious and will be similarly impossible to meet without an economy-wide price on carbon. No one likes taxes, but the reality is that, without them, it will be impossible for any of the world's industrial democracies to achieve carbon emission reductions that are consistent with the quantum of their Paris targets. Therefore, the question isn't whether we need to attach a national price to carbon, but rather *how* to do so. Most agree that any such national measure must be broadly applied and that it must increase in stringency in a measured and predictable way. It must be designed to build on existing provincial carbon-pricing initiatives, and it must be developed in concert with our North American trading partners to avoid damaging Canada's competitiveness. And perhaps most obviously, unless it is demonstrably revenue neutral, it is unlikely to find much support with Canadian taxpayers.

Canada has been slowly moving in this direction for more than a decade and has in fact been a cauldron of experimentation when it comes to carbon pricing. More than 85 percent of the Canadian economy is now subject to carbon-pricing initiatives—albeit through provincial measures. British Columbia's revenue neutral carbon tax (discussed shortly) is widely regarded as the most successful such initiative in North America, but the cap-and-trade system in place in Quebec and planned for in Ontario and Manitoba are also important steps forward. Alberta, which was the first jurisdiction in North America to attach a price to industrial carbon emissions, will introduce a broad-based (although not revenue neutral) carbon tax in 2017.

The New Democratic Party (NDP) government in Alberta

has also put in place a controversial carbon "levy" on transportation and heating fuels to be paid by consumers, starting out at $20 per tonne in 2017, then increasing to $30 per tonne in 2018. The government says that about two-thirds of the revenues generated—$6.2 billion of the estimated $9.6 billion over the first five years—will be used to fund green technologies and renewable energy projects, and the balance will assist lower-income Albertans in the form of consumer rebates and support to communities where coal plants will be closing.

Canada also participates in a number of international and continental initiatives that are focused on global efforts to actually put a price on carbon. Canada is a member of the Carbon Pricing Leadership Coalition that was struck in Paris. Quebec, British Columbia, Ontario and Manitoba are members of the International Carbon Action Partnership, and Quebec is also a partner in the Partnership for Market Readiness program of the World Bank.

Discussions have also begun among Canada, the United States and Mexico on what a harmonized continental carbon-pricing mechanism might look like. American leadership is obviously important in any such initiative. Mexico already has a national carbon tax, and the focus in Canada will increasingly be on how to harmonize our many provincial initiatives. Frankly, the fairest and most efficient way to arrive at an acceptable outcome is to work together with the United States and Mexico to arrive at a continental approach to carbon pricing. Each country is becoming increasingly aware that a national carbon tax is inevitable. Canada needs to lead in developing policies that will protect its own consumers and ensure that our country is not disadvantaged from a trading perspective.

Jim Prentice *with* Jean-Sébastien Rioux

The need to attach a price to carbon is best illustrated by looking at hydrocarbon-based fuels. The vast majority of the carbon emissions occur when fuel is burned by the consumer. As described in the previous chapter, a wells-to-wheels life cycle analysis of the carbon emissions of transportation fuels shows that more than 75 percent of the emissions are accounted for by tailpipe emissions. Although the industrial processes by which the fuel is produced and the transport of fuel are important, they account for less than 25 percent of overall emissions. Therefore, when we attach a price to industrial carbon emissions or design a regulatory system to constrain them, we are addressing only 25 percent of the problem. If we are serious about abating emissions, we must inevitably deal with the end-use consumption of hydrocarbons.

British Columbia's carbon tax is levied on all emissions from fuel combustion as defined by Environment Canada's National Inventory Report, with very few exemptions. It is a tax that consumers pay—for example, at the gas pump or in their monthly natural gas bill. It is currently set at $30 per tonne, which works out to about seven cents per litre of gas at the pump. The feature of BC's carbon tax is that it is "revenue neutral," meaning that the revenues generated by the province through it were used, in equal amounts, to reduce other taxes. Making hydrocarbon-based fuels more expensive prompts consumers to lower their consumption. And the levy appears to be working since fuel use has dropped 16 percent since 2008, when the tax was implemented.

None of this will be easy, as illustrated by the first meeting between Prime Minister Trudeau and the premiers in March 2016. We have, however, reached the point that an economy-wide tax on carbon consumption is inevitable. The important questions now surround the design, implementation and neutrality of such a national initiative.

190

CANADA'S ELECTRICITY SYSTEM— PHASING OUT COAL

If you are concerned about carbon emissions, by definition you must be concerned about the combustion of coal to produce electricity. By 2030, as the International Energy Agency notes, 41 percent of the anthropogenic carbon emitted into the atmosphere will still come from burning coal.[3] Those emissions rise as emerging economies seek inexpensive sources of electricity to pursue their industrialization.

Judged against that standard, Canada's performance is among the very best in the world. We burn very little coal and we are steadily burning even less. Canada's system of electricity generation, transmission and distribution is already one of the cleanest in the world—81 percent of the country's electricity system generates no carbon whatsoever. Most of our electricity comes from either hydroelectricity (62.5 percent) or nuclear energy (16.8 percent), and those sources that do emit carbon, including thermal coal, diesel and natural gas, account for barely 19 percent of Canada's electricity generation and a declining percentage of our GHG emissions. Coal itself accounts for only 14.7 percent of Canada's total electricity generation. This is a remarkable achievement.[4]

The United States, by contrast, depends heavily on coal—it accounts for more than 38 percent of that country's electricity generation. Although the US electricity industry has begun the conversion to natural gas, almost 600 coal-burning thermal electricity plants operate in the United States and, taken together, annually contribute 1,417 megatonnes of GHG emissions. This is 23 times more than the GHG emissions of the entire Canadian oil sands, which produce 62 megatonnes. In fact, a number of American states emit more carbon dioxide than the entirety of Canada's oil sands complex.

China is much worse. As the world's largest producer, importer and consumer of coal, China uses almost half the world's annual coal production to fuel its growing economy. It produces more than 70 percent of its electricity from coal and is the world's largest emitter—responsible for about as much CO_2 as the United States, the European Union and India combined. The Chinese government recognizes the public health dangers of burning so much coal and is also leading the world in the growth of renewable electricity generation—although starting from a minuscule amount.

Canada, meanwhile, is not resting on its laurels and is taking concerted action—at both the federal and provincial levels—to phase out its remaining coal-burning electricity plants. Canada's national policy framework, the thermal coal policy of 2012, is complemented by decisions of the Ontario, Nova Scotia and now Alberta governments to close all their coal-burning facilities over time. Saskatchewan is the only other province that burns coal to generate electricity, and it will proceed with concurrent investments in carbon capture and storage (CCS).

The reductions in GHG emissions have been immediate. Ontario moved quickly with the closure of several facilities and has reduced its electricity generation emissions by 68 percent (23.6 megatonnes) since 2005. All but one of the province's plants had been taken out of service by the beginning of 2014. Alberta has also moved forward with the closure of coal-burning units—869 megawatts of coal-burning generation were initially targeted to be taken out of service by 2020 and another 2,893 megawatts removed by 2030. The current Alberta government is now moving to accelerate those closures, although it has learned in the process that phasing out existing capital stock can be contentious and costly. Certainly, the task is a trap for the unwary. Nova Scotia will phase out its coal-burning units concurrent with the commissioning of Newfoundland and Labrador's new Muskrat Falls hydroelectric project, which will ensure that Newfoundland and Labrador, Nova Scotia, New Brunswick and Prince Edward Island have one of the cleanest electricity systems in the world.

Canada has received little credit at the international climate change table, even though these world-leading initiatives are already delivering emission reductions. In fact, emissions from Canadian electricity generation peaked in 2000, when the sector generated 131 megatonnes of CO_2 equivalent. By 2013, that figure had declined to 88 megatonnes, and it continues to progress steadily downward. No other industrial democracy will be able to assert that it is on track to phase out its entire coal-burning electricity fleet by 2030.

Canada's record of achievement in phasing out coal was underpinned, in part, by good luck—most of our coal-burning units needed to be phased out anyway. As such, the discussions that led to Canada's thermal coal policy originated in the recognition that the country's fleet of coal-burning electricity plants, which consisted of 53 coal-burning units housed in 21 individual facilities, was nearing the end of its economic life and would demand reinvestment or replacement. In fact, all but 10 of those units were scheduled to reach the end of their 40-year economic life by 2025, with most of the remaining units destined to turn over between 2020 and 2030.

Shortly after I became Canada's minister of the environment, the companies that owned those facilities began pressing for certainty surrounding the long-term reinvestment decisions that they needed to make. From their perspective, the federal government's policy position on GHG emissions represented the critical unknown. Should they reinvest in those coal-burning units or convert them to a cleaner fuel source, such as natural gas? One of industry's principal concerns was to avoid stranding assets that had not yet reached the end of their useful life. A critical concern of everyone at the table was to maintain stable electricity prices while ensuring a cleaner future. In effect, our government was presented with a unique opportunity. We quickly seized on an approach, which I described as "capital stock turnover," that allowed for a gradual conversion of each facility—as it reached the end of its useful economic life—to a cleaner energy source. It had the added advantage of being smart economic policy.

The thermal coal policy allowed emissions from existing plants to remain at existing levels until the end of their economic life (50 years), at which time they were required to meet a more stringent performance standard, based on that of a "natural gas combined cycle" facility. The policy effectively precluded the construction of "dirty" plants by artfully requiring new facilities to achieve the higher performance standard of a new natural gas facility. As each existing coal unit reached the end of its defined economic life, the owners were required to convert the unit to natural gas or replace it with some other form of electricity generation. No public funds, subsidies or tax incentives were involved. The policy itself was ultimately rolled out by my successor in 2012, and although it was modified slightly in response to industry pressure, it remains the same as the one negotiated between the CEOs of Canada's electricity industry and the minister of the environment—who used to be a coal miner—in 2009 and 2010.

Implementation was carried out with the co-operation of Alberta, Saskatchewan and Nova Scotia. All three provinces ultimately signed GHG regulatory co-operation agreements with the Government of Canada, negotiated to ensure "equivalency." Saskatchewan, the hardest case, required some added flexibility since the province had few other generation options. Ultimately, the three provinces were allowed to move toward an alternative "CCS-ready clean coal" standard. In effect, Canada defined a national standard but allowed each province to devise its own regulatory plan and timetable to get there.

The thermal coal policy had a number of objectives. It was intended to reduce Canada's electricity sector emissions by 33 percent by 2020, and by 77 percent by 2030. In that sense it helped move Canada toward our international targets, and it will be invaluable as we look toward our Paris objectives. But it had a greater strategic purpose: It was intended to help silence Canada's international critics on GHG emissions because no other industrial democracy in the world has the capacity to build an electricity system that emits less carbon than Canada's. The fact that Canada is constructing one of the cleanest electricity systems in the world gives pause to even our toughest critics. To get there, all we need to do is stick to the plan.

Canada's thermal coal policy is a demonstrable illustration of global leadership in the battle to reduce carbon emissions. Unfortunately, we have failed to tell the world about it, and it needs to be a centrepiece of the Canadian story as we move forward.

IMPROVING THE PERFORMANCE
OF CANADA'S OIL SANDS

Canada's oil sands are both our greatest resource opportunity and our greatest environmental responsibility. There is no way around that reality. We have trumpeted the fact that they are one of the world's largest hydrocarbon deposits, but we have completely failed in our efforts to convince the world that we are developing them in a sound and environmentally responsible manner. Whether it is fair, the world will continue to devote a disproportionate amount of attention to Canada's oil sands and their associated carbon footprint. The question now is what to do about it.

The oil sands are also the elephant in the room when it comes to Canada's greenhouse gas emissions. Canada's increased GHG emissions in the time since 1990 correlate with the increase in oil production from the oil sands since that time.

I am not suggesting that our environmental performance is poor—far from it. Few people in Canada have spent more time explaining and defending Canada's oil sands to the international community than I have. On every occasion, I have emphasized that our environmental performance measured against other jurisdictions that produce oil and natural gas is exceptional. Our regulatory regime is robust. It is science based. We are protective of air sheds and watersheds. Our reclamation standards are among the highest in the world, and we lead the world in controlling methane emissions. And when it comes to climate change, Alberta was one of the first jurisdictions in the world to attach an industrial price to carbon. In fact, other jurisdictions such as British Columbia, when confronted with the hard choices surrounding industrial emissions, have chosen to pursue a regulatory framework modelled on the one Alberta put in place more than a decade ago.

No one in the world seriously contends that the environmental standards or carbon policies of other jurisdictions that produce oil and natural gas are better than Canada's. Yet Saudi Arabia, Russia, Venezuela, Mexico, Iraq, Iran, Libya, China and

Colombia all seem to have been granted the right to be held to lower standards than Canada.

Moreover, there is no material difference between Canada and those other Western democracies that produce hydrocarbons when it comes to environmental standards and industrial carbon emission regulations. The United States, Norway, the United Kingdom and Australia all produce energy under regimes comparable with Canada's. Each country can justifiably make the claim that it is best in class in some respects. Certainly, Canada can. While it is true that the oil produced from Canada's oil sands has a higher carbon footprint than the oil of some other countries, the difference is marginal. When the comparison is confined to the heavier oils that the world is increasingly producing, we see no significant difference. Why then has Canada been singled out? More importantly, what do we do about it?

It is useful to think about where we are from both a strategic and a tactical perspective. Tactically, it is tempting to say we are in this predicament because we failed to lead and because we failed to communicate. Undoubtedly both responses are true, but the deeper reality is that we have never really agreed on what it is we are communicating or who is going to lead. We've had no plan, at least not one that everyone agreed on, resourced and carried out.

The Government of Alberta, in particular, has lurched from message to message. For a period, Albertans led the crusade against climate science, abandoning that posture only when it became so embarrassing that it threatened the province's market access initiatives. After that, the Alberta government's official position was that the United States needed Alberta's oil and would be compelled to approve the Keystone XL Pipeline whether it liked the oil sands or not. Many Albertans even resorted for a time to the argument that we should instead export our oil to China—overlooking the fact that we don't yet have any export routes to the Asia Pacific countries. Belatedly, Alberta returned to the message that the province is an environmental leader, with a solid record of effort in the reduction of emissions on an "intensity" basis. Is it any wonder that our critics are emboldened and our supporters confused?

Industry has been largely acquiescent through this entire piece, although it did invest in a national communication campaign between 2009 and 2014. That campaign did help consolidate Canadian—although not international—public opinion. In the end, one would have to say that Canadian industry lacks the credentials—and arguably the cohesiveness—to successfully pursue an international advocacy campaign defending the development of Canada's oil sands.

The federal government has itself struggled for a consistent message surrounding the oil sands. Success was achieved in the battle over the European Fuel Quality Directive. However, relations with President Barack Obama continued to deteriorate on the topic of energy and the environment, and Canada's attempts to regain its footing on the international stage continue to be dogged by criticism over the oil sands, unabated and for the most part un-rebutted in any meaningful way over the past 20 years. Thus, the reputational damage is now largely done.

In my view, our current circumstances demand national intervention. As noted earlier, the federal government is going to need to pursue a national agenda that repositions Canada on the international stage as an environmental leader. New oil and gas regulations, including regulations that apply to the oil sands, are going to have to form part of that agenda, and they are going to have to be tough enough to position Canada on the road to regained credibility. At a minimum, they will need to withstand unrelenting public scrutiny.

Provincial equivalency, as noted, will need to be accommodated. In the context of the oil sands, this goal is quite achievable because only two jurisdictions, Alberta and Canada, need to reach a consensus on the best way forward. Also, Alberta's regulatory framework is a good one on a conceptual or "architectural" level, and there is no reason to dismantle it. The challenge is to strengthen it without destroying the competitiveness of the sector that has been the engine of the Canadian economy for the past 15 years. The federal regulations will need to be obligatory, and they will need to create a pathway for Canada's oil- and gas-producing provinces to

- become leaders in responsible energy use and production, and in the transition to a greener energy economy;
- emerge as trusted partners in defining and meeting Canada's climate change commitments;
- become leaders in North America in setting continental standards that will achieve market-based approaches to reducing the carbon intensity of production and use; and
- achieve the 2020 reduction target and be on a pathway to absolute reductions in emissions by 2040.

To its credit, Alberta's left-leaning NDP government has made some advancement on this file, publishing its Climate Leadership Plan, which toughened the province's rules for industrial emissions, in time for the 2015 Paris COP 21 meeting. Alberta was the first jurisdiction in North America to attach a price to industrial carbon, by way of the Specified Gas Emitters Regulation, which was enacted in 2007. Large industrial facilities emitting more than 100,000 tonnes of CO_2 in a year were required to reduce the intensity by 12 percent below their established baseline emissions. Compliance mechanisms included reducing on-site emissions; purchasing Alberta-based emissions offsets or performance credits; and paying a levy of $15 per tonne into a "technology fund" mandated to reduce GHG emissions or improve the province's ability to adapt to climate change.

Under the new climate plan, large industrial emitters will continue to be subject to this framework until the end of 2017, at which time the province will transition to product- and sector-based performance standards. The NDP's steps to increase both the stringency and the carbon price had been preceded by several years of concerted effort between the Alberta government and industry. Most controversial of all has been the provincial government's commitment to cap total oil sands emissions at 100 megatonnes per year. (As noted, oil sands currently emit 62 megatonnes annually.)

The Canadian energy industry remains bitterly divided over the collaborative steps taken by Suncor, Canadian National Resources Ltd. and Cenovus Energy to work with the Alberta government on climate change. The decision by those companies to endorse the government's move in 2015 to cap oil sands emissions has been a particularly difficult issue on which there is little consensus. Certainly no other energy-producing jurisdiction in the world has agreed to limit its oil production or associated emissions. Those who support the initiative emphasize that the emissions, not the production, are being capped. For my part, I don't believe that capping emissions from the oil sands was prudent in the absence of a commitment from our continental partners to do the same. The United States, with whom we compete every day in the energy business, has yet to even put a price on industrial carbon emissions, let alone agree to cap their output.

The real challenge is to advance the agenda without damaging the competitiveness of Canada's oil and gas industry. Frankly, the changes we are speaking of need to be accompanied by an agreement with the United States and Mexico to pursue a continent-wide low-carbon fuel standard that would apply to every barrel of oil produced by or landed on one of the three countries. The best way to protect the environment while preserving Canada's ability to compete is to subscribe our production to a continental system that has a level playing field. We have now placed ourselves in a perilous position, having both attached a price to Alberta's industrial carbon emissions and agreed to cap that output, while our main competitor and most vocal critic has done neither.

In sum, Canada must continue to support the production of oil from the Canadian oil sands. They are one of our greatest resource endowments and hold the promise of being a driving engine of the Canadian economy, ensuring prosperity and a high quality of life for our children and grandchildren. The Governments of Canada and Alberta must ensure that the oil sands are developed in an environmentally responsible manner. The goal must be to confront that challenge, not to retreat from the development of a resource that is unparalleled in the Western democratic world.

The oil sands and their environmental footprint have become an international issue that transcends the interests of any single province or corporation. What is at stake on the international stage is our reputation as a country and, increasingly, our ability

Jim Prentice *with* Jean-Sébastien Rioux

to do business. Accordingly, we need to up our game in terms of both our environmental performance and our communication and advocacy efforts at home and abroad. Industry will need to be an essential part of that effort, but national leadership is required. The world looks to national action and national policies.

CONTINUING IMPROVEMENTS IN ENERGY EFFICIENCY

Another area of emphasis, also recommended by the International Energy Agency (IEA), is a continued focus on energy performance standards for buildings, lighting, appliances, heating and cooling equipment, and industrial motor systems and transportation vehicles. As the IEA points out, this focus has the potential to deliver significant greenhouse gas reductions. The agency urges that every country make this a priority, and here, too, there is no reason why Canada cannot assert itself as a leader. The IEA estimates that more stringent energy-efficiency measures could reduce global energy–related emissions by 1.5 gigatons—1.5 billion tons—by 2020, a level equivalent to all of Russia's GHG emissions.

Frankly, this initiative is the heavy lifting of regulatory standardization and harmonization. It is slow going and not always exciting, but it produces results and can be done without compromising our standard of living. It is also an area where consumers have the final say and can bring their individual leadership to bear.

The key is for Canadian governments, at every level, to work together with industry to harness new technologies and innovation to reduce consumption, eliminate waste and improve fuel efficiency in every way possible.

Progress also lies in the elimination of the "tyranny of small differences" that sometimes divides Canada and the United States. Our two countries often develop regulatory standards that reflect minor differences that complicate manufacturing and ultimately work to the disadvantage of consumers, usually Canadian consumers, by driving up costs. These different standards have been particularly problematic in the automobile industry. When I was Canada's minister of industry, I used to ask why we needed different fuel consumption standards in Canada than the United States when we drive the very same cars; or, for that matter, why we needed slightly different standards for the width of seat belts or the impact tolerance of bumpers. The same issues exist across a broad range of electricity-related consumer goods. Shouldn't we be working across the border to achieve common standards that are best in class? No one in the world is better positioned to make gains in this area than Canada.

Our two countries share a common economy. We are a common market for goods and services, and one of our continuing challenges is to deal with the proliferation of minor differences in standards and regulations. The elimination of those differences will make us more efficient, make us more competitive and, in the context of our present discussion, ensure that we achieve superior environmental outcomes on everything from building codes to transportation fuel–efficiency standards. Frankly, our relative size means we often take a lead from the United States on such standards. In the interests of economic efficiency and improving environmental outcomes, we should aggressively pursue harmonization with the United States wherever possible.

That is exactly what we did in 2009, when Canada and the United States agreed on North America–wide standards for passenger vehicles and light-duty trucks. Conceptually, it was easy. When Carol Browner (director of the White House Office of Energy and Climate Change Policy) and I first met in February 2009, during President Obama's first visit to Ottawa following his election, we readily agreed that we shared a common transportation system and should harmonize fuel efficiency standards on a continental basis. We agreed that the first step would involve light-duty trucks and passenger vehicles, and we would follow with working groups for all other vehicle classifications—heavy trucks, buses, tractor trailer units and so on. In the two years that followed, we did exactly that. The new standards were ultimately rolled out in April 2010, at a Ford dealership in Ottawa.

I emphasize, however, how demanding, time-consuming and labour intensive such harmonization can actually be. I was amazed at the time and energy required, since the approvals involved multiple government departments, including Environment, Industry, Transport and Foreign Affairs. The entire effort took more than a year, and I recall at least five trips to Cabinet to secure approvals. Add in the complexities of consulting industry and securing the approval of all the provinces and states, and you get some appreciation of the challenges. But we stuck with it, and it remains the most important accomplishment of both the Obama and Harper administrations in the reduction of greenhouse gas emissions. The important lesson is that Canada and the United States can do the same thing across a broad range of consumer and industrial goods.

Canada should be at the forefront of these kinds of changes and innovations. This is true whether we talk about fuel economy standards for motor vehicles; LEED (Leadership in Energy and Environmental Design) standards for the sustainable design and construction of commercial buildings or building codes for residential structures; or ENERGY STAR standards for the full array of household appliances. Working together with our American partners, we have made considerable progress in this manner. We must maintain those efforts.

REDUCING METHANE EMISSIONS

While the major public discourse and international treaties focus on carbon dioxide (CO_2) emissions as a proxy for "greenhouse gas emissions," methane (CH_4) is, in fact, one of the greenhouse gases that play a large role in human-made climate change. Methane is the primary component of natural gas, and it is well understood by people working in the energy and environment fields that its short-term impact on atmospheric warming is possibly 34 times more powerful than CO_2; hence, the importance of controlling methane in addition to carbon dioxide.

Because methane gas is often found alongside gas and oil deposits, some CH_4 is emitted into the atmosphere during the production, processing, storage, transmission and distribution of natural gas, as well as during the production, refinement, transportation and storage of crude oil. In addition to some seepage from gas wells, it can also be released by disturbing muskeg, for example. Finally, methane is also released "naturally" by livestock. For example, according to the Department of Agriculture and Agri-Food Canada, a lactating dairy cow releases about the same amount of methane (by "cow farts," in the immortal words of the late Ralph Klein) in one year as a mid-sized vehicle driven 20,000 kilometres.

On the issue of methane emissions, Canada is a world leader. We were one of the six countries that launched the United Nations

Environment Programme's Climate and Clean Air Coalition to Reduce Short-Lived Climate Pollutants (CCAC) in 2012. The purpose of this coalition, which was later joined by seven other countries, is to limit pollutants such as methane, black carbon and hydrofluorocarbons, which account for about one-third of current global warming. Our expertise is recognized by international organizations such as the World Bank, which selected Alberta as the world leader in the management and reduction of natural gas flaring. In 2012, the World Bank formed the Global Gas Flaring Reduction Partnership and adopted Alberta's best practices on and regulatory approach to flaring management, to share with other countries. This partnership between the World Bank and Alberta was renewed in 2015, when I was the premier.

In addition to upstream oil and gas expertise, Canada is well positioned to share its knowledge in agricultural methane management as well. For example, Genome Canada is working with universities to genetically select dairy cattle with the traits needed for more efficient feed conversion, which will lead to lower methane emissions in livestock. Technologies developed in Canada could be exported and used worldwide.

Returning then to the opportunity for Canadian leadership on climate change, it is very encouraging to note that of the four urgent policy recommendations proposed by the International Energy Agency to help curb greenhouse gas emissions, Canada is already a world leader in at least three. We are phasing out coal-fired plants that generate electricity; we do not have fossil-fuel subsidies for consumption; and we are a global leader in managing methane emissions. On the fourth, which is adopting more stringent energy-efficiency measures, we can and should be making improvements. These are successes that we can leverage internationally, emphasizing our credentials as a respected world citizen who simultaneously excels in the protection of the environment and in the production of renewable as well as non-renewable energy.

PART FOUR

Canada's First Nations

The Pacific Northwest: Why Canada's Coastal First Nations Are the Key to Canada's Asian Gateway

I have enjoyed a close relationship with Canada's indigenous peoples my entire adult life. That journey began in the late 1980s, when I was a young lawyer and negotiated treaty land-entitlement settlements in northern Alberta, settlements that eventually became precedents for dozens of similar negotiations across western Canada. Later, I would serve as a commissioner and co-chair of Canada's Indian Claims Commission for close to a decade.

In 2006, as a new minister in a new Conservative government, I drew on that background in working together with Aboriginal leaders I had come to know and respect. Phil Fontaine, the national chief of the Assembly of First Nations, and I surprised many by successfully negotiating the Residential Schools Settlement Agreement in 2006, employing former Supreme Court of Canada Justice Frank Iacobucci as a go-between. Several modern-day treaties in British Columbia followed in 2007. I worked with Premier Gordon Campbell and the British Columbia First Nations of Maa-nulth and Tsawwassen to achieve agreements in principle. Later in 2007, we forced a reluctant federal bureaucracy to adopt a package of reforms described as "Justice at Last," which effected changes to Canada's land claims process that had languished since Prime Minister John Diefenbaker first attempted them in the 1960s.

In 2009 and 2010, while I was the minister of the environment, we worked with Canada's indigenous peoples, including the Inuit, in the creation of many of Canada's new national parks. In British Columbia we were able to do something that everyone said was impossible. We struck a partnership with the Haida and created the Gwaii Haanas National Marine Conservation Area, in effect Canada's first undersea national park, protecting the ecosystem of a portion of Haida Gwaii (formerly the Queen Charlotte Islands) from the bottom of the continental trench to the tops of the coastal mountains.

It wasn't always easy, and every one of these advancements faced internal and external opposition. But I have worked alongside First Nation, Inuit and Métis peoples more or less constantly since 1986, and I have seen our country change for the better over that time. Unfortunately, that progress has been uneven, and it saddens me to say that the crushing weight of poverty among Canada's indigenous peoples remains the greatest challenge facing Aboriginal communities and, indeed, our country.

Through it all I have come to love and respect indigenous peoples. Their future is our future. I admire their resilience in the face of overwhelming odds, and I believe fervently that modern Canada will never achieve its full potential unless we make the reforms and the investments necessary to advance the interests of

Aboriginal Canadians, especially in the education of indigenous children so that they may share equally in that future.

It is impossible even to think about a book on Canada's energy future without discussing the central role that First Nation, Métis and Inuit peoples must play as full partners in that economic development. Decades ago, I counselled First Nation leaders that the day would inevitably come when resource development in Canada would be impossible without their real involvement and meaningful economic participation. That day has now arrived. Stated simply, Canada will never be able to export its oil or natural gas into the Asia Pacific Basin unless it is by way of pipelines and port facilities that are owned, at least in part, by First Nation partners.

Travelling the Pacific Northwest

In March 2016, I travelled along the coast of Canada's Pacific Northwest, that beautiful expanse of ocean and verdant rain forest that comprises the northern coast of British Columbia. These lands and waters are the ancestral home of many of the coastal First Nations who are central to the debate swirling around Canada's energy future. I went there to visit them, accompanied by my good friend Miles Richardson, a respected Haida leader.

The First Nations along the Pacific Northwest coast include the Haida, who occupy the islands of Haida Gwaii, where archaeologists have discovered the earliest evidence of human inhabitation of North America, dating back some 15,000 years. Then, the continent was entombed in ice, and these very islands defined its barren Pacific coastline. The rich oral history of the Haida supports their contention that they are the direct descendants of those first peoples, and that they were here even before the cedar trees—in fact, 5,000 years before. The Haida were always the most warlike of the indigenous peoples along this coast, and today they apply that assertiveness to the protection of the Haida Gwaii, a magical archipelago of 150 islands that defines Canada's most westerly coast.

The Nisga'a, the people of the Nass River Valley, live on the mainland along the Nass River, and they too have been here since time immemorial. The Nisga'a courageously set themselves apart from most of British Columbia's other First Nations in 1999, when they signed Canada's first modern-day treaty. Today, as a result, they exercise legal and governance dominion over the Nass Valley and some 2,000 square kilometres of their ancestral lands.

To the south of the Nisga'a are the Tsimshian peoples, the most populous of the indigenous peoples along the northern Pacific coast. The Tsimshian tribes are allied by history and ancestry and today consist of the First Nations of Lax Kw'alaams, Metlakatla, Kitkatla, Gitga'at, Kitsumkalum, Kitselas and Kitasoo. They are collectively known as the Allied Tsimshian Tribes.

And further inland are the proud Gitxsan, known as the Coast Tsimshian peoples; and to the south the Haisla, who occupy the lands at the head of the beautiful Douglas Channel, adjacent to the community of Kitimat.

* * *

The First Nations of British Columbia's Pacific Northwest intrigue and confound outsiders. Their culture, history and politics are among the richest and most fascinating in Canada, and their art, which is manifested in their totems, masks and blankets, is celebrated internationally and has become an important part of Canada's self-image. For those interested in Canada's energy future, these First Nations are also among the most important in Canada because virtually all the liquefied natural gas (LNG) facilities, oil ports and energy terminals proposed along the west coast have been sited somewhere in the territorial lands of the Nisga'a, Tsimshian, Coast Tsimshian and Haisla peoples. The corridors that have been proposed for the natural gas and oil pipelines that would feed those export facilities also traverse the territories of these First Nations, as they do the territories of other First Nations further inland in British Columbia and Alberta. Moreover, the Asia-bound tanker traffic associated with those projects, whether carrying oil, natural gas or refined petroleum products, will need to pass through the waters adjacent to Haida Gwaii. The only substantial energy project on Canada's west coast that is located elsewhere is Kinder Morgan's important Trans Mountain Pipeline, which is built along an existing pipeline alignment and terminates in the Port of Vancouver. That exception aside, the Tsimshian, Coast Tsimshian, Haida, Nisga'a and Haisla peoples find themselves today at the very centre of Canada's energy landscape.

I had returned to the Pacific Northwest coast to gather the research to finish the chapters of this book that speak to the role of Canada's First Nations in the country's energy future. Obviously, these are not the only indigenous peoples who are important to our future in energy and the environment. The reality is that every major energy project in the country has an impact on one or more of Canada's 634 First Nations. Enbridge's proposed Northern Gateway Pipeline, for instance, traverses the territorial lands of 65 First Nations; Kinder Morgan's Trans Mountain project another 15; and TransCanada's ambitious Energy East project a remarkable 155. But I have chosen to start here, in the Pacific Northwest, because these First Nations are critical to the future of Canada's Asia-bound energy exports.

The Pacific Northwest is Canada's closest and most proximate gateway into the energy markets of the Asia Pacific Basin. Tragically, for most of the past 15 years, Canada simply assumed that the First Nations who live here would cheer the arrival of energy mega-projects along the coast that they depend on and have occupied since time immemorial. We would come to learn how flawed that assumption was and understand that, without the environmental support and economic participation of those First Nations, there would be no LNG facilities, oil terminals or energy exports.

The Gateway to Asia

One cannot understand the energy picture of British Columbia's Pacific Northwest coast without some understanding of its intimidating terrain. The landmass of the region is defined by the Coast Mountains, which drop hard against the Pacific Ocean to create a mystical and impenetrable wilderness where ocean, mountain, coastline and weather merge into one. The shoulders of the mountains are steep, and they define two of the province's most pristine and important watersheds, the Skeena and the Nass, which snake inland and have sustained Aboriginal peoples since before recorded time. It is a very remote and very beautiful place.

Travel here is difficult, since distances are magnified by impenetrable mountains and long, meandering coastal inlets. Energy infrastructure, especially linear infrastructure, invites environmental controversy and is expensive to construct, requiring complex and circuitous routing up and down narrow mountain valleys. And while the Haisla, Tsimshian, Coast Tsimshian and Nisga'a peoples live in proximity to one another as the crow flies, their communities are in fact worlds apart, separated by substantial travel distances, whether by boat or land vehicle.

The Pacific Northwest is also a place that has been inundated and eventually convulsed by competing proposals to build more than 25 major energy projects over the past decade. The proposed projects are so numerous that the Government of British Columbia wisely created a website, a racing form of sorts, to inventory and explain the many that are under discussion. Most of the proposed projects will never get built but, in the time since 2000, the world's largest energy companies have expended billions of dollars here planning and designing LNG ports, natural gas pipelines, oil export terminals, oil pipelines and the associated transportation, electricity and marine infrastructure.

The most controversial of the projects has been Enbridge's Northern Gateway Pipeline, a 1,180 kilometre pipeline that would have carried 525,000 barrels of oil per day from Alberta's oil sands to a marine export terminal at Kitimat. The history of the project has been troubled and, while the major regulatory approvals for that project were secured in 2015, they were subsequently struck down by the Federal Court of Appeal in 2016. More importantly, 15 years after the project was conceived, its proponents continue to struggle to secure a coastal First Nation as a partner for the port facility.

Most of the other projects proposed along the Pacific Northwest coast involve LNG. Canada has long been one of the world's largest natural gas producers, using that gas for both domestic consumption and export to the United States. However, since the year 2000, new drilling and fracking technologies have harnessed ever-larger North American natural gas reserves, with the result that both Canada and the United States now have more natural gas than they can realistically consume. This is especially true of Canada, where even our proven reserves are several hundred times larger than our annual domestic needs, ignoring consideration of other enormous frontier natural gas basins that remain untouched and largely unexplored.

In the years since 2000, Canada has therefore been at the centre of a bonanza of proposed projects, designed to liquefy western Canadian natural gas at facilities on British Columbia's Pacific coast and to export that LNG into the hungry markets of the Asia Pacific Basin. The race to develop LNG export facilities is a global one, with Canada's main competition coming from the United States, Australia and Qatar. However, Canada's massive resource base, our open-for-business environment and our reliability as a country that can be counted on to fulfill its contractual commitments over a long period have all meant that we have been at the centre of a deluge of competing project proposals. More than 20 LNG projects have been proposed along the British Columbia coast, but the most substantial are located in the Pacific Northwest, in one of three locations: along the Douglas Channel near Kitimat; in the vicinity of Prince Rupert; or farther north, along the Portland Inlet. Premier Christy Clark astutely recognized the economic potential of LNG, and her government has been singularly focused since 2011 on the goal of having three LNG facilities in operation by 2020. Unfortunately, the strategy has failed.

To describe the activity surrounding all these proposed projects as frenetic would be an understatement. For a decade, many of the world's largest energy corporations have been active in the Pacific Northwest, negotiating with the province and First Nations to secure terminal locations and pipeline rights of way. Myriad consultation agreements, access and benefit agreements, participation agreements and business partnerships have been concluded among the project proponents, the Government of British Columbia and the many First Nations in the region. Billions of dollars have been expended on project design and approval. Shell alone will have invested more than $2 billion before it makes the final decision on whether to proceed with its $40 billion proposed LNG project. The pressure on British Columbia's coastal First Nations to keep pace with these proposed developments has been enormous.

The young chief of the Kitselas First Nation, Joe Bevan, who is a financial wizard, met me in Terrace and described how his First Nation was forced to go from standing still to employing a staff of 25 and an army of consultants, all to manage their negotiations on 24 different energy projects. In a speech I gave to the Tsimshian chiefs in 2010, I warned them that, when it comes to dealing with the world's largest energy companies, "you don't get what you deserve—you get what you negotiate." Joe Bevan thanked me for that advice and gave me a quick inventory of the economic advancements he had secured for the Kitselas people. I was not surprised to hear later that, among the many project proponents, the word is that if you are meeting with Kitselas, you'd best have done your homework.

When it comes to First Nation participation in resource development, the Pacific Northwest has been Canada's cauldron of innovation. Nothing on this scale has happened before in Canada. In fact, nothing on this scale has happened for indigenous people anywhere in the world, since few other indigenous people in the world enjoy the legal and constitutional rights of most of British Columbia's First Nations. For more than a decade now, the

Pacific Northwest coast has been inundated with Canadian energy companies such as TransCanada, Enbridge and Progress Energy, together with global players such as Petronas, Shell, Woodside, BG and ExxonMobil—all working hard to define a new collaborative future with Canada's First Nations.

As discussed elsewhere in this book, the economic case for pipelines and ports on Canada's west coast, affording access to the Asia Pacific Basin, is self-evident. That is where the future market lies for incremental volumes of Canada's oil and natural gas. The Government of British Columbia recognizes the opportunity that this situation represents, and Premier Clark has been an unrelenting supporter of British Columbia's future as an LNG exporter. Her government has been less supportive of Alberta's need to export its oil into the Asia Pacific Basin, employing her so-called five conditions to forestall that discussion while British Columbia focuses on what it understood to be the more immediate LNG opportunity.

Unfortunately, Canada's progress on LNG has been halting. Once again we misplayed our hand, failing to recognize that the task was to secure a global advantage as the "first mover"— the jurisdiction with the largest invested capital base, able to withstand the ups and downs of the global natural gas market. We were slow off the mark and lost critical time in finalizing a competitive fiscal framework. Federal and provincial regulatory approvals have been slow in coming, as has First Nation support to finalize terminal locations. Petronas continues to be frustrated by its inability to secure the regulatory and fiscal certainty it requires to proceed on its Lelu Island LNG terminal site, and problems persist on other proposed terminal locations. The international companies at the centre of these proposed projects have continued to warn the federal, provincial and First Nation governments of their frustrations.

We were overconfident at first, seemingly oblivious to the reality that the world is awash in natural gas and that the largest energy corporations have alternatives and can readily shift their capital investments from Canada to competing locations. In late 2015, Canada's new Liberal government introduced yet another level of environmental scrutiny, questioning the climate change merits of LNG, seemingly oblivious to the fact that exports of North American natural gas into Asia are likely the single-most advantageous thing that Canadians can do to help reduce global greenhouse gas (GHG) emissions emanating from Asia.

Our timing couldn't have been worse. In the time since 2014, the global LNG market has cooled, as demand softened, supply increased and prices plummeted. Demand from Asian markets, which comprise 70 percent of the global market, has stagnated. LNG exports to China actually declined in 2015, for the first time ever. At the same time, global supply from Qatar, Australia, Russia and the United States has expanded dramatically—outpacing demand, sending prices spiralling downward and forcing project proponents, including those in Canada, to re-evaluate the scale, timing and merits of their proposed investments.

And, of course, our competitors in the United States, Australia, Qatar and Russia have not stood still. The United States, once our largest natural gas customer, has become our most successful natural gas competitor on every front. Americans have moved speedily to re-engineer existing LNG import facilities to allow them to export large volumes of new "surplus" American natural gas, essentially capturing much of the available Asian market. Cheniere Energy's sprawling LNG terminal at Sabine Pass in

Texas began exporting in 2016, with an initial export capacity of 27 million tonnes per annum (3.8 billion cubic feet per day). The company's regulatory approvals allow it to more than double those export volumes.

It is the Australians, however, who have truly schooled Canada. The Australians seized on the LNG opportunity a decade ago and, with the opening of Chevron's monster Gorgon facility in March 2016, are well on their way to surpassing Qatar to become the world's largest LNG exporter by 2019. Australia has commissioned four new LNG projects since 2014, with three more to come, completing a $200 billion investment boom. By 2020, Australian LNG exports will exceed 85 million tonnes per year. With a bit of luck, Canada may have one project under construction by then.

Even front-running Canadian projects such as Shell and Petronas have repeatedly delayed their so-called final investment decisions. Shell's most recent delay will defer the decision into late 2016, although some speculate that the company is unlikely to make a final investment decision until as late as 2020. Petronas has now also deferred its own final investment decision, highlighting the continuing controversy surrounding its proposed terminal site at Lelu Island. Most of the other proponents appear content to defer final investment decisions, pending greater clarity on regulatory issues and the ability of the international market to absorb a greater LNG supply.

None of this is necessarily fatal to Canada's long-term LNG ambitions. Energy investments on this scale are made on the basis of long-term fundamentals and, despite our attempts to "get in our own way," those fundamentals favour Canada. Ironically, Australia's success also favours Canada, as international LNG consumers focus on the need for diversification in their LNG supply chains. But the gold rush phase of the LNG bonanza has certainly drawn to a close and, in the face of a global supply glut, regulatory delays and siting confusion, coupled with continuing opposition from environmental opponents and some First Nation leaders, skeptics have begun to ask whether any of British Columbia's projects will ever proceed. The Fraser Institute estimates Canada's annual export losses at close to $25 billion per year for oil exports alone.[1] Realistically, no one ever expected all 20 of the proposed projects to proceed. The global LNG market is capable of absorbing two, or at most three, world scale Canadian LNG facilities on our Pacific coast, and attention has now turned to which projects will survive.

Nonetheless, it is embarrassing that, despite 15 years of effort, Canada has no new oil pipelines or energy shipping terminals under construction in the Pacific Northwest and, despite close to 10 years of effort, there is not a single LNG terminal or natural gas pipeline under construction either. In the same period, Australia has transformed itself from a middling natural gas producer to becoming the world's largest LNG exporter, and the United States has gone from being a rapacious consumer of imported natural gas and oil to an exporter of both. By comparison, Canada is standing still, needing to reach new and growing markets in Asia yet lacking the infrastructure that is required. This situation has gradually clouded our prospects and, one by one, the world's major energy players have begun to focus on opportunities elsewhere.

Progress with the coastal First Nations of the Pacific Northwest has been decidedly uneven. Oil remains the more difficult topic, and opposition to Enbridge's Northern Gateway project continues to be intractable, even though among some First Nations a sense of inevitability seems to have settled around the project. The most significant problem continues to be the terminal location. The Haisla First Nation remains virulently opposed to oil tanker traffic on the Douglas Channel, and therefore it opposes the approved terminal location near Kitimat. The First Nation initiated the legal proceedings that led to the quashing of Enbridge's regulatory approvals.

Most coastal First Nations support LNG exports. The Haisla First Nation, for example, has been an outspoken advocate of Shell's LNG Canada project and has pressed the federal government to avoid further regulatory delays that could imperil it. The other First Nations along the coast are also now generally supportive of LNG as a cleaner and greener alternative to oil exports.

The Pacific Northwest LNG project proposed by Petronas enjoys wide First Nation support on a conceptual level, but the decision to construct the facility on Lelu Island, near Prince Rupert, continues to trouble the project. The Tsimshian oppose Petronas' decision to site its terminal on Lelu Island, concerned that it would threaten critical nursery habitat for juvenile salmon, and confusion and controversy continue to swirl around the supposed "billion dollar offer" that Lax Kw'alaams voted down in a community referendum in November 2015.

The First Nation now has a new chief, John Helin, who is generally supportive of the project and has indicated a willingness to revisit the community's decision. Chief Helin has been frustrated, however, by the substandard quality of the environmental baseline work done surrounding the Lelu Island site. Several other Tsimshian First Nations, most notably Metlakatla and Kitsumkalum, also continue to question the suitability of the site and, more problematically, question Lax Kw'alaams' right to choose it on their own. The Metlakatla and Lax Kw'alaams First Nations share the same history, ancestry and territories. As Chief Harold Leighton, the soft-spoken and respected leader of Metlakatla, puts it, "If we can't do this together, we are all going to lose out."

Leaders of the Tsimshian First Nation recognize that the proposed LNG projects could bring long-term economic benefits to their communities. Chief Harold Leighton speaks of the opportunities for investment in marine infrastructure, such as tugs and barges, together with opportunities to advance clean energy projects such as hydroelectricity. Several of the project proponents have been moving in this same direction, showing a willingness to use their projects to finance First Nation investments such as hydro-electric facilities. Chief Helin of Lax Kw'alaams is also an outspoken advocate of First Nation project ownership, and he speaks passionately about the need to pursue the economic opportunities surrounding the LNG projects, on their own terms—as "owners."

Chief Helin and Chief Leighton are right in that the status quo on resource development no longer holds, and Canada is now charting a new course. How we manage our way forward in the Pacific Northwest will play a major role in determining Canada's economic and social future, especially as it relates to resource development and the Asia Pacific Basin. Embedded in this shifting reality are challenging constitutional and legal issues related to the role of First Nations in west coast energy corridors, terminals, shipping routes and marine management. These are areas of responsibility that undoubtedly require careful government regulation and, ultimately, important federal and provincial marine safety investments. But importantly, they also require the negotiation of economic partnerships with First Nations.

In a sense, it is frustrating that non-Canadians have been able to see the way forward more clearly than we have. Global multinationals such as Shell and Petronas, and even some of the Chinese state-owned enterprises, have moved quickly to embrace First Nations as their partners. I know from my time as a banker that many international players have approached the reconciliation of economic interests with Canada's First Nations more quickly and with a broader perspective than have our own Canadian companies. International players seem to have taken a much longer-term perspective on the need to build sustaining relationships with coastal and corridor First Nations.

To be sure, all such negotiations are challenging. Pipeline companies in particular must continue to advance right-of-way negotiations in a complex and politically sensitive setting. Yet those who have been successful, such as Kinder Morgan's CEO Ian Anderson, have recognized that the inclusion of First Nations in the development process is about far more than observing and minimizing the constitutional duty to consult and accommodate. Rather, it is about getting traction on economic terms by viewing First Nations as business partners.

I have repeatedly said that west coast access, for both oil and natural gas, is a national imperative for our country. Canada will remain a satellite supplier of energy to the United States unless and until we can sell our oil and gas into the global marketplace at global prices. So what better time and what better place to advance both Canada's economic interests and those of its First Nations? Put another way, if we cannot achieve a sensible rebalancing of the economic interests of First Nations and the rest of Canada on something as important and profitable as Canada's energy exports, where can we achieve it?

Today, thanks to our abundance of natural resources, we stand on the verge of a new era of growth and development. It represents a game-changing opportunity for the First Nations of Canada's Pacific Northwest. No other country in the world has such an opportunity to bring on energy projects at the pace or scale of Canada. We are talking about billions of dollars in major resource developments that are currently—or will be—taking place on or near First Nation communities.

And so, as my good friend Miles Richardson and I met the Haida, Tsimshian and Nisga'a peoples who are so critical to our energy future, we posed these very questions. What do they think of Canada's energy future? Do they oppose or support the export of Canada's oil and natural gas? What do they envision as the role of the First Nations?

Among the First Nations of the Pacific Northwest, these are divisive questions and consensus remains elusive. There are still many, especially among the young, who oppose any association with Canada's hydrocarbon economy. But others see the economic opportunities associated with the many proposed projects, especially those related to LNG, and have begun to envision a different future. Most leaders quietly admit that their communities are poorer than they should be and that they need long-term, sustainable jobs and economic opportunities.

Oil and bitumen remain a tougher sell, but even there a sense of inevitability has begun to settle over the Pacific Northwest, and leaders in every First Nation have begun to strategize quietly on how they might take advantage of the economic opportunities available to their own First Nation. It is generally understood that most of the proposed projects will not proceed, and the First Nations who "land" an LNG terminal or an oil port will quickly become among the wealthiest communities—Aboriginal or otherwise—in North America. Some deplore such a future.

Others have begun to reach toward it. All are highly motivated by a desire to protect the environment, especially the riverine and coastal ecosystems that have sustained them. A competition of sorts has also begun to develop among the First Nations, arousing dangerous jealousies between people who have been linked by ancestry, marriage and culture since time immemorial.

All in all, it is a fascinating and exciting time. One thing is certain: The coastal First Nations of Canada's Pacific Northwest are the key to Canada's energy future, and there will be no access to the growing markets of the Asia Pacific unless they are full partners in that endeavour.

CHAPTER 11

It's Not about the Money: A First Nation
Perspective on Jurisdiction, the Environment and Energy

To visit the Nass River in the spring of the year is to witness what the wilderness of North America must have looked like before the arrival of the first Europeans. While Canada can be justifiably proud of many remote and wonderful places, few can rival the beauty and startling fecundity of the Nass. The Nass River rises from the mountains in north central British Columbia and drains south and west, opening into the Pacific Ocean at the Portland Inlet, immediately south of Alaska. The name Nass comes from the Tlingit word for "food depot," referring to the rich marine resources of the river. The people who have been the stewards of these lands are the Nisga'a—"the peoples of the Nass River"—who have been here since time began.

Early spring is the time when the Nass returns to life. The eulachon run begins then, and the small fish are coursing up the Nass by the millions to spawn, and then to die. They are accompanied by an entire ecosystem that depends on them as their life source—seals, sea lions, whales and birds . . . and more birds. It is as though every seagull in the Pacific Northwest has congregated here, flocking together in pursuit of the eulachon, the small, oily fish that the Nisga'a sometimes call the "saviour fish" because it is the first food source to arrive after the long, wet winter.

I have travelled the length and breadth of North America, but I have never before seen gulls in the millions—flocks so dense that they seem to crowd the azure sky. Ravens and bald eagles are everywhere. On one sandbar, near Kincolith where the Pacific Ocean and the Nass merge, eight eagles caucus haughtily together on a cedar stump in a sandbar. Upstream, along the river, seals and sea lions bob playfully, glistening in the sun as they break the surface of the water. It is an extraordinary sight, all the more poignant because the eulachon, once plentiful along every major river system on the west coast of North America, are now endangered elsewhere. Only on the Nass do you get a sense today of what it must have once been like.

Gerald's Eulachon Grease Camp

In March 2016, I headed to Greenville to meet with Mitch Stevens, president of the Nisga'a Lisims Government. But first, my friend Miles Richardson and I wanted to witness the eulachon run along the Nass and visit one of the camps where the Nisga'a produce the valuable eulachon oil that has traded among the indigenous peoples of North America since before recorded time. The eulachon is a very oily fish, so oily that it is also known as the candlefish because, when dried, it will light and burn like a candle. The oil or grease from the eulachon has been a staple among

Aboriginal people across western North America for as long as anyone remembers; the early trails across the Pacific region of North America were known as grease trails. Today, the Nisga'a alone continue that harvest, and Mason jars of their eulachon oil trade among the First Nations of the Pacific Northwest as would the finest European olive oils.

We were invited to visit Gerald Robinson's camp at Fishery Bay, near Black Point on the Nass River. I was exposed to eulachon oil years ago, while a commissioner of Canada's Indian Claims Commission, during an inquiry into the claims of the Lax Kw'alaams First Nation, but I hadn't been to one of the storied fishing camps where the harvest takes place. Miles had never seen one either, even though he is well known in these parts and knew Gerald's father, Rod Robinson, a famous Nisga'a elder. The Haida and the Nisga'a are friendly rivals, and the Nisga'a have skilfully employed their eulachon grease, which the Haida covet, as the currency in the relationship. On the way to the camp, Miles regaled us with stories of his youth and the inspiration that Nisga'a leaders such as Frank Calder and Joe Gosnell provided to his generation of Haida leaders.

Gerald's eulachon camp was a colourful and untidy assortment of tents, tarps and scattered propane tanks. A rich, pungent odour hung over the place, and warm steam and the sound of voices wafted out from beneath an orange tarpaulin at the centre of this tiny makeshift village. Children dodged happily in and out among the propane tanks scattered here and there. Beneath the orange tarp was a steaming, bubbling tub of boiling eulachon. The vat was being stirred by two men in overalls, smiling and wielding homemade paddles.

The men introduced themselves as Ernie and Mansel. They

welcomed us enthusiastically and eagerly shared the intricacies of rendering eulachon grease. It is a laborious process, and the two men were nearing the end of the day's batch. Every 24 hours, several hundred pounds of eulachon are mixed with water from the Nass and loaded into a big cedar vat, and the long process of distilling them into grease begins anew. It seems a poor end for a eulachon, but most have now spawned and would die anyway. Ernie told us that he intended to be there for a full month.

As the fish are boiled, they release their oil, which floats to the surface of the vat to be skimmed, filtered, filtered again and then bottled. It was early in the season, and so the first oil was clear and light, the colour of olive oil and with a similar texture, but possessing a fishy aftertaste. I was told that as the season progressed and the giant tubs of eulachon fermenting outside ripened, the oil would become darker, richer and more flavourful. That day's product, however, was described as the "first cut." It is an acquired taste, not really my own, but when Gerald generously offered Miles a Mason jar full of the early-season product, he was moved beyond words. For hundreds of years the Haida have depended on eulachon grease to moisten the dried salmon that they live on through the long winter months. All in all, it was a remarkable glimpse into a traditional harvest that once flourished along the Pacific coast.

Canadians who know of my background and history with First Nations often ask me, "What do First Nations want? Why can't someone just figure it out and pay them whatever it is, so that we can get on with building pipelines?"

The trip along the Nass reminded me how very difficult such questions are to answer. Aboriginal and non-Aboriginal Canadians barely know each other, and as Canada becomes an increasingly urban multicultural nation, fewer and fewer Canadians have spent time among those First Nations and Inuit who are still close to the land, leading lives that are modern in some ways yet reflective of the values of their ancestors in others. I don't question the goodwill of Canadians toward Canada's First Nations. I believe it exists and is stronger than ever. But few Canadians have ever travelled to the Arctic or the Pacific Northwest or northern Labrador and eaten muktuk, wild goose or moose-nose soup. Few have taken part in a caribou hunt, or been inside a sweat lodge, or seen a eulachon grease camp. We live in very different solitudes.

As Miles Richardson and I travelled among the Haida, the Tsimshian and the Nisga'a, we asked what they thought about Canada's future when it comes to energy and the environment. Do they oppose or support the export of Canada's oil and natural gas? What do they envision as the role of First Nations?

There are no easy answers to such questions because every First Nation in Canada is different, occupying its own territorial place. Each has a well-established right to be here, and each has survived, and indeed flourished, in the face of enormous odds. Their communities, languages, cultures and traditional practices survive to varying degrees, and they are vocal, united and intractable in their insistence on their right to be heard and to participate in the economic development of the lands and resources that surround them. And our legal system, led by Supreme Court Chief Justice Beverley McLachlin, has supported those assertions.

In sum, the modern aspirations of Canada's First Nations reflect all these complexities. There are no easy answers to the question "What do Canada's First Nations want?" Entire libraries have been written on the subject. This is one account, and others will undoubtedly follow.

The debate over Canada's energy future has convulsed our country for more than a decade, and Canadians should, by now, broadly understand at least three important things about Canada's First Nations on the Pacific Northwest coast.

BC's First Nations and Inherent Jurisdiction

First of all, British Columbia's First Nations are self-governing indigenous peoples or "nations" that exist within the context of the overall Canadian federation. As such, they enjoy a nation-to-nation relationship with both the federal and provincial governments. Miles Richardson is one of Canada's most forceful and articulate First Nation leaders on this topic. A respectful nation-to-nation relationship must start, in his view, with the recognition that each First Nation has "inherent jurisdiction" to govern itself and continues to hold legal powers that it has never surrendered. In the context of British Columbia, this perspective is deeply held since most of the province's First Nations never signed a treaty and have therefore never ceded their inherent jurisdiction, nor surrendered their Aboriginal title. Their inherent rights are protected under the Royal Proclamation and the Canadian Constitution, and they retain the authority to negotiate the extent to which they are prepared to compromise their inherent jurisdiction in working together with other levels of government. This authority obviously introduces complexities in the modern governance of British Columbia, with which other provincial governments have limited experience.

Joe Gosnell, the legendary Nisga'a leader, is said to have summoned the courage of his people in the 1960s by warning them that, unless they rose up in defence of their inherent jurisdictional and Aboriginal title, "All that they will leave us is a sea of dead stumps. They will take every last log. They will take every last fish. They will leave us nothing." When asked by Prime Minister Pierre Trudeau what he meant when he spoke of "Aboriginal title," Gosnell stormed back, "It means we own it all—lock, stock and barrel."

Joe Gosnell led the Nisga'a First Nation in its long struggle to conclude a modern treaty with Canada and British Columbia. It came into effect in 2000 and is premised on these very concepts of inherent jurisdiction and Aboriginal title. The rights of the Nisga'a differ somewhat from those of First Nations who have not signed such a treaty, but their inherent position is strengthened by the jurisdiction they have maintained over matters such as the environment and, further, by the legal certainty that accompanies their position under their treaty. Their rights are enshrined in their treaty, and that treaty, in turn, is protected under the Canadian Constitution. Their dominion over their Nisga'a lands is absolute.

The Stewards of the Coastal Environment

The second thing that Canadians need understand about Canada's First Nations, including those on the Pacific coast, is the importance that indigenous peoples attach to the environment. This is true across Canada, but here in the Pacific Northwest, it is clear that Canada's coastal First Nations will never compromise the marine environment of our west coast.

Canada's coastal First Nations are closer to and more protective of the environment than most Canadians can ever understand. For hundreds of years, the natural environment has sustained Canada's indigenous peoples in the face of crushing poverty and government neglect. This is particularly true along the rich ecosystems of the Pacific coast. Not surprisingly, therefore, the indigenous peoples who live here are suspicious and unyielding in the face of any threats to the very resources that have sustained them. In the specific context of Canada's Pacific Northwest, the Nisga'a, Haida and Tsimshian peoples have been sustained by the marine resources of the Pacific Ocean since time immemorial—and there are few who would not readily lay down their lives to protect the environment from those who might, even inadvertently, despoil it. The rest of us say that we understand this devotion, but we really don't.

Aboriginal Title and the Right of Economic Participation

A third reality in the Pacific Northwest is that Canada's First Nations fully expect to participate in the economic benefits arising from their possession of "Aboriginal title." Outsiders struggle with this notion, since the legal boundaries of the concept of Aboriginal title remain uncertain; but the reality for the coastal First Nations of British Columbia is that they have never signed a treaty, never surrendered title, nor abrogated their rights as the holders of the Aboriginal title that underlie this part of British Columbia. Their Aboriginal title has value and, while they may be prepared to negotiate a monetary exchange in return for infringements on it, they are not prepared to give it away. Why would they? A corporate CEO who gave away a valuable asset without recompense would be fired, and a non-Aboriginal politician—say a premier—who did so would be impeached. And so, not surprisingly, Canada's First Nations have fought aggressively to translate their title right to be "consulted and accommodated" into financial benefits such as bonus payments, property taxes, access and benefit agreements, financial overrides and, increasingly, partial project ownership. Ironically, international companies have more readily adapted to the implications of this position than have Canadians.

So what do Canada's coastal First Nations want? They expect to be treated respectfully as self-governing peoples within the Canadian federation. They demand that the environment be protected. They expect to be treated respectfully as self-governing peoples within the Canadian federation. And they expect to negotiate financial benefits as a consequence of infringements on their Aboriginal title.

INHERENT JURISDICTION

British Columbia's First Nations are self-governing indigenous peoples, or "nations" that exist within the context of the overall Canadian federation. They insist on a government-to-government relationship with both the federal and provincial governments, which is premised on the fact that they have never given up their inherent jurisdiction to govern themselves.

Every First Nation citizen in Canada enjoys a legal and constitutional relationship with the federal Crown that is unlike that of any other Canadian citizen. Few Canadians understand why this is the case, and most are astonished to learn that the claims of Canada's First Nations to Aboriginal title are grounded in an ancient document called the Royal Proclamation, which was passed by King George III in 1763 at the end of the long-forgotten European conflict known as the French and Indian War. The proclamation recognized that the Indian tribes on the frontier of America enjoyed certain inalienable land rights, and it prohibited anyone except the Crown from extinguishing those rights and, even then, only by way of a formal treaty. In the several hundred years that followed, successive British, then Canadian, governments signed hundreds of such treaties. The proclamation was a controversial document even in its day, and it was one of the many grievances that eventually ripened into the American Revolution. Today, the Royal Proclamation is regarded as the constitutional wellspring of the long line of modern Supreme Court of Canada decisions that reinforce and strengthen the Canadian concept of Aboriginal title. Visualize it as the Magna Carta of Canada's indigenous peoples. In a very real sense, the United Nations Declaration on the Rights of Indigenous Peoples and its requirement of "free, prior and informed consent" is a modern articulation of the Royal Proclamation.

The concepts contained in the Royal Proclamation of 1763 are now embedded in section 35 of Canada's Constitution, and these rights have a special importance in British Columbia because it is in that province that the concept of Aboriginal title retains its fullest legal vitality. For more than 250 years, successive British Columbian governments refused to sign treaties with the province's First Nations, ignoring the proclamation itself, the pleas of the First Nations and the advice of their own lawyers. All that eventually changed in 1992—but modern treaty-making is laborious, and progress has been limited to the Nisga'a Treaty of 1999 and the two treaties with the Maa-nulth and Tsawwassen First Nations that were signed in 2007 by Premier Gordon Campbell and me, during my tenure as Canada's Indian affairs minister.

There are obviously differing perspectives on the legal and political boundaries of the concept of inherent jurisdiction. However, when it comes to energy and resource development issues, the concept is relied on by Canadian First Nations to achieve three broad outcomes. First of all, First Nations view resource development in their traditional territories as an opportunity to exercise their inherent jurisdiction. In fact, most view it as an aspect of their obligations as "stewards" or "watchmen" over their traditional resources. Second, virtually all First Nations view resource development in their traditional territories as subject to an overriding obligation to protect the environment and the sustainability of the resource base that remains. In this context, they begin by assessing the risks that the proposed activity entails, coupled with an assessment of the concurrent benefits. This calculus may lead them to oppose the project altogether, but it may equally invite a willingness to examine and negotiate toward trade-offs of benefits and costs. Third, every First Nation expects to derive full value for infringements on their Aboriginal title. What that value is will depend on the nature of the infringement, and on the scale and sustainability of the economic opportunities that are available as compensation.

This latter point is an important one and, from a practical perspective, all First Nations wrestle with challenges of poverty and capacity, and they expect that project proponents will accord them the time, patience and resources required to arrive at informed decisions. They will not be rushed, and they demand transparency and consensus in grappling with the alternatives before them. But they do so as an order of Canadian government, not as a stakeholder, and they expect to be treated with the respect which that entails. And they reserve, as any government must, the right to say no.

The Nisga'a Treaty is the most modern codification of the concept of inherent jurisdiction. The Nisga'a people fought for more than 130 years to assert their right to Aboriginal title over the Valley of the Nass, eventually securing Canada's first modern-day First Nation treaty with the Governments of Canada and British Columbia in 1999. Their struggles to conclude a treaty with the Crown are chronicled elsewhere—for example, in Tom Molloy's fine book, *The World Is Our Witness*. It is one of the most remarkable stories in Canadian history, beginning with the short, humiliating meeting between the premier of British Columbia and the Nisga'a in 1887, when they were turned away with the explanation that they were "little better than wild beasts of the field." It concluded in December 1999, with the ratification of Canada's first modern-day treaty in the Canadian House of Commons, as the world watched in fascination.

The Nisga'a were not unique among First Nations in their resiliency during the long, dark years from the end of the 19th century until the mid-20th century, but they were certainly the first to skilfully invoke British common law and the Canadian courts to assert their claims. In 1967, their tribal council, led by then-president Frank Calder, instructed Vancouver lawyer Thomas Berger to begin legal proceedings against the Province of British Columbia asserting the existence of their Aboriginal title to the Nass Valley. The resulting decision of Canada's Supreme Court, some seven years later and known as the *Calder* case, was ambiguous, but it marked the genesis of the long line of modern Canadian judicial decisions that now recognize the legitimacy of the claims of British Columbia's First Nations.

Modern Canadian history would henceforth turn on the simple yet inescapable truth asserted by the Nisga'a and validated by the Supreme Court of Canada—the Nisga'a had neither surrendered nor ceded their Aboriginal title and, under the Royal Proclamation of 1763 and later, section 35 of the *Constitution Act, 1982*, it remained intact.

Land claim negotiations with the Nisga'a began in 1976, a few short years after the Calder decision, and, after two decades of effort, culminated in the Nisga'a Treaty in 1999. During those years the Nisga'a were led by a legendary figure, Tribal Council President Joe Gosnell, who was indefatigable in his pursuit of a modern treaty.

The Nisga'a Treaty was controversial from the outset. It was challenged by Reform Party politicians on the premise that it gave too much to the Nisga'a, and it was criticized by Aboriginal leaders who thought that the Nisga'a had given away too much. Time has, however, validated the Nisga'a Treaty. It remains the precedent against which all other modern treaty-making efforts are judged, and the rights and benefits conferred under it ensure that the Nisga'a are today masters of their own fate, exercising modern governmental authority over 2,000 square kilometres of the Nass Valley, from the upper reaches of the river to the open waters of the Portland Inlet of the Pacific Ocean.

STEWARDS OF COASTAL ENVIRONMENT

I admit to feeling strongly about the inadequacies of Canada's marine safety and emergency response system on our west coast. I worked with the Haida to create the Gwaii Haanas National

Marine Conservation Area, Canada's first undersea national park, and, like them, and I believe Canada should make the necessary marine infrastructure investments to protect it. I continue to hold the view that not a drop of Canadian oil should move off Canada's Pacific Northwest until the Government of Canada has created a world class coastal regime in full partnership with the Government of British Columbia and the province's First Nations. That, rather than a tanker ban, is what we truly need, and it is to be hoped that Canada's new Liberal government will undertake the five years of heavy lifting required to create such a regime. Promises are not enough.

The 2014 incident of the *Simushir* proved this point beyond all doubt and, in the process, galvanized the thinking of First Nation leaders on our west coast.

* * *

On October 17, 2014, the Russian cargo vessel *Simushir* lost engine power off the west coast of Canada and began to drift helplessly toward the shores of Haida Gwaii. Gale-force winds would eventually bring the ship and its dangerous cargo of paint, aerosols, batteries, propane tanks and bunker fuel to within 5.6 nautical miles of one of Canada's ecological treasures—Gwaii Haanas—the only place in the world where the coastal ecosystem is protected as a national park from the tips of the Coast Mountains to the floor of the Pacific ocean. The ensuing race to prevent the *Simushir* from crashing ashore transfixed the entire country. Disaster was ultimately averted through shifting weather, Coast Guard heroism and good old-fashioned luck, but the crisis has forever changed the perspective of Canada's coastal First Nations.

The *Simushir* wasn't a particularly large ship—135 metres long, 17 metres wide, and with a draft of 7.12 metres and a gross tonnage of 6540 tonnes. This is smaller than most of the international cargo vessels that ply Canada's west coast, and the ship could only be described as "miniature" when compared with the international vessels that carry oil and LNG. By comparison, the largest VLCCs (very large crude carriers) that carry two million barrels of crude oil can be as large as 470 metres long and 60 metres wide, and can carry more than 330,000 tonnes. Indeed, the *Simushir* is shorter than the ocean-going tugs used to push and pull the giant VLCCs. So the stricken Russian ship wasn't especially big and, for a nation with a world class marine safety and emergency response system, it shouldn't have presented much of a problem. Unfortunately, Canada isn't that nation.

All mariners know of the dangers of "leeward shores," and the leeward shores of Haida Gwaii can be among the roughest in the world when the weather is bad. When the *Simushir*'s engines failed, the ship was some 20 nautical miles off the coast and, as the crew struggled to repair the engines, the ship drifted shoreward, slowly at first but with alarming speed as the weather worsened. The captain seemed initially optimistic about the ability of his crew to restart the ship's engines, but by midnight on October 16 the weather had begun to deteriorate markedly. Winds of 40 to 50 knots thrust the ship toward the rugged shore of Haida Gwaii as it was pummelled by 5- to 6-metre ocean swells. Shortly after midnight, the powerless *Simushir* was rolling heavily, heading inexorably toward the rugged coast of Gwaii Haanas. The captain, by then badly injured from a fall, called for the assistance of the Canadian Coast Guard.

By then the race to reach the *Simushir* before it could crash ashore had begun in earnest. By good fortune, the Canadian Coast Guard ship *Gordon Reid* was some 13 hours away in Hartley Bay, across the Hecate Strait, and Captain Michael Shuckburgh set out across the dangerous strait as soon as he received the call. A second Canadian Coast Guard ship, the *Wilfrid Laurier*, was diverted to the scene as it sailed from the Aleutian Islands homeward to Victoria. The Americans joined in the effort, and their Coast Guard vessel *Spar* was diverted from Ketchikan, Alaska, and their Jayhawk helicopter and Hercules aircraft were quickly flown into the Sandspit airport on the east side of Haida Gwaii. After some confusion, the closest ocean-going tug, the *Barbara Foss*, was hired and redirected from the Hecate Strait to the west coast of Haida Gwaii.

The real question was whether anyone could reach the *Simushir* before it crashed on the shores of Gwaii Haanas National Park. Canadian authorities estimated on the basis of the prevailing winds that they had until 11 the next morning to reach the ship. After that, it would be too late. The Haida First Nation, in particular, watched helplessly.

It would be 13 long hours before the CCGS *Gordon Reid* arrived, battered by its own perilous trip across the Hecate Strait, and by then the *Simushir* was drifting treacherously close to the coast, rolling badly and less than two-and-one-half hours from the coast. Fortunately, as the entire country watched, the storm off the coast of Gwaii Haanas began to abate.

The *Gordon Reid* was never intended to be a tugboat. It is what is known as a mid-shore patrol vessel. It is only 50 metres long and, although it had 5,000 hp engines, it had no realistic chance of towing the *Simushir* completely out of danger. The plan, instead, was to attach a tow line to the *Simushir* and keep it from drifting any closer to the coast, pending the arrival of the ocean-going rescue tug *Barbara Foss*.

The *Gordon Reid*'s own tow line snapped on its first attempt to tow the drifting vessel. A second attempt, employing the *Simushir*'s tow line, also failed. Inexplicably, it too snapped. A third attempt using the *Simushir*'s mooring line held in the early evening of October 17, and the *Gordon Reid* began to coax the crippled vessel slowly out to sea. That third tow line would eventually break the next morning, but by then the *Simushir* had been moved 40 kilometres back from the coast.

The situation was not fully resolved until the late afternoon of October 18, 2014, when the American tugboat *Barbara Foss* finally arrived on the scene, fully 41 hours after the incident began. That the *Barbara Foss* was available at all was pure happenstance. The tug had been headed south from Ketchikan, Alaska, and was able to divert from the Prince Rupert harbour, some 170 kilometres and 28 hours away. The *Barbara Foss* is an ocean-going tug and is designed for such work, and it secured the *Simushir* and towed it safely away from the coast of Haida Gwaii, to Prince Rupert.

Protecting the Pacific Coast—What Comes Next?

The *Simushir* incident was a wake-up call for all of Canada. The truth is that Canada is neither equipped nor prepared for a major marine disaster off its northwest coast, and this has been known for some time. It is one thing to talk about Canada having a world class tanker-safety system, and it is quite another to have one. The *Simushir* incident laid bare the inadequacies of Canada's marine protection system.

Repeated studies have underscored the risks to Canada's coast-line. A 2002 Oil Spill Task Force jointly commissioned by the US Coast Guard, the American Pacific states and British Columbia identified the remote west coast of Haida Gwaii as the highest-risk area on the entire Pacific coastline. The problem is its remoteness, coupled with the fact that ocean-going rescue tugs are not always readily available nearby. There are fewer than 80 ocean-going tugs that are capable of severe weather rescue on the entire west coast of North America between Cook Inlet, Alaska, and San Diego, California. None are stationed in ready proximity to Haida Gwaii. There are few such tugs along Canada's Pacific Northwest coast, and neither the Canadian Coast Guard nor the Canadian Forces have one. Even the private tugs operating out of CFB Esquimalt are less than one-third the size of the *Barbara Foss*.

In sum, Canada owns no tugs capable of recovering a drift-ing ship such as the *Simushir*—and the obvious and embarrassing question is how the Canadian Coast Guard can possibly fulfill its mandate of "Protecting the Marine Environment" without such equipment. The British Columbia coast is daunting in size, some 1,000 kilometres from north to south, and its inlets and channels add up to 25,000 kilometres of coastline.

By contrast, the Americans are ready for such an eventual-ity. Alaska and Washington—the two states that border British Columbia—have dedicated rescue tugs on call to respond to emer-gencies. Washington maintains an industry-funded rescue tug at Neah Bay, and the Alaskan government now maintains similar emergency towing capacity, after a near miss in 2007 at Unalaska.

The *Simushir* incident also had a galvanizing effect on the coastal First Nations who saw the full measure of risk they face given Canada's poor state of preparedness—with or without a

Canadian oil pipeline. The Haida, in particular, now recognize how completely helpless they were in the face of the *Simushir* crisis. While they have fought hard to exert jurisdiction over Haida Gwaii, they are completely bereft of the resources necessary to protect it. No boats. No ocean-going tugs. No rescue ships. No rescue response capability. No life-saving equipment. No emergency towing equipment. No emergency plan. No spill prevention equipment. No spill containment equipment. No money. In short—not much of anything.

The outspoken head of the Haida First Nation, Peter Lantin, led his community through the traumatic hours of the incident and afterward lamented their complete helplessness: "We would have spent 12 hours watching this thing wrecking on the beach and no one would be able to do anything, including us. We weren't prepared."

Moreover, the coastal First Nations now recognize that the protection of the marine environment of the Pacific Northwest isn't just about Enbridge's proposed Gateway project. The truth is that there are already hundreds of oil tankers of various sizes moving up and down the west coast of North America. There are, for example, loaded tankers servicing the Trans-Alaska Pipeline System between Valdez, Alaska, and Puget Sound, Washington. Others move northward along the coast, en route to Asia, having originated in Venezuela, Mexico, Ecuador and now even the American Gulf coast. The 2013 British Columbia *West Coast Spill Response Study* estimated that some 110 million cubic metres (691 million barrels) of petroleum move in vessels along British Columbia's west coast every year. Leaving aside bunker fuel movements, the largest single source of petroleum shipments is Alaska. Each year, more than 38 million cubic metres (239 million barrels) of Alaska North Slope crude oil move southward to US refineries in Washington. Another 25 million cubic metres (157 million barrels) of petroleum move up and down the coast from various sources.

What Canada's coastal First Nations want is what the federal government continues to promise—the creation of a world class system to prevent a marine disaster, together with the necessary infrastructure investments to contain a spill should one happen.

Interestingly, the *Simushir* incident has also brought many First Nation leaders to an appreciation of the marine opportunities that are embedded in the energy projects now proposed along the Pacific Northwest coast. Elvis Davis, a hereditary chief of the Haida in Old Massett, put it this way when I met with him and Elder Francis Ingram: "We woke up two years ago. I saw that we are so vulnerable to disasters that I had to start thinking differently. We had to negotiate with the devil and we had to stop saying 'no' to everything and grab the opportunity to be part of safety." Another hereditary chief, Robin Brown, added: "We are now looking at signing up with Northern Gateway as an Aboriginal equity partner because we want tugs and jobs and we want to be able to protect ourselves. When the *Simushir* was crashing we couldn't do anything. It was heart wrenching. Women were crying. There was going to be a disaster and we couldn't do anything. Nothing." Two other prominent members of the Haida First Nation, Wilson Brown and Roy Jones, Jr., now work with Northern Gateway and are pressing for Haida ownership of ocean-going tugboats and full participation in the marine safety system, along with Canada and British Columbia.

I am not suggesting that the Haida First Nation is now in favour of the Northern Gateway project. Far from it—both

Skidegate and Old Massett are still festooned with "Stop Enbridge" signs. But there are fewer signs than there used to be, and quietly many in the community are seriously discussing how to secure the marine investments so there will be no repeat of the *Simushir*. More than 6,000 vessels ply up and down the west coast of Haida Gwaii annually, many of them carrying oil, and sooner or later another will lose engine power in a storm. For some in the community, as Wilson Brown put it, "a line has been drawn in the water."

The frustration, of course, is that Canadians know what needs to be done. In 2010, the federal commissioner of the environment and sustainable development released a report that raised concerns about the current state of preparedness to respond to ship-source oil and chemical spills in Canadian waters. In 2013, the Standing Senate Committee on Energy, the Environment and Natural Resources completed a report on the subject. Also in 2013, Nuka Research completed a report for the Government of British Columbia: *West Coast Spill Response Study*. Douglas Eyford highlighted the existence of all these reports in his 2013 report to Canada's prime minister: *Forging Partnerships, Building Relationships: Aboriginal Canadians and Energy Development*.

In 2013, Transport Canada released its comprehensive report, *A Review of Canada's Ship-Source Oil Spill Preparedness and Response Regime—Setting the Course for the Future*. A fine piece of work, it provides 45 recommendations on exactly what Canada needs to do to live up to its stated ambition to have a world class tanker-safety regime. The Government of Canada, working together with the Government of British Columbia and the coastal First Nations, needs to get on with this work. The study highlights the need for years of preparation, consultation and investment before Canada can be said to be world class. Frankly, the coastal First Nations will never consent to exports of Canadian energy from Canada's shores until we have done so.

IMPORTANCE OF ECONOMIC PARTICIPATION

The third and final reality that must be recognized about Canada's First Nations is that they fully expect to participate in the economic benefits arising from resource development and major projects within their traditional territories.

Those expectations are predicated on the legal concept of Aboriginal title and on section 35 of Canada's Constitution, which impose legal obligations on the Crown and project proponents who "infringe" on Aboriginal rights and title to ensure that the affected First Nations share in the economic benefits associated with the development. The precise legal boundaries of the concept of Aboriginal title are uncertain, and always will be, but the reality for most of the First Nations of British Columbia is that they have never signed a treaty and never surrendered title; nor have they abrogated their rights as the holders of the Aboriginal title that underlies most of British Columbia. Their Aboriginal title therefore has an intrinsic value; and frankly, absent agreement between those First Nations, the Crown and the project proponents, it is virtually impossible to secure the legal certainty that investments on the scale of major energy projects require.

Canada's First Nations have fought aggressively to assert the right associated with "Aboriginal title," but it is here in British Columbia that the underlying legal concept enjoys its strongest footing. Not surprisingly, therefore, First Nations across the province, including those in the Pacific Northwest, have translated their title right to be "consulted and accommodated" into financial benefits such as bonus payments, property taxes, access and benefit agreements, financial overrides and, increasingly, partial project ownership.

These rights of economic participation pave the way to alleviating the challenges of poverty, at least, among the communities that are proximate to economic development.

The challenges of Aboriginal poverty are impossibly complex, involving as they do more than 600 individual First Nations and well over a thousand different communities across Canada. There are no simple solutions, but one thing is incontestable: First Nations, Métis and Inuit communities need functioning local economies and jobs.

I am passionate about the involvement of Aboriginal Canadians in resource development, especially the energy industry, because jobs and economic opportunity are critical to the future of those families and those communities. I have been to every corner of this sprawling country of ours and have visited hundreds of First Nation and Inuit communities. I know from experience that those communities where Aboriginal men and women are able to participate meaningfully in the economy and secure jobs and contracting opportunities are flourishing and successful communities. Challenges certainly remain, as they do for any community, but I know from experience how different those communities are from others where there is little or no economic activity. We know from experience how quickly the pathologies of poverty, despair and hopelessness dissipate once people have jobs and economic opportunity.

I remember a time in our country when the notion that First

Nations should have a right to participate in the economies surrounding them was exactly that—a notion—and so it was moving for me to spend time with leaders such as Chief Harold Leighton of Metlatkatla and Chief John Helin of Lax Kw'alaams.

Chief Leighton is one of the respected elder statesmen of the Tsimshian peoples, and he carries himself with the soft-spoken and quiet dignity of one who knows. He chooses his words slowly and carefully as he describes the work that his community has undertaken with energy companies such as Nexen, Exxon and Petronas. He speaks proudly of how successful the people of Metlakatla have been in securing employment and how excited they are by the prospects of investments in marine infrastructure and hydroelectricity, should one or more of the proposed LNG projects—which they support—proceed.

John Helin is the new chief of Lax Kw'alaams, and he too is an outspoken advocate of the need for First Nations to pursue their own economic future, buoyed by the opportunities surrounding new energy projects. Chief Helin also speaks softly, describing the weight of the Lelu Island controversy and his struggles to ensure that the science surrounding the salmon habitat is reliable and fully shared with the people of his community. He is optimistic that he can repair the situation but recognizes that he will require the support and inclusion of the elders and hereditary chiefs of the wider Tsimshian communities to move forward. He is mindful of his obligations surrounding the protection of the coastal environment but also speaks passionately of Aboriginally owned and controlled energy assets.

We know that this is possible, and we know that it has worked especially well in the energy industry. I recently read Rick George's book *Sun Rise*, which recounts the progress that leading Canadian companies such as Suncor have made through an assertive commitment to Aboriginal employment and contracting, even recruiting First Nation business leaders to serve on the company's board of directors.

Today, many of Alberta's most successful business leaders are Aboriginal men and women who are now carving their own paths to success and, in the process, creating economic opportunity for other Aboriginal Canadians. Some of that success is individual; in other cases it is collective—nowhere more successfully than at the Fort McKay First Nation where Chief Jim Boucher has created a multi-billion-dollar energy success story. Other First Nations in Alberta, British Columbia and Saskatchewan have flourished as the owners of energy resources, as producers and as contractors supporting the local energy industry.

Critics of Alberta's oil sands development fail to point out that the economic activity in northeastern Alberta has created more economic opportunity for Aboriginal Canadians than in any other place in Canada. Nor is this a singular case. Communities, including Aboriginal communities, that have jobs and access to economic opportunity succeed. I have seen this time and again across Canada. The Snap Lake, Diavik and Ekati diamond mines of the Northwest Territories are another illustration, since much of the workforce is made up of Aboriginal Canadians. The resulting prosperity has been felt across the Northwest Territories. Another illustration is the Voisey's Bay nickel mine in Labrador, where Vale has patiently built up a labour force that is largely Inuit—also producing healthier families and communities.

I have seen enough to know that the answer to the social challenges of Canada's Aboriginal peoples requires leadership and education, but it also demands economic opportunity. The energy industry is an important part of that future. It is the main economic driver across much of western Canada, and many of the jobs that the industry creates lend themselves to Aboriginal employment since the resource plays and associated infrastructure are located near Aboriginal communities. Moreover, the areas where energy development is taking place are generally the ones where First Nations enjoy collective rights of economic participation. In areas where First Nations have signed a treaty, those benefits generally take the form of impact and benefit agreements. In British Columbia, where the First Nations and the Government of Canada never concluded treaties, First Nations have an even greater say in resource development. The economic benefits available to those First Nations go well beyond impact and benefit agreements and increasingly include some degree of collective economic participation. The same is true "north of 60", where the comprehensive claim settlements that have been negotiated in Canada over the past 50 to 75 years have afforded land ownership, together with specific participatory rights, to indigenous peoples.

Every chief I meet in the Pacific Northwest speaks of the importance of jobs for the young people in their communities. The Canadian reality is that we need workers to maintain our ambitious pace of growth. Canada is short of workers and depends heavily on immigration to continue to meet our labour shortages. It is a paradox that Canada has the highest immigration intake of any G7 country and yet has experienced its highest unemployment rates among its fastest-growing population segment—young Aboriginal men and women. The median age of the Canadian population is 41, yet among Aboriginal Canadians it is only 28. This is a striking difference and one that brings challenges, but also opportunities. Those young Aboriginal people are disproportionately overrepresented among the unemployed, the underemployed and those who lack the requisite education to take on jobs. Surely, this is one of our country's greatest challenges and it is one where the energy industry can continue to make a difference.

Over the decade ahead, some 400,000 Aboriginal youth will enter the job market. This is the very definition of potential—not only for Aboriginal communities, but also for Canada. Their success in greater numbers could define the beginning of a new age and a new way of life for Aboriginal Canadians. It is therefore important that we invest in their future, and in their ability to succeed. That means working to increase high school graduation rates, which are currently half those of the non-Aboriginal population, as well as post-secondary graduation rates, which are currently no better than one-third. Education will be the key to economic progress, and it will be how greater numbers of Canada's First Nation, Métis and Inuit youngsters will come to succeed as skilled workers, professionals, entrepreneurs and business leaders. It will continue to be important for us to find opportunity in our country's skills shortage and help equip young Aboriginal workers with the expertise they'll need to get ahead.

If we cannot work out partnerships between Aboriginal peoples and industry and government in the energy industry, then where can we? Canada is in the energy business. The economic opportunities and jobs created by oil, natural gas, pipelines, LNG terminals, ports, wind farms and hydro facilities are proximate to the very Canadians who live where those jobs are and, in most cases, who have a legal basis on which to negotiate some element of participation.

The stakes for Canada are high, and that is why I am so

encouraged to see leaders such as Mitch Stevens of the Nisga'a, Harold Leighton at Metlakatla, and John Helin of Lax Kw'alaams at the negotiating table with the country's biggest energy companies. They represent a new generation of indigenous leadership— smart, aggressive, well-educated and successful in their own right before becoming chiefs. They have an intimate understanding of how great the stakes are for their communities and view the energy projects that have inundated their traditional territories as an opportunity to advance the economic opportunities of their people. They know that the interference of outsiders is the greatest risk they face. Chief Joe Bevan at Kitselas recently warned Canada's minister of transport, Marc Garneau, not to "cut the throat" of his First Nation by imposing a blanket tanker ban on the Pacific Northwest coast. Others apparently made similar comments.

While progress seems slow, I am encouraged by just how dramatically our country has changed over the past 25 years, as responsible Canadian corporate citizens, multinational companies and Canadian entrepreneurs embrace a new future. It isn't always easy, and there have been failures. Some project proponents have stumbled, failing to recognize the importance that indigenous Canadians attach to the protection of the natural environment. Others have moved too quickly or clumsily, failing to establish the necessary trust at the community level. The embattled Northern Gateway Pipeline project illustrates the challenge of rebuilding trust with Aboriginal peoples once it has been lost.

But there have also been success stories, and the economic empowerment of the James Bay Cree in northern Quebec is one example. So, too, are the successes of the First Nations in and around the Alberta oil sands. Nor is that success limited to the oil sands region, since most of the First Nations in Alberta and many in Saskatchewan and in northern British Columbia are in the energy business in one way or another.

Progress in the Pacific Northwest, spurred on by many proposed energy projects, has been especially profound. I am struck by the vision, thoughtfulness and breadth of experience of the First Nation leaders with whom I met.

It is the Nisga'a and the Haida, together with the Tsimshian tribes of the Pacific Northwest, who are now best positioned to change the future of Canada. They and they alone have the ability to open a gateway to export Canada's oil into the Asia Pacific Basin, and in that sense they are critical to Canada's future as a global energy power. Without them, we will never get there. With them, as full and equal partners in the ownership of an export pipeline, together with the associated export terminal and marine infrastructure, all things are possible. It is to that new First Nation proposal that we now turn.

PART FIVE

The Asia Pacific Basin

CHAPTER 12

A New Proposal for Oil Exports to Asia:
Why First Nations Must Become Economic Partners

I magine a country whose proven oil and natural gas reserves are the largest of any industrial democracy in the world but which has failed after 15 years of sustained effort to construct a single oil or natural gas pipeline, a single port or a lone liquefied natural gas (LNG) terminal to connect those resources to the expanding markets of the Asia Pacific. Such a country does exist, and we should be embarrassed to admit that it is our own—Canada.

Canada's failure to resolve the complex issues surrounding west coast access has frustrated Aboriginal and non-Aboriginal Canadians alike. It has strained the bonds that tie us together as Canadians, damaged our international reputation as a reliable place to invest and sown lasting bitterness across western Canada. The public and private cost, tangible and intangible, has been immense and will only worsen with time. To add further uncertainty, the only such project to have received federal Cabinet approval, the Northern Gateway Pipeline, has now been struck down by the Federal Court of Appeal.

Yet, despite all this, I remain an optimist. The current impasse can be resolved, and I know from past experience that Aboriginal and non-Aboriginal Canadians can achieve remarkable things when we decide to do something together—respectfully, and as partners.

Canada's Asian Advantage

Canada cannot turn its back on the Pacific Rim. We are a Pacific Rim country, and our competitive advantage in the energy world of tomorrow stems from that simple reality. We have a tendency to overlook this fact, focusing instead on the history and trading relationships that tie us to Europe. Our European nexus is undeniably important, but it is equally true that the linkages between Canada's west coast and the Asia Pacific are profound. We share the Pacific Ocean with countries such as China, Japan, South Korea, Taiwan, Thailand, Indonesia, India and Singapore. These are the markets where demand for energy continues to grow, and they are the very markets where Canada enjoys a competitive advantage.

The most likely markets for Canadian crude oil and natural gas are in Northeast Asia: China, South Korea, Japan and Taiwan, and the dominant suppliers in each of those markets are currently from the Middle East. The opportunity for Canada lies in the sheer size of those markets and in the fact that Canadian crude oil and LNG involve shorter shipping distances to get there. Furthermore, Canada can provide much-needed diversity of supply in the Asia Pacific region, in the case of oil, limiting the market dominance of OPEC.

Canada's competitive advantage in shipping distance is quite striking. For example, a round trip from Kitimat, British Columbia, to Shanghai, China, is 8,082 nautical miles. By comparison, a return trip from the Arabian Gulf to Shanghai is 13,277 nautical miles; and from Nigeria, 21,931 nautical miles. Ironically, we think of Australia, rather than Canada, as an Asian Pacific country, and yet the distance between Prince Rupert, British Columbia, and Tokyo is 3,702 nautical miles, compared with 3,887 nautical miles between the natural gas fields of Carnarvon in northwestern Australia and Tokyo. And while it is true that Canada does not enjoy the same absolute transportation advantage in the markets of southeast Asia, such as India, Canadian oil and LNG are nonetheless very competitive in those markets.

Nor is our competitive advantage limited to geography. The growing economies of the Asia Pacific value their historic and cultural linkages to Canada and our Pacific coast. Taken together, the Chinese languages (Mandarin and Cantonese) are the third most-spoken in Canada, and the influence of Asian culture and commerce in British Columbia is undeniable. And Canada's close relationship with India is deep and a source of pride in both countries. One cannot travel in the Asia Pacific without acquiring a strong sense of the respect that Canada enjoys there and, equally, an appreciation of the desire to do business with Canada and Canadians. Remarkably, more than 300,000 Canadian citizens reside in Hong Kong.

In recognition of these realities, Canada has continued to strengthen its trading relationships in the region. We concluded a trade deal with South Korea and, in September 2012, signed a Foreign Investment Promotion and Protection Agreement (FIPA) with China. We have also signed the Framework Agreement on the larger and potentially more important Trans-Pacific Partnership, which is a proposed trade agreement under negotiation among 12 countries on all sides of the Pacific Ocean: Australia, Brunei, Chile, Canada, Japan, Malaysia, Mexico, New Zealand, Peru, Singapore, the United States and Vietnam. Many of our west coast First Nations have also established important cultural and business linkages into the Asia Pacific.

The growth in energy demand in Asia will dominate global markets over the next 50 years. To begin with, most of the countries of the Asia Pacific are not energy producers themselves and therefore depend on imported energy sources. The region currently consumes more than 30 million barrels of oil per day (bpd) but produces less than eight million bpd, and most of that production is in China. Canada's inability to build pipelines, ports, LNG facilities and oil terminals on the west coast is met with incredulity throughout the energy world, but nowhere more so than in Asia, where government and business leaders see Canadian energy as an important source of reliable supply.

The Essential Problem: How Canada Got in Its Own Way

There are many reasons why Canada has failed in its efforts to achieve west coast access for its energy exports. While there is more than enough blame to go around, our failure must be said to be a collective one. One is left, however, with the sense that at some level the country isn't working and that Canadian federalism isn't functioning the way it should. Most recently, Canada's Federal Court of Appeal has strongly expressed the view that the federal government, and indeed the Harper Cabinet, failed in the discharge of the constitutional obligations that they owed to the First Nations of British Columbia.

Many have vilified British Columbia's Premier Christy Clark on account of the so-called five conditions that she enunciated as the preconditions to British Columbia's support of a west coast oil pipeline. In fact, Premier Clark's conditions merely stated the obvious. To be sure, Premier Clark's relationship with Alberta Premier Alison Redford was never good, and the five conditions exploded onto the scene in 2012, as Premier Clark's response to Premier Redford's blandishments that she needed to support the Northern Gateway project because it was in the national interest. In the months that followed, Premier Clark carefully outlined the requirements that would need to be met before British Columbia could support any pipeline linking Alberta's oil sands to the Pacific coast:

1. successful completion of the environmental review process— in effect, a positive recommendation from the National Energy Board Joint Review Panel;
2. world-leading marine oil-spill response, prevention and recovery systems for British Columbia's coastline;
3. world-leading practices for land oil-spill prevention, response and recovery systems;
4. resolution of the issues surrounding Aboriginal and treaty rights, ensuring that First Nations have the opportunities to participate in and benefit from such projects; and
5. British Columbia receiving a fair share of the fiscal and economic benefits of a proposed heavy oil project that reflects the level, degree and nature of the risk borne by the province, the environment and taxpayers.[1]

Relations between the two premiers soured irreversibly at that point. A *Globe and Mail* article published in the days following the delineation of British Columbia's five conditions accurately captured the depth of the impasse: "Premier Christy Clark is threatening to block the controversial $6-billion project unless her province gets an unspecified 'fair share' of the windfall, a cash call Alberta Premier Alison Redford is flatly rejecting."[2] The article went on to quote Premier Clark, saying that "if Alberta is not willing to even sit down and talk, then it stops here."[3] Certainly, by the time of the Council of the Federation meetings in Halifax in July 2012, the two premiers were barely on speaking terms.

Premier Clark was not, in fact, opposed to the construction of a pipeline linking Alberta's energy resources to the Pacific coast. She and I discussed the subject of oil pipelines at length during my time as premier of Alberta. Viewed from her perspective, the conditions were an attempt, admittedly an aggressive one, to provide a pathway forward, in her words, "a way to get to yes."

I have never viewed British Columbia's five conditions as the real issue. Four of the five conditions relate to the environment, and they are all obvious and compelling. Surely the Governments of Canada, British Columbia and Alberta are united in their insistence that any such project must adhere to world class environmental standards. Those standards must apply to the protection of both the terrestrial and marine ecosystems, and it would be absurd to ask the Province of British Columbia or its taxpayers to bear those costs and risks on their own. The fourth condition, underscoring the need to reach agreement with British Columbia's First Nations, merely states the obvious: Every pipeline corridor and export terminal under consideration in British Columbia has an impact on the unresolved land claims of BC's indigenous peoples, and progress without their agreement is legally and constitutionally impossible. The Federal Court of Appeal's subsequent decision to quash the Northern Gateway Cabinet approval surely underscores the accuracy of Premier Clark's point.

The real issue was, is and will always be the reconciliation of the interests of the project proponents and the First Nations of British Columbia. The Governments of British Columbia and Canada are obviously more than mere bystanders in that process since they owe shared constitutional obligations to the First Nations of British Columbia, but the final decision-making authority resides with the First Nations and not with either government. Put simply, a project that enjoys the support of both governments—but not the First Nations—has no future, and by parity of reasoning, a project that enjoys the full support of the affected First Nations will be hard for either government to block.

What then is the status of Canada's attempts to export our energy resources into the Asia Pacific?

LNG—Canada Misplays Its Hand

It would be an understatement to say that British Columbia has been inundated with competing LNG proposals over the past decade. Unfortunately, not a single one of those proposals has yet come to fruition by way of a positive final investment decision.

The small community of Kitimat has been at the very centre of Canada's energy debate, beginning with the controversial Enbridge Northern Gateway Pipeline. But it is also the nexus of several proposals to export liquefied natural gas to Asia. Of the four projects on the books there, one of the largest is the LNG Canada project, proposed by a partnership between Shell Canada Limited and a consortium of Chinese, Korean and Japanese off-takers: PetroChina, Korea Gas Corporation and Mitsubishi Corporation. These are among the largest corporations in the world, and they have proposed a project that is equally massive in scale.

The capacity of LNG facilities is measured by the export capacity they are designed to achieve. The LNG Canada facility would be capable of exporting 24 million metric tons of liquefied natural gas every year (mmtpa). To appreciate the scale of that proposal, take the time to look up images of Chevron's monster Gorgon facility in Australia, which is slightly smaller and capable of exporting 15.6 mmtpa. The LNG Canada project would require a natural gas feed of 3.7 billion cubic feet per day, and natural gas for the project would come from northeastern British Columbia and from Alberta. The sheer scale of these facilities, their massive capital cost and the 50-year time horizon over which they are designed to operate explain why LNG is the exclusive preserve of the world's largest energy corporations.

Other projects include Kitimat LNG, designed as a 10 million tonne per year export facility. A third project, Triton LNG, a partnership of AltaGas and Idemitsu Kosan, appears to have been abandoned. The Haisla First Nation, which has been at the centre of these various projects, has proposed its own LNG facility, the Cedar LNG project, which involves a partnership with several industry participants. The project is much smaller than the others—it would liquefy 850 million cubic feet of natural gas per day and be capable of exporting 6.4 million tonnes of liquefied gas per year.

Prince Rupert has also been the focus of a number of competing LNG projects. The largest and most advanced is Pacific Northwest

LNG, proposed by the Malaysian energy giant Petronas together with its partners Sinopec/Huadian, JAPEX, Indian Oil and Petro-leumBRUNEI. It is a world scale facility proposed for Lelu Island that would export 12 mmtpa. The proponent, Petronas, is owned by the Government of Malaysia, and the plan to build this $36 billion facility in Canada represents a conscious and strategic decision to tie Malaysia's future natural gas needs to Canada's supply.

ExxonMobil has also proposed a massive project, WCC LNG Ltd., on Tuck Inlet near Prince Rupert, capable of exporting 30 million tonnes of LNG per annum and requiring feedstock of four billion cubic feet of natural gas per day. Other projects proposed near Prince Rupert include a BG (British Gas) proposal called Prince Rupert LNG, on Ridley Island at the Port of Prince Rupert, designed as a 21 mmtpa export facility, but the future of the project is clouded by Shell's corporate acquisition of BG in 2015. It is fair to assume that Shell will not proceed with two LNG facilities at the same time, and the company's plans for either will remain unclear until 2017, at the earliest.

Other projects proposed in the vicinity include the 24 mmtpa Aurora LNG project originally proposed by Nexen Energy (now owned by CNOOC) together with its partners INPEX and JGC. Australian energy giant Woodside Energy proposed a 20 mmtpa facility, Grassy Point LNG. Other projects include the New Times Energy facility and the Watson Island project, the latter in partnership with the City of Prince Rupert. A substantial floating facility, described as Orca LNG, has been proposed to export 24 mmtpa.

The BC coast north of Prince Rupert has also been the subject of a number of LNG proposals. The Nisga'a First Nation has proposed a facility known as Nasoga Gulf, on the Mylor Peninsula, along the Portland Inlet. Several hundred kilometres further up the Portland Inlet, at the head of the Alice Arm, Kitsault Energy has proposed a 20 mmtpa export facility. In addition, a large floating facility, described as the Canada Stewart Energy Project, has been proposed further up the Portland Inlet at Stewart.

The LNG bonanza in British Columbia is not confined to the province's northwest coast. A sizable facility, Steelhead LNG, has been proposed on Huu-ay-aht land at Sarita Bay, at the southern end of Alberni Inlet on Vancouver Island. At Delta, another small facility, described as WesPac, has been proposed by WesPac Midstream Vancouver. A very small facility, described as the Woodfibre LNG project, has been proposed for Squamish; and yet another company, by the name of Quicksilver Resources, has proposed a facility at Campbell River on Vancouver Island.

In spite of all this activity and in spite of a 2013 provincial election fought and won on LNG being the economic future for British Columbia, not a single project has proceeded. Instead, through our own folly, Canada now serves as a safe "bank" for the next generation of projects, approved and held by the world's largest energy multinationals pending changes in the global supply-demand balance. Our LNG ambitions have been relegated to the next wave of LNG projects, in five, 10 or 15 years' time.

Oil—Canada Misplays Its Other Hand

The situation is equally frustrating when it comes to the competing proposals to construct oil pipelines and ports across British Columbia.

Canada has only one existing pipeline that carries oil to the west coast—the Kinder Morgan Trans Mountain Pipeline, which transports crude oil and petroleum products from Edmonton, Alberta, to Burnaby, British Columbia. The Trans Mountain Pipeline also collects crude oil from northeastern British Columbia and northwestern Alberta, via an interconnection operated by the Pembina Pipeline Corporation, which connects into the Trans Mountain system at a terminal near Kamloops, British Columbia. The Trans Mountain system, consisting of 1,150 kilometres of existing pipe, has been in operation since 1953 and is capable of transporting 300,000 barrels per day through to its Burnaby terminus. The system also connects to Anacortes, in the state of Washington.

The Trans Mountain Pipeline is, in effect, the only Canadian pipeline transporting Canadian oil products to a west coast Canadian port facility and, not surprisingly, it is completely oversubscribed, all the time.

The terminus of the Trans Mountain Pipeline is the Westridge Marine Terminal in Burnaby, and from that terminal products move into the Greater Vancouver area and into the Puget Sound area in Washington State. The Westridge Marine Terminal is located within Port Metro Vancouver and has been in operation since 1956. It is a critical piece of infrastructure in the distribution of oil and petroleum products in the City of Vancouver and to facilities such as the Vancouver International Airport. It services approximately five tankers per month.

The Westridge terminal suffers from a critical limitation: Vessels loaded there must transit the length of the Vancouver Harbour and must be small enough to pass beneath both the Highway 1 Port Mann Bridge and the Lions Gate Bridge. In the result, the terminal can load only coastal tankers (300,000 barrels) and Aframax tankers

(750,000 barrels). It cannot handle Suez Max tankers, the so-called VLCCs (very large crude carriers) or the ULCCs (ultra large crude carriers) that are necessary to link Canadian oil supplies to Asia. The gigantic vessels that carry LNG are even larger and also, obviously, out of the question.

The Westridge Marine Terminal is essential because it links western Canadian oil production with Pacific coast consumption, but it will never suffice as the key portal for Canadian exports to Asia. Most of the oil currently transported on the Kinder Morgan system is, in fact, consumed in Canada and along the coast of Washington and California.

In April 2012, Trans Mountain Pipeline announced its intention to expand the pipeline, a $5.4 billion proposal. The Trans Mountain Pipeline Expansion project (TMX) would expand the existing pipeline system between Edmonton and Burnaby as well as the Westridge Marine Terminal. The expansion would include 981 kilometres of new pipeline, new and modified facilities such as pump stations and tanks, and the reactivation of 193 kilometres of existing pipeline.[4] Importantly, some 73 percent of the proposed expanded pipeline will follow the existing right-of-way.[5] On December 16, 2013, Trans Mountain filed a formal Facilities Application to the National Energy Board seeking permission to build, operate and maintain the necessary facilities required for the proposed project.

The Kinder Morgan project has been led by Ian Anderson, a self-effacing although visionary leader who has skilfully developed support for the Trans Mountain project among the many First Nations along the alignment.

Kinder Morgan's proposal to expand the Trans Mountain Pipeline is an important project, and it is to be hoped that both the National Energy Board and the federal Cabinet ultimately approve the project in 2017. The project continues to be hampered by significant opposition to *any* oil pipelines or ports being built in British Columbia and, given the depth of the opposition among both Aboriginal and non-Aboriginal citizens in the province's Lower Mainland, it is unlikely the issues surrounding it will be resolved within the existing regulatory processes. The underlying opposition is primarily political, not regulatory. The construction of the Trans Mountain Project will ultimately depend on the political intervention of Canada's national government, and on the resolution of the court proceedings that will inevitably follow.

However, the Trans Mountain project doesn't solve Canada's problem because Canada's critical limitation is, in fact, the absence of world scale oil-export facilities on our west coast. The real issue is that we don't yet have terminals capable of operating at a global scale to export our oil and natural gas into the markets of the Asia Pacific. We are close to resolving that limitation when it comes to LNG, but the absence of an export facility for oil remains our greatest challenge.

The Northern Gateway Project

The Northern Gateway project was intended to rectify that very problem, through the construction of a new pipeline connecting to a new oil terminal in Kitimat, British Columbia. The project, which was proposed by one of Canada's most successful pipeline companies, Enbridge, involved the construction of a 1,177 kilometre twinned pipeline between Bruderheim, Alberta, and Kitimat. The westbound pipeline was designed to transport 525,000 barrels of oil per day and the eastbound pipeline was intended to transport an average of 193,000 barrels of natural gas condensate per day back to Alberta. Condensate is a liquid that is recovered from natural gas reservoirs and used as a diluent to thin Alberta's heavy oils to facilitate pipeline transport. The terminal at Kitimat was designed to include two ship berths and 19 storage tanks, with a capacity to serve about 220 ship calls per year and include a radar-monitoring station and first-response capabilities.[6]

Enbridge began studying the feasibility of the Northern Gateway Pipeline in 1998, and the project was formally launched in 2004.[7] In 2005, Kitimat was chosen as the marine terminal site.

The Northern Gateway project has been anything but easy for Enbridge. The environmental and political controversy surrounding it was intense from the beginning and, in the wake of the Federal Court of Appeal's quashing of the project approval in June 2016, it would have to be said that virtually everyone involved with the project and its review failed to appreciate the regulatory and legal complexities of the undertaking.

Enbridge formally submitted its application for the development of the Northern Gateway Project on May 27, 2010. The Joint Review Panel (JRP) hearings began on January 10, 2012, in Kitamaat Village (located just south of the town of Kitimat) and lasted 18 months, until June 2013. In the 180 days of hearings, 1,179 oral statements were given; in addition, 9,400 letters of comment were filed and analyzed by JRP staff. In its decision, eventually handed down on December 19, 2013, the panel recommended that the federal government approve the project, subject to 209 conditions, and concluded that *"opening Pacific Basin markets is important to the Canadian economy and society (. . .) [and] that the project would bring significant local, regional, and national economic and social benefits* [emphasis mine]."⁸ It is important to note that Enbridge did offer the First Nations and Métis communities along the alignment an opportunity to become equity partners, affording them a collective 10 percent equity interest in the project, in addition to more than $1 billion of associated economic benefits.

In the time between 2010 and 2014, the project continued to polarize Canadians, dividing them along ever-deeper fault lines— left versus right; Liberal versus Conservative; Aboriginal versus non-Aboriginal; Albertans versus British Columbians; those in the energy industry and business community versus everyone else. It became one of the defining political differences between the Conservative government of Prime Minister Harper, who supported the project unequivocally if clumsily, and the Liberal Party of Justin Trudeau, for whom opposition to Northern Gateway became a mantra. The project divided Albertans and British Columbians so deeply that it eventually destroyed British Columbia's Premier Christy Clark's relationship with Alberta's Premier Alison Redford, and the undercurrents surrounding the project and the alternatives to it were almost certainly determinative of the 2012 BC provincial election.

Enbridge was ultimately successful in obtaining a positive recommendation from the Joint Review Panel in December 2013, and a project approval from the Harper Cabinet followed in June 2014; but, in the absence of support from British Columbia's First Nations, the project has remained moribund in the years since. Throughout that time, Enbridge and its shipping partners remained steadfast in their commitment to the project and soldiered on in their attempts to rebuild a First Nations coalition around the project. In the meantime, the First Nations who opposed the project, led by the Haisla who have been virulent in their opposition, continued on with their legal challenges to the legitimacy of the federal approval. On June 30, 2016, they succeeded as the Federal Court of Appeal quashed the approval of the Harper Cabinet on the basis that the federal government had failed in its obligations to consult with and accommodate the concerns of those First Nations, particularly the Haisla. The Northern Gateway Pipeline must now be said to be officially dead.

Sadly, the federal government knew, or should have known, what needed to be done. In late 2012, I attracted the government's ire by publicly criticizing its approach to Aboriginal consultations and warning that Ottawa was putting the project's approval at risk. Moreover, in March 2013, the government appointed a respected British Columbia lawyer, Douglas R. Eyford, as Canada's special federal representative on west coast energy infrastructure with a broader mandate "to identify Aboriginal interests in and opportunities related to the development of west coast energy projects."[9] Following eight months of engagement with Aboriginal communities in Alberta and British Columbia, industry and local and provincial governments, Eyford published a Report to the Prime Minister: *Forging Partnerships, Building Relationships: Aboriginal Canadians and Energy Development*. Within the report, Eyford presented four key observations and a series of recommendations based on four themes: building trust, fostering inclusion, advancing reconciliation and taking action. The key observations were that

1. Canada and Aboriginal communities need to build effective relationships and this is best achieved through sustained engagement;

2. Aboriginal communities view natural resource development as linked to a broader reconciliation agenda;
3. Aboriginal communities will consider supporting natural resource development if it is undertaken in an environmentally sustainable manner; and
4. these projects would contribute to improving the socioeconomic conditions of Aboriginal communities.[10]

Of the 29 recommendations in the report, perhaps the most substantial involve Canada's approach to Aboriginal consultation, with five recommendations that focus on "relationship-building, engaging outside the consultation process and addressing Aboriginal interests beyond project specific issues."[11] Furthermore, the report encourages the formation of a Crown–First Nations tripartite energy working group that would "create an open and sustained dialogue and action on energy projects" in response to an identified "need for Canada to build its internal capacity and to adopt an integrated approach to address Aboriginal interests in relation to west coast energy projects."[12] In the wake of the Federal Court of Appeal's quashing of the Gateway approval, Douglas Eyford's advice must be said to be prophetic.

Other Proposals

The landscape of energy projects proposed in and around northern British Columbia is further complicated by the presence of other projects, some further along than others. For example, two separate groups have proposed the construction of refineries near Kitimat that would export gasoline or diesel instead of oil sands bitumen. The idea is that such refineries would increase the likelihood of obtaining "social licence" for hydrocarbon exports to Asia. One such project is the Pacific Future Energy, with several prominent First Nation leaders serving as executives and advisers. It seeks to build a 200,000 bpd facility to transport neatbit (undiluted bitumen) by heated rail cars from Alberta, to be refined in British Columbia and then exported to Asia as refined product. Newspaper publisher David Black has proposed another refinery for the area. Called Kitimat Clean, it is estimated to cost $22 billion and would also import bitumen by rail to be refined and exported. Neither of these projects contemplates getting its oil from a pipeline, and neither one enjoys any real support among energy industry leaders.

Another proposal, by a group called G Seven Generations (G7G), would build a 2,400 kilometre rail line carrying 1.5 million barrels per day of bitumen in heated rail cars from Fort McMurray, Alberta, through northern Alberta and British Columbia, to Delta Junction, Alaska, where the bitumen would be transferred to the Alaska oil pipeline and exported from Valdez. This project touts strong support from First Nations along the route—including a formal endorsement by the Assembly of First Nations. The estimated cost of the project is $34 billion.

So this is where things stand today—after 15 years of effort, Canada has yet to approve or construct a single pipeline or port facility to export Canadian oil and bitumen to markets in the Asia Pacific.

A New Approach

Canada still has the time to assert itself as a global energy player by connecting our energy resources to the expanding markets of the Asia Pacific. The economic and political consequences of our failure to make this happen as of yet are now apparent for all to see: Despite a resource base that is the envy of the democratic world, we have diminished our economic and political potential and limited our future to that of a captive supplier of discounted energy resources to the United States.

It is instructive that the Americans have refused to marginalize their energy resources in the way that we have and are instead aggressively pursuing a future as a global exporter of natural gas and, to a lesser extent, oil. For many Canadians, this is a little disorienting. After all, wasn't it the president of the United States who convinced many Canadians that we shouldn't be in the energy business at all, or at least not in the oil sands business? Yet somehow it is now the Americans who have bested us—with new and expanded export terminals, energy jobs, profits and tax revenues. By contrast, Canada finds itself on the sidelines, searching for a new approach and a new routing to the global markets of the Asia Pacific.

It is now obvious that the indigenous peoples of Alberta and British Columbia are the key to Canada's global energy ambitions, and we must embrace them as full partners in our quest for access to global markets. The pipeline and port facilities that will link Canada to the Pacific Rim will need to be economically and environmentally sustainable, and they will need to be constructed and regulated to the highest environmental and safety standards.

However, they must also be owned, in part, by the indigenous Canadians who are making way for them. The indigenous peoples who are affected by those pipelines and port facilities, whose territories will be crossed, whose Aboriginal title will be infringed on and whose way of life will be exposed to significant increases in marine traffic must be full partners in this enterprise. They must share in the ownership of these projects, and they must share in the environmental solutions that underpin them.

This is not a question of merely accommodating or mollifying the First Nations along the pipeline corridor or on the Pacific coast. They are not just stakeholders. Under the Canadian Constitution they are the owners of the underlying Aboriginal title. Frankly, the imposition of energy infrastructure on this scale, without their ongoing consent, is a practical, if not legal, impossibility. The task at hand is therefore to achieve an alignment of interests—an alignment of Canada's national interest with the financial interests of the project proponents and the legal and community interests of the affected indigenous peoples. Everyone's capital, whether financial or political, must be brought to the investment.

Absent such a balance of interests, Canadian oil and natural gas will never access the expanding markets of the Asia Pacific. If the experience of the past 15 years has taught us nothing else, it has surely taught us that. Not everyone sees it this way, and some will remain on the sidelines, denying Canada's constitutional history, deploring the capabilities of Canada's indigenous peoples, disparaging the missteps of Northern Gateway and the Governments of Alberta, British Columbia and Canada. But those on the sidelines will be relegated to the past, because Canada has found the courage and ambition to move forward.

I am confident that Canada will find a way to export its oil and natural gas into the Asia Pacific and that we will do so with Canada's First Nations as real partners in that cause—as full partners in both the protection of the environment and the economic uplift arising from Canada's emergence as a global energy force.

Why am I so confident? And what then does that future look like? Frankly, it looks a lot like the future that the Nisga'a First Nation chose a generation ago when it had the courage to conclude a modern treaty with Canada and British Columbia.

The best location for an energy terminal connecting Canada to the Asia Pacific is along the Pacific Northwest coast of British Columbia. Not surprisingly, most of the proposed LNG projects are sited along that coastline, north of the Douglas Channel. This is because the most direct routing from Canada to Asia is, in fact, from Prince Rupert or, alternatively, from a new port along the coast to the north. Prince Rupert itself is an ideal port, but the deeply incised Skeena River Valley makes pipeline access to it very difficult. A port at Kitimat remains a theoretical possibility but one that seems unlikely in view of the vociferous objections of both the Haisla First Nation and Canada's Liberal government to tanker traffic on the Douglas Channel. In addition, because of the length of that channel, Kitimat is several days' more distant from Asia than ports to the north. There are, in fact, superior sites elsewhere.

The obvious partners in such a project are the First Nations along the Pacific Northwest coast. The Haida are also an important ally since all the preferred tanker routings entail a crossing of the Hecate Strait, past the northern tip of Haida Gwaii and then onward to Asia. While all this may seem obvious, bear in mind that, despite 15 years of effort, no Canadian energy company has yet concluded an agreement with a First Nation for the siting of an oil terminal on Canada's west coast.

An energy terminal big enough to link Canada to the Asia Pacific is a large undertaking. It must have the immediate capacity to export one million barrels of Canadian oil per day, and it must be designed and constructed in a manner that allows for its expansion over time. The energy markets of the Asia Pacific are large enough to accommodate new Canadian supply of one million barrels of oil per day and, in time, as much as two to three million barrels per day. To China, India and other countries, Canada's oil represents a welcome diversification from their dependency on the Middle East.

Such a port will also allow Canada to export more than just oil and natural gas. It must be constructed as a full energy port, designed and built to a global scale. It will have to be a deep-water facility, capable of loading the largest tankers in the world. And it must be supported by world class marine tugs and barges and services.

Two things are critical to such a future. The first is an ethic that starts with the protection of the environment as the first and inviolate principle. The second is an ownership structure that includes the indigenous partners as significant owners in the pipeline, the ocean terminal and the marine infrastructure supporting it.

Beginning with the environment, it is critical that we remain true to the ecological ethic that is so important to the indigenous peoples of the Pacific Northwest. The environmental objective must be to build and operate a pipeline, together with storage and port facilities, that is sustainable and designed and constructed to the highest environmental and safety standards. The facilities must represent an enhancement to the quality of life of the indigenous partners and strengthen their ability to protect the ecosystems that are valuable to them. And while a terminal that exports hydrocarbons can never be truly carbon neutral, every effort must be undertaken to "green" the project, through renewable energy initiatives and an operating philosophy that limits access to the port to shippers who ascribe to the highest possible safety and environmental standards. This overall commitment to the protection of the environment must apply equally to the coast and to the corridor linking Alberta and British Columbia.

These energy facilities should be a source of pride to Canadians. Does anyone seriously advocate that they should be designed and built to anything other than the highest possible standards?

Understanding the lessons of the *Simushir*, the federal and provincial governments, working together with the coastal First Nations, must seize this opportunity to design and implement a world class coastal management system. If there is to be a tanker ban off Canada's west coast, it must be temporary, pending the delineation of a new regime that incorporates regulatory, pilotage and financial requirements that are as tough as any in the world. For its part, the federal government must make the requisite Coast Guard investments in the vessels and equipment that are necessary to protect Canada's west coast. This is, after all, its constitutional responsibility. The coastal waters surrounding Haida Gwaii can no longer be known as the most exposed and least protected waters on the west coast of North America. All this is possible. We have studied the issues and we know what needs to be done.

To those who say that Canada cannot afford the costs associated with the creation and operation of a world class environmental regime, there is a simple answer: Then we shouldn't be shipping oil at all. The Government of Alberta and the Canadian energy industry must understand this reality and must participate in the cost of this effort. Neither the First Nations along the corridor or those on the coast, nor the taxpayers of Canada or British Columbia specifically, should be expected to finance or underwrite unacceptable environmental risks. Either we do this properly, or we don't do it all.

The same philosophy must apply to the economic partnership at the heart of the enterprise. The First Nations who are affected by the pipeline and port must also participate in the economic opportunities created by those facilities. This has traditionally meant the kinds of employment and contracting benefits that are available to First Nations under agreements known as IBAs (impact and benefit agreements). That won't work in this case. The pipeline and facilities under discussion will be among the largest industrial facilities on the west coast of the continent, and it is unrealistic to expect the First Nations of British Columbia to agree to the siting of them on their lands without more meaningful economic participation. The scale of the opportunity that west coast access represents is well known, and the time has surely come for Canada's indigenous peoples to participate more fairly in the prosperity that flows from the ownership of Canada's infrastructure and resources. I happen to agree with that perspective, but even those who do not agree must surely arrive at the same conclusion through enlightened self-interest. The bottom line is this: When it comes to the export of Canada's oil, the affected indigenous communities along the energy corridor and at the coastal port must be owners. Otherwise, those facilities aren't going to get built.

I have long believed that indigenous ownership is the best option. As owners, Canada's indigenous peoples will share in both the benefits and the risks associated with these projects, and their interest will be fully congruent with those partners who have risked their financial capital. It is that alignment of interests that is so critical to our future success.

The precise quantum of the indigenous ownership in the port, the pipeline and the associated marine opportunities will depend on the negotiations of the parties. The ownership consortia of the pipeline and the port need not be the same, since the objective is to achieve an alignment of interests among those affected by the construction and operation of the different facilities.

For instance, the quantum of the ownership interest in the pipeline connecting Alberta and the west coast and its break-down between the affected First Nations and Métis groups along the corridor will depend on the project routing and the extent of the infringement on Aboriginal title, together with an assess-ment of the specific risks and mitigations proposed. Returning to the algorithm of Miles Richardson, why would a "corridor" First Nation, whose Aboriginal title has been confirmed time and again by Canada's highest courts, compromise that title without full compensation?

The port facility requires similar considerations but involves different parties and an entirely different scale of infringement on those adjacent to it. An oil terminal capable of handling one to three million barrels of oil per day and requiring adequate draft to accom-modate VLCC and ULCC tankers is no small matter. Then, too, there is the need for some eight million barrels of on-site storage. The port will be located on First Nations land, and the negotiations surrounding the ownership of that enterprise will need to reflect the scale and complexity of the facility, the First Nations that are affected either directly or indirectly, and the risks and mitigations proposed. Also relevant are the many economic opportunities surrounding the marine infrastructure and the barges, tugs and other vessels that will sustain high-quality employment opportunities for generations to come.

None of this is without its complexity. None of it is entirely new either: Imperial Oil and TransCanada negotiated equity arrangements with the Aboriginal Pipeline Group on the Mackenzie Valley Pipeline project a decade ago. More recently, in the context of the Northern Gateway project, Enbridge has been working to craft an equity proposal with its own Aboriginal Equity Group. Surprisingly, however, Canadian political and corporate leaders have failed to recognize that indigenous ownership and the alignment of interests that it represents is the critical key to unlocking the challenges of west coast access. Without it, nothing will happen. With it, all things are possible.

The coastal and corridor First Nations await the discussion. Visionary chiefs such as Mitch Stevens, Harold Leighton and Mayor John Helin are more than prepared for it. The real question is whether Canada is ready. Is Canada's energy industry up to the challenge? Are Canada's pipeline companies and port operators? Is the federal government prepared to help facilitate the creation of indigenous equity through a creative financing measure such as a loan guarantee? Are the financial intermediaries who will be called on to finance such a massive project prepared to embrace a future of joint ownership with Canada's indigenous peoples?

Most participants say that they are, and their resolve is about to be tested. Virtually every indigenous community between Alberta and the coast of British Columbia has cut its teeth in negotiations with the world's largest LNG companies, and so they are more than ready. The negotiations will be interesting because, as they say about the First Nations of the Pacific Northwest, "If you are negotiating with them, bring your A game."

Canada can access the Asia Pacific and can become a global energy player, but we will get there only if we are prepared to include our indigenous peoples in that dream—as owners and as our partners. For me, that is a dream and a future worth having.

PART SIX

The Canadian Common Market and the Atlantic Basin

Unfinished Business: Energy East and the Importance of Canada's Common Market and the Atlantic Basin

A s Canada celebrates the 150th anniversary of Confederation in July 2017, we can agree that we have come far as a country. Canada is a modern democracy, a member of the G7 club of the most advanced industrial economies in the world, and regularly classified by the United Nations as one of the best countries in which to live. But remarkably, 150 years after Canada's founding, our Confederation remains unfinished. We still don't have a true internal common market where goods and services from one province can freely move and be sold in other provinces. The proposed Energy East Pipeline, which would link western Canadian oil with eastern Canadian consumers, now finds itself at the centre of that very debate.

The work of constructing a true Canadian common market for our own goods and services has been under way since Confederation itself. Indeed, that is exactly what the union of the British Canadian Provinces was intended to achieve in 1867. And yet,

150 years later, myriad regulatory and legislative differences across the provinces create walls that impede the free flow of people, goods, services and investments among Canadians. These "walls" damage our own competitiveness and increase costs for Canadian businesses. By a recent estimate, "internal trade liberalization could add as much as $50 billion to $130 billion to Canada's overall GDP—in line with the government's own estimates of $50 billion in potential gains."[1] To put that number in perspective, the amount lost to these internal trade barriers—$50 billion—is very close to the entire annual budget for the Province of Alberta.

What is all the more remarkable about this sad state of affairs is that Canada is one of the world's most successful international traders and has been a global leader in advancing the cause of bilateral and multilateral trade liberalization and in negotiating advantageous free trade agreements with other countries. Our support of trade liberalization is unqualified—except here at home, where ridiculous barriers persist; for example, penalizing the sale of craft beers in Alberta if they are produced in Saskatchewan, or restricting the interprovincial labour mobility of nurses, lawyers and hairdressers. Most egregiously, new barriers are now being erected to restrict the flow of energy. In the past few years, interprovincial rivalries and local politics have conspired to frustrate the construction of new interprovincial pipelines, even though the jurisdiction for examining and approving or rejecting these project proposals is held by Ottawa.

In the face of this parochialism, I remain optimistic that TransCanada will eventually secure the regulatory and political approvals required to build the Energy East Pipeline. On January 14, 2015, I gave a speech reflecting that optimism at the Albany Club in Toronto.

I was the guest speaker at the dinner commemorating the 200th anniversary of the birth of Sir John A. Macdonald. The Albany Club was founded by Canada's first prime minister and, more than 150 years later, it remains the place where Conservatives in Ontario congregate to discuss the politics of the day and, of course, to plot the politics of tomorrow. The biggest event of the year is always the Sir John A. Dinner, and the 200th anniversary was obviously special. I was then the premier of Alberta and, following the ill-fated defection of most of the members of the Wildrose caucus to my government the previous month, everyone wanted to hear what I had to say. The main ballroom was sold out. So, too, was the overflow room, and so, too, was the overflow room from the overflow room.

I put a lot of work into my speech and, to prepare for it, I reread Donald Creighton's two extraordinary biographies of our first prime minister: *The Young Politician* and *The Old Chieftain*. Those two books remain the definitive pieces on Sir John A. Macdonald and, while they are less often read today, they remain among Canada's finest biographical writings.

My speech was long, but I needed time to knit together the essential narrative of Sir John A.'s life and the essential narrative of Canada. On its face, the speech wasn't about energy policy or about pipelines—but in reality it was about Energy East.

The breadth and scope of Macdonald's ambitions for Canada were audacious. This one man willed Canada into existence— defying geography, race, language and the financial limitations of a sparsely populated colony. His vision of Canada was impossible in its sheer breadth—the creation of a single country from the Atlantic to the Pacific, and then northward to the Arctic.

Sir John A. knew that a country as massive as Canada would

need to be perfected by economic infrastructure, and he aggressively asserted federal authority over railways, ports and other public works, pushing aside the provincial rivalries that have always complicated, and on occasion threatened, Canada. That evening, I reminded the Albany Club's members that we must rise above diminished ambition when provincial rivalries jeopardize the nation-building infrastructure that ties us together as Canadians—railways and highways, transmission lines, and of course pipelines and ports. We must reject the notion of a smaller and weaker Canada and rely on the example of our first prime minister, who would have refused to countenance the provincialism that increasingly surrounds the opposition to Energy East.

I wasn't the premier of Alberta for much longer, and my speech at the Albany Club was, in fact, my last major, substantive speech. But in the months that followed, I did begin the process of rebuilding the relationship between Alberta on the one hand and Quebec and Ontario on the other. Those relationships are critical to the future of Energy East.

* * *

It is hard to imagine a project more perfectly suited to fulfill the promise of Canada's energy future than Energy East, a proposed pipeline running 4,500 kilometres to carry 1.1 million barrels of oil per day from western Canada to New Brunswick, announced by proponent TransCanada on August 1, 2013. The merits of that project are difficult to refute when one considers what the project means to Canada, to our energy industry and to our country's broader ambitions to become a global energy power. Imagine a project that will enhance Canadian energy security; allow us to export our oil into the Atlantic Basin; strengthen and diversify the supply base of our refining industry; and simultaneously create much-needed employment and investment opportunity in Atlantic Canada. And while there are those who disagree, the project will also improve, rather than detract from, overall global environmental outcomes. In a nutshell, Energy East will be one of the world's longest pipelines, perfecting the Canadian common market when it comes to oil and affording Canada advantages that no one else in the world can compete with—in terms of the environment, energy security and our industrial capacity. If the Energy East proposal didn't already exist, there would be calls to invent it because it helps solve many pieces of Canada's energy puzzle.

First is the important matter of energy security. Canada may be one of the world's top five oil producers but, surprisingly, when it comes to oil we remain dependent on foreign suppliers. We produce more than four million barrels of oil per day, but our refineries in eastern and Atlantic Canada simultaneously import more than 730,000 barrels of foreign oil every day, most of it now coming from the United States, but also from Saudi Arabia, Nigeria and Algeria. Energy East will change that, by linking those eastern and Atlantic Canadian refineries with western Canada's massive supplies of oil, making Canada the only major industrial democracy in the world that is actually energy independent.

Then there is the fact that Energy East will allow Canada to export its oil into the Atlantic Basin, extricating western Canadian oil from what I have described previously as the continental trap. The project will have the capacity to move 1.1 million barrels of oil per day from western Canada to a deep-water port in Saint John, New Brunswick, providing western Canadian oil with full access to the Atlantic Basin for the first time. The European energy marketplace is one of the largest in the world and, while it is also very competitive, Canada's stature as a reliable and historic trading partner with countries such as the United Kingdom, France and Germany will undoubtedly benefit us. The project will also facilitate Canadian exports to other markets—including the eastern seaboard of the United States, which has traditionally relied on crude oil borne by tanker or rail and has been largely inaccessible to western Canadian crude oil, whether in its raw form or as refined petroleum product.

Finally, the project will strengthen Canada's refining industry by broadening and diversifying its supply sources, all at open, competitive prices. Our industrial base will be strengthened by the expansion of port facilities and marine infrastructure on our east coast. And it is impossible to dispute that the Canadian federation will undoubtedly be strengthened by a broader regional sharing of the industrial and employment benefits arising from the development of Alberta's oil sands. In that context, the many First Nations that will benefit from the construction and presence of the pipeline across their traditional lands also warrant participation. The project will cross through the traditional territories of 150 First Nations, and the TransCanada Corporation will be required to ensure that those First Nations benefit from the economic activity surrounding the project.

So, then, what is the problem, and why has this project aroused such fervent Canadian opposition? This opposition to shipping western Canadian oil eastward did not begin with Energy East. TransCanada's main competitor in the pipeline industry, Enbridge, had previously encountered similar issues in relation to its so-called Line 9B project.

Enbridge's Line 9B

Enbridge's Line 9 pipeline runs from Sarnia, Ontario, to Montreal. It is a 30-inch-diameter pipeline with a capacity of 240,000 barrels per day, and Enbridge had operated it since 1976. The oil in the Line 9 pipe originally flowed eastward, supplying refineries in Ontario and Quebec with crude oil from North American sources. Then, in 1998, Enbridge decided to reverse the flow of the pipeline, responding to changing global market conditions that made oil from West Africa and the Middle East cheaper and more plentiful than North American supplies. In the result, Line 9 carried "foreign" oil from Montreal to Sarnia from 1998 until 2015.

As North American production increased in the years between 2000 and 2010, the absence of eastbound pipeline capacity left much of it stranded in the mid-continent, driving prices downward. Responding to that market dynamic, Enbridge elected to re-reverse Line 9 back to its original flow—from west to east— to carry 300,000 barrels per day of North American crude oil to North American refiners, essentially supplanting foreign oil from places such as Nigeria and Saudi Arabia. Concurrent with that decision, the company decided to upgrade the pipeline.

Enbridge submitted its application for the second phase of the project to the National Energy Board (NEB) in November 2012. Enbridge's public filings included detailed engineering studies on the integrity and safety of the pipeline, together with a comprehensive Environmental and Socio-Economic Impact Assessment (ESEIA) of the project. The next 10 months would prove to be busy for both Enbridge and the project's detractors because, stunningly, this straightforward proposal to reverse the flow of an *existing* pipeline back to its *original direction* met with outraged opposition from environmental groups in Ontario and Quebec.

The public hearings in Montreal and Toronto were especially raucous, leading eventually to the arrest of 32 protesters in Montreal on October 10, 2013. A week later, in Toronto, the protests were so disruptive that the NEB was forced to shut down the final day of hearings, forcing Enbridge to submit its final "oral argument" . . . in writing!

Enbridge would eventually secure approval for the Line 9B reversal, but it took much, much longer than anyone expected, the process was more rancorous than anyone could have imagined, and western Canadians were taken aback by the virulence of the opposition to the Line 9B reversal. This was, after all, a proposal merely to reverse the flow of an *existing* pipeline linking western Canada and eastern Canada. What would the response be to an even more ambitious project—one carrying larger volumes of Canadian oil across the expanse of the country to refineries and tidewater in eastern Canada? That question would soon be answered.

Energy East

The Energy East project involves the conversion of one of Trans-Canada's existing "Mainline" natural gas pipelines into an oil pipeline. The project is therefore predicated on converting 3,000 kilometres of TransCanada's existing natural gas pipeline into an oil pipeline, running from Hardisty, Alberta, to Montreal. An additional 1,460 kilometres of new pipeline would then be built from the terminus of the existing natural gas Mainline in Montreal to Saint John, New Brunswick. Energy East would be one of the world's largest pipelines, running 4,460 kilometres across Canada.

The Atlantic Basin is one of the world's largest and most important oil markets and, while demand there is not growing, as it is in the Asia Pacific, Canada does have important trading relationships in Europe. Although most of the refineries in Europe are not configured to refine heavier crude oils and are therefore not a natural market for the Canadian oil sands, the Atlantic Basin is nonetheless a very important one, and access to tidewater is undeniably beneficial. Moreover and arguably more important, Energy East will allow western Canadian oil to access the US Gulf coast via tankers loaded in New Brunswick. Although the routing is obviously circuitous and more costly than a continental pipeline (Keystone XL, for example), it would allow Canadian heavy oil to compete with international alternatives.

The project is therefore an important one to western Canadians and, indeed, to all Canadians. I have personally supported the project since its inception, but I had no idea how quickly I would be dragged into pipeline diplomacy once I became the premier of Alberta.

Pipeline Diplomacy, Canadian-Style

Getting big things done in Canada can be complicated and, as premier of Alberta, I was but one of the many players involved with the Energy East file. Although the National Energy Board is charged with the examination of interprovincial pipelines, this technical jurisdiction is no longer sufficient to get a pipeline approved. We live in a new world, and a lot of politics and diplomacy are required. So I began meeting my counterparts across the country to engage them.

The first premier to reach out to me on the Energy East project was Premier Brian Gallant, the newly elected (Liberal) premier of New Brunswick, who visited Alberta within two weeks of being sworn into office. Brian Gallant is bright and articulate, and he grasps the importance of the Energy East project to New Brunswick generally and to the large Irving refinery operation that is the heart of the economic and industrial base of that province.

We met at my office in October 2014, discussed the project and held a joint press conference at which the premier spoke of the need for the project and its importance to the country and to his province.

Gallant recognized the importance of the project as a potential export route into the Atlantic Basin for both Canadian oil and Canadian natural gas. Not the least bit timid about pipelines, he also advocated the twinning of the line as a natural gas route, providing export feed to the Canaport LNG terminal in Saint John. The Canaport terminal opened in 2009 as an LNG import facility, purchasing natural gas from major natural gas exporters such as Qatar and Trinidad. The dramatic increases in North American natural gas production dictate that a brighter future for the project involves its conversion to a North American LNG export terminal. The provincial government has approved exactly that plan.

Premier Gallant acquitted himself well in all his dealings with Alberta, forcefully advocating on every occasion for the best interests of New Brunswick but doing so in a way that would strengthen, rather than weaken, the country as a whole. Both he and Premier Stephen McNeil of Nova Scotia, with whom I also met, are exceptional individuals. Both have a bright future in Canadian politics.

Alberta's relationship with Ontario and Quebec were, however, to prove more challenging on this file.

Quebec's Seven Conditions

By this time, in 2014–15, Quebec had been going through several years of difficult internal debates on oil and gas issues, so the context was challenging for a premier of Alberta talking about sending oil eastward.

The beginning of that challenging context could be traced to 2008, when Quebec joined California in the Western Climate Initiative to create a cap-and-trade system, while the federal Harper government had skewered the Liberal leader, Stéphane Dion, on his "Green Shift" plan as a "tax on everything." So Canada and Quebec were heading in opposite directions on that front by 2008.

Two years later, as small exploration companies began exploring the Utica shale gas formation lying under the St. Lawrence Valley between Montreal and Quebec City, local protests erupted against companies drilling exploratory wells using hydraulic fracturing. Soon after, the provincial environmental regulator—the Bureau d'audiences publiques sur l'environnement (BAPE)—issued a moratorium on exploration drilling while it studied the problem. In 2014, it eventually decided that hydraulic fracturing should not be carried out in Quebec until a more robust regulatory system was in place along with greater social acceptability of hydrocarbon development; in effect, the regulator imposed a moratorium. Call this strike two for the oil and gas industries in Quebec.

Recall that, during this period, Enbridge's Line 9B proposal was being examined, with the 2010 Kalamazoo River spill as a backdrop. Then, the incomprehensible tragedy of Lac-Mégantic occurred on July 6, 2013. Forty-seven people were killed when a tanker train full of light crude oil exploded in the middle of town, devastating families and destroying the entire downtown. Strike three for the image of petroleum in Quebec.

Therefore, by the time TransCanada was proposing its Energy East project, the social context—or, as Quebeckers say, the social acceptability of hydrocarbon projects—was severely compromised. Moreover, the project had the endorsements of Premier Alison Redford of Alberta, Premier David Alward of New Brunswick and Prime Minister Stephen Harper—who by then was not popular in Quebec. All English Canada, it seemed, was promoting the project, before getting any buy-in from Quebeckers.

In this context, Quebec's environment minister, David Heurtel, sent a letter to TransCanada CEO Russ Girling on November 18, 2014, containing seven conditions the company would have to meet, including a demand for a provincial environmental review.[2] It is still unclear to me whether Quebec Premier Philippe Couillard was aware of the letter before it was sent, but it reflected a deep and widening distrust in Quebec toward TransCanada and the Energy East project.

Quebec's seven conditions were problem enough, but a few days later, on November 21, 2014, following a joint meeting of the provincial cabinets of Ontario and Quebec, the two provinces stunned the country by jointly announcing seven joint conditions attached to their support for the Energy East Pipeline. The expressed conditions borrowed heavily from Minister Heurtel's letter to TransCanada.[3] The notion that the country's two largest provinces would impose provincial conditions on a nationally regulated project was breathtaking. Even more alarming, however, was the suggestion by Ontario Premier Kathleen Wynne that neither the Energy East project nor the development of Alberta's oil sands was in Ontario's interest, given the climate change aspirations of her government.

The seven conditions were a surprise to me, to Saskatchewan Premier Brad Wall and to BC Premier Christy Clark. All of us were caught badly off guard. There had been no warning that Ontario or Quebec was about to impose provincial "conditions" on a national project.

The conditions concerned matters that the National Energy Board would need to consider anyway. In addition to demanding that TransCanada look at whether the pipeline would increase greenhouse gas (GHG) emissions, the two provinces insisted that the company consult First Nations and other local communities, and that they consider all environmental and economic risks and the needs of natural gas consumers, especially those in Quebec where a significant commercial dispute between TransCanada and Gaz Métro was bubbling away. Frankly, failure on the part of the National Energy Board to fully consider all these matters would have been unthinkable.

This wasn't really about the regulatory process, however. It was about politics. It was about the two provincial governments speaking to the discomfort of their own citizens about the oil sands and the GHG emissions associated with the development of that resource. The seven conditions were clearly inflammatory to western Canadians, and the Governments of Ontario and Quebec should have considered that before issuing them. I would later ask Premier Couillard to reflect on how Quebeckers would respond to demands by Albertans concerning their reservations over the impact of a large-scale Quebec hydro proposal, or in Premier Wynne's case how the people of Ontario might respond to an Albertan challenge to the construction of an

Ontario nuclear facility. Neither, of course, would have a defensible answer.

How, then, to respond?

I sat at the centre of Canada's national government for more than five years, and one of the roles the prime minister asked me to fulfill was that of a problem solver. I have always found that the best way to solve difficult issues is through face-to-face discussion, relying on reason rather than public confrontation. Don't get me wrong. The media can serve a valuable purpose from time to time, but it is a blunt instrument and especially dangerous when longer-term interests are at risk.

The Energy East project is important to both Saskatchewan and Alberta, but Alberta is the larger partner and the more immediate target of those in eastern Canada who oppose the energy economy. It seemed to me that the greatest risk in the so-called seven conditions lay in the eruption of a public schism between Alberta on the one hand, and Quebec and Ontario on the other. In my view, Alberta already had more than enough trouble in its simmering dispute with British Columbia.

I spoke at length with Russ Girling, the CEO of TransCanada, and in the days that followed I sought the counsel of a number of other people I respected, including several from Quebec. Those discussions confirmed my intuition that an open and acrimonious war of words between Alberta and Quebec and Ontario would be a big mistake, potentially setting the project back many years. Saskatchewan could afford to take a different position. Alberta couldn't.

In the longer term, Alberta was going to require both provinces as partners in the rebranding of Alberta and its energy industry. I had felt for years that the climate change file was the key to all that, and my plan was to strike a partnership between Alberta and Quebec to move our province forward. We had been working internally on exactly that approach since I became premier, and I wasn't going to allow the ill-considered seven conditions to blow all that good work apart.

While the matters raised by Ontario and Quebec in their seven conditions were already being addressed through the NEB regulatory process, two substantive issues required clarification.

First, were Ontario and Quebec actually contending that they, rather than the national government, had jurisdiction over the regulatory process surrounding Energy East? Quebec's position, that it shared regulatory authority with Ottawa, didn't surprise me, since the province has long contested its constitutional boundaries with Ottawa over the environment. But Ontario? If the Canadian federation had reached the point where Ontario no longer respected the constitutional jurisdiction of Ottawa over national infrastructure, then it would seem that Canada's national government existed in name only.

Second, we needed to ascertain whether Ontario and Quebec were seriously contending that they were going to use Energy East as the rationale for convening provincial regulatory inquiries into the cumulative levels of GHG emissions from Alberta's oil sands. Alberta was prepared to address that very issue, but only in the context of a national inquiry.

At about the same time, I received a private call from Premier Greg Selinger of Manitoba, who was then facing his own leadership challenges, forewarning me that he intended to bring forward his own list of 10 conditions that the project would have to satisfy to meet the needs of Manitoba. The discussion was terse, and I reminded him that he was, in fact, a western Canadian premier and the premier of an oil-producing province. And so, on it went—a slow unravelling of the political and institutional bonds that hold us together as Canadians. (Fortunately, Premier Selinger never issued his set of conditions.)

Brad Wall and I spoke again, and he indicated that he intended to respond aggressively. In the days that followed, he did exactly that. I don't fault him for doing so. I respect him enormously and the "good cop, bad cop" routine that followed actually worked out pretty well. I pointed out that Alberta had a longer game to play with Ontario and Quebec, and I had no intention of destroying my ability to work with them, especially with Premier Couillard, until I had provided the opportunity to disagree with what I was proposing. From my perspective, the better solution was to engage in "pipeline diplomacy," and so my office immediately put plans in place to travel to Quebec City and Toronto to meet with both premiers.

Premier Couillard and I met at his office at the National Assembly on December 2, 2014. He and I hit it off from the outset. He is smart, articulate, a fiscal conservative and a passionate federalist. It is easy enough to be a federalist elsewhere in our country, but in Quebec it takes courage. Premier Couillard has that quality, and I consider him one of the critical players to the future of our country.

We explained our positions, and I outlined my plan to have Alberta and Quebec work together on the "road to Paris" as we began the long process of rebranding Alberta as a leader in the environment and technology. I outlined how our two provinces could work together, and I explained our plan to launch an environment technology fund using both Alberta's carbon fund and a small allotment from the province's Heritage Fund as seed money.

I invited him to consider Quebec's participation in this joint initiative, which we might announce at the Quebec climate change conference he was hosting in May 2015.

We met for an hour and continued our discussion over lunch. We then held a joint press conference, conducted in both French and English, where he and I explained that we had arrived at a mutual understanding.[4] Premier Couillard acknowledged that Quebec could not, and ought not, be seen to be trying to regulate Alberta's oil sands. He clarified that Quebec's environmental impact assessment agency would consider only GHGs produced by the Quebec segment of the pipeline project, excluding any consideration of emissions resulting from expanded oil sands production, stating, "It would be ideological to do otherwise because whatever the future of the TransCanada project, extraction will take place."

I left looking forward to the beginning of a new partnership between Alberta and Quebec. Sadly, I was unable to keep my end of the bargain.

Ontario

The meeting with Premier Wynne the following day, December 3, 2014, was even more challenging.

Premier Wynne and I met in her office at Queen's Park in Toronto. We had never met previously, although we had spoken several times over the phone. Given our different backgrounds, different politics and the recent Energy East controversy, the pleasantries were very limited. I was clear in pointing out that Alberta and Alberta alone would make decisions concerning the development of the Alberta oil sands, and I went to some lengths in describing the record of our province on climate change and the environment. I also questioned Premier Wynne on why Ontario would be challenging what was clearly a national project, adding that, other than Alberta, the biggest beneficiary of the construction of the project would be Ontario, since the General Electric turbines required for the project were going to be fabricated in Peterborough. Moreover, Ontario is the province where most of the oil sands' capital assets are fabricated and the place where the Canadian energy sector is financed.

We discussed the so-called seven conditions. Premier Wynne emphasized that, in her mind, these conditions were intended to allow us, in her terms, "to get to yes." The contentious matter was, of course, not the pipeline, but the oil sands. Premier Wynne acknowledged as much, and I pointed out that I was well aware of the problem and for that reason I had reached out to her and Premier Couillard to forge a Canadian partnership that would allow Alberta to renew its climate change policies and begin the arduous work of rebranding our province. I underscored that Premier Couillard and I were working to that same end and that I planned to attend the climate change conferences that Quebec and Ontario were hosting in the spring of 2015. I invited her collaboration on the journey to Paris and explained my views on how Alberta and Ontario and Quebec could work together. I emphasized repeatedly, however, that Alberta would not and could not submit to the direction of another Canadian province on environmental issues relating to the oil sands.

Premier Wynne grew more cordial as the meeting progressed. It became increasingly obvious to me that whatever she might have said over the previous several days, she had no intention of damaging her future working relationship with Alberta on environmental matters. I think she concluded by the end of the meeting that we could work together and that she should take me at my word on Alberta's commitment to move toward a broader, more pan-Canadian approach to energy and the environment.

The real purpose of the visit was, of course, the joint press conference that followed. It was brutal. I was no stranger to the media, particularly the central Canadian media, but I was accustomed to some degree of decorum and respect surrounding the relationship between elected officials and the press. Not so in Toronto.

Premier Wynne spoke first, welcoming me to Ontario, without addressing the specifics of what we had discussed. I knew that I needed the position she had shared with me privately on the public record, so when it came my turn to speak I provided an overview of what we had agreed on. Premier Wynne was then afforded an opportunity to respond but was unable to get through her commentary as members of the media shouted her down, calling out that she had "flip-flopped," "backed down" and "broken her word." It was pandemonium. As she tried to speak, journalists catcalled her and scurried about the room caucusing in disgust and comparing tweets on their mobile phones. I had never seen anything like it, and I resisted the temptation to insert myself into the commentary.

To her credit, Premier Wynne stood her ground, and I admired her for doing so. Again, as in the previous day's discussions with Premier Couillard, I considered this a good day for Alberta when Premier Wynne stated that "Premier Prentice and I both agree that this is a project of national importance" and that we would "work together" to advance a common agenda. She added that her government would not consider upstream greenhouse gas emissions when deciding whether Ontario would back the pipeline. Rather, the broader discussion on climate change would be discussed as part of the National Energy Strategy summit planned for July 2015.[5]

Where to, then, from here?

I acknowledge that the project's many critics have raised legitimate environmental concerns that must be addressed. Some doubt the merits of the project and, in fact, challenge the overall public and environmental safety of pipelines. Their concerns must be examined, and the project will obviously have to live up to exacting, modern regulatory standards. Surely a country as sophisticated as Canada is capable of regulating the construction and operation of such a pipeline.

The National Energy Board could, of course, refuse to issue a certificate, and the federal Cabinet could also refuse to approve it, but that seems unlikely. A country that opposes the construction of its own pipeline, across its own territory, to consume its own oil, isn't much of a country, or at least not one with much of a future. A country that produces four million barrels of oil per day but refuses to construct the infrastructure necessary to do anything but transport it to the United States so it can be refined, up-priced and transported back for Canadian consumption would be a bit of a laughingstock. Sadly, that is what our critics in the energy world already say about us. Energy East will allow us to prove them wrong.

Among most Canadians there is therefore a growing sense that what our country is missing is national leadership and, on this issue, most of us quietly hope we see some of it before it is too late. As the controversy surrounding Energy East drags on, one is left with the disquieting feeling that somehow Canada is failing, or that Canadian federalism is failing. Canada has always had its complications, but most Canadians have always assumed that, at a minimum, we are a common market of sorts. What can stronger leadership do to ensure that this national infrastructure project can move ahead?

First, the prime minister of Canada must show his support for the National Energy Board and recognize that it is a respected regulator. It does a tremendous disservice to the NEB's mission, morale and reputation to undercut it, as Prime Minister Trudeau has done in the past. The NEB was created as an independent tribunal in 1959 to take politics away from the technical and commercial analysis required for the approval of these complex projects. Dismissing its findings is counterproductive.

Second, the provincial premiers must recognize the federal jurisdiction of the inter-provincial pipeline approval process. Provinces can act as intervenors and state their case. But pretending, for local political purposes, that they can issue "conditions" and veto NEB decisions is the wrong approach.

Third, pipeline proponents have their work to do as well. The social and political environment is different from what it was a generation ago, and people seek answers to their questions. Their tolerance for risk and their evaluation of benefits have shifted. It's no longer simply about the number of construction jobs advertised on the project's website. It's about protecting groundwater, crossing streams and rivers, responding to spills and compensating landowners. Citizens do not wake up in the morning and say, "I think I'd like a 36-inch pipeline crossing my backyard today." These projects are high profile and generate angst; the companies must do a better job setting up the need for pipelines. Pipelines do serve a need, and this fact is rarely articulated. Before they grant "permission" to build a pipeline, people want to know that the solution being proposed to fill a need is the best possible one.

Finally, we need to rethink the way benefits accrue to various jurisdictions. We have heard British Columbia, Ontario and Quebec, as well as many municipalities, oppose pipelines because they face 80 percent of the risks (such as spills) but receive little or no benefits. Out west, we always retort that the benefits are called "equalization payments"—strong economies in British Columbia, Alberta and Saskatchewan benefit all of Canada. This point does not resonate. Another model has to be created—one that also benefits First Nations.

Certainly the politics surrounding Energy East remain complex. I am optimistic, however, that our national and provincial governments will see the wisdom of the project. Most sensible Canadians, including those in the province of Quebec, agree with Sir John A. Macdonald's vision of Canada, and they too dream of a larger, rather than smaller, country.

CHAPTER 14

Conclusion: Looking Confidently Toward a Better Future

The many questions raised in this book can be boiled down to a single, fundamental choice: *Does Canada want to be a leader or a follower in the transformation that is now sweeping the global energy marketplace?* It is really a question of whether we have the courage to pursue global leadership.

We have everything we need to lead. Our resource base, both renewable and non-renewable, is undoubtedly the envy of the world. When it comes to hydrocarbons, no other major industrial democracy has the ability to be at once energy independent and, at the same time, one of the world's largest exporters of oil and natural gas. When it comes to renewables such as hydroelectricity, our resource base is equally immense—affording us the ability to build a national electricity grid that has negligible carbon emissions, with surplus clean electricity available for export. No other country in the world has these possibilities. We have the labour and capital markets to succeed, and we are well known for our abilities in science and in the application of new technologies to our industrial output. We are also a trading nation, unafraid of the gale-force winds of competition, respected and admired by the very international players who need a dependable, free-market energy supplier such as Canada.

Yet we are not leading and we are, most assuredly, not global. We have allowed ourselves to drift into a dependency as a supplier of discounted energy resources to the United States, selling massive quantities of our oil and natural gas into the continental marketplace at a value far below global prices. We do so because we have no other customers. Indeed, despite almost 15 years of effort, we lack any of the pipeline or port infrastructure that would allow us to reach other global customers for our oil and natural gas. In fact, when it comes to oil, we don't even have the pipelines in place to reach our own eastern Canadian customers. It is quite remarkable, really. We are the world's largest overall energy producer but we exist as a provincial outlier, completely disconnected from the global marketplace. The talented young engineers, geologists, geophysicists, technicians, bankers and lawyers who represent the future of Canada's energy industry are as disconnected from global opportunities as are the young citizens of Britain in the wake of Brexit. Global opportunities in the energy world reside elsewhere, not in Canada.

It will be obvious by now that my perspective is that of a Canadian nationalist. I never thought it was particularly prudent that Canada had only one customer for its oil and natural gas. Now that the United States is both our only customer and our most successful competitor, it seems just plain dumb. I don't say this as a criticism of the United States. I admire and respect our American neighbours, but I also understand how free markets function when they are oversupplied. So, too, do the Americans, and they have moved with lightning speed to export their surplus oil and natural gas into the global market to realize higher global prices. They are fully aware of the folly of dumping their surplus resources into a saturated continental marketplace. We aren't. Or at least until now, we haven't been.

There are other consequences to a failure to access global markets. We deny ourselves the geopolitical authority that is implicit with our status as one of the world's largest energy producers. We deprive ourselves of the trade advantages and market penetration opportunities that accompany having a strong hand internationally. It is true that Canada and the United States share a continental economic partnership, but it is also true that we are close allies with a shared commitment to global free markets, energy security and the stability that comes from balanced and diversified global energy markets. Canada should stand confidently alongside the United States and our other international allies when it comes to the global geopolitics of energy. We have instead become a satellite to the United States and its energy revolution, seemingly indifferent to the fact that the jobs, investment opportunities and future are increasingly American and not Canadian, as the United States dominates global markets for both refined petroleum products and liquefied natural gas.

Our production from the oil sands continues to escalate inexorably, and our dependency on the United States as the sole customer for our oil continues to intensify. The 2016 American presidential primaries and the election that followed have underscored that vulnerability. We all now see that the denial of a presidential permit for a new pipeline is far from the worst thing that could happen to Canada. The confluence of rising US protectionism and escalating environmental activism makes Canada more vulnerable than ever, and the activist debate in the United States has shifted unmistakably and ominously from the granting of new pipeline permits to questions surrounding the renewal of permits and approvals for existing infrastructure. We will need to be measured in our response to rising US protectionism, but we will also need to be shrewd about protecting Canada's own interests.

In the face of these challenges, I remain an optimist. This book is about Canada's energy future, and that future, like any economic future that is bright, limitless and prosperous, must be a global one. We are after all one of the world's great free traders. There is a growing recognition that Canada has lost its way when it comes to global energy markets, but there is also a growing recognition that we need to learn from mistakes and change our ways.

Foremost among the lessons that we have learned is the essential nexus between leadership on energy and leading on the environment. We have learned the hard way that Canada's future as a global energy supplier will be truncated unless we are also seen to be a leader on the environment generally and climate change specifically. And why shouldn't we lead in both areas? One of the great challenges of the next hundred years lies in meeting the energy needs of human civilization while averting the worst consequences of rising carbon emissions. In that struggle, Canada should be a leader, not a follower.

There is also a growing recognition that we will need to work together with Canada's indigenous peoples to reach the Asia Pacific and that Canada's First Peoples should be our partners, rather than our adversaries, in that pursuit. We can still seize the opportunities that lie ahead and make better choices that will convert Canada's vast energy resources into a secure, prosperous and environmentally responsible future. There is much that we need to do to regain that vision. But we can press forward if we move beyond the mistakes of the past and become more strategic in our vision, wiser in our choices, more collaborative within our confederation, assertive in our energy sovereignty and in our role in world markets, and open to new ways of working with indigenous peoples.

For me, the story of the Raven Totem illustrates how we can put the mistakes of the past behind us, pressing forward to a more confident future.

The Raven Totem Pole

Jasper is one of the most spectacular tourist destinations in Canada and, for more than a century, visitors had marvelled at the giant Raven Totem Pole standing at the front entrance to the railway station on the main street. I first saw it when I was a boy of 13 in 1969, after my family had moved to the small Alberta coal-mining town of Grande Cache in the heart of the Rocky Mountains. Jasper was our first stop when we reached the Rockies, and I remember staring up in awe at this incredible pole, astonished by its height, wondering about its meaning and believing that it symbolized the spirituality of the Rocky Mountains. It did, in fact, have a spiritual meaning but, as it turned out, not one relating to the Rockies.

You see, what few people knew was that this extraordinary piece of Canadian history and culture had been pirated away from the Haida on Haida Gwaii (then the Queen Charlotte Islands), almost a century before. The Grand Trunk Railway, whose success depended on attracting tourists from all over the world, had moved the Raven Totem to Jasper in 1916 as a tourist attraction. And so, the big pole stood in Jasper, beside Canada's national rail line, for more than 93 years.

It was not until 2008, when I was Canada's environment minister and the minister responsible for Parks Canada, that I learned that the Raven Totem was one of Canada's most brazen acts of cultural piracy. It had been taken from Old Massett on Haida Gwaii, where it had stood as a memorial pole marking the life of a beloved chief of the Raven clan. The pole had been carved in the 1870s from a 500-year-old red cedar. Parks Canada had inherited the pole when it purchased the historic Jasper train station from the Canadian National Railway and, learning of its history, had contacted Chief Sdiithldaa Frank Collison of the Haida Nation and my good friend Guujaaw, then the president of the Council of the Haida Nation.

The Haida obviously wanted to see the Raven Totem Pole repatriated to Old Massett. This was, of course, never in doubt, and we began planning the return of the giant totem to Haida Gwaii. But I was not prepared for what came next. Several weeks later, Guujaaw phoned and explained that the Haida had spoken among themselves and decided, "There's been a Haida pole in Jasper for the last one hundred years and we think there should be a Haida pole in Jasper for the next one hundred." It was a simple yet profound gesture that illustrated what I have always admired about the Haida: their confidence in themselves and in their relationship with the rest of Canada. These are, after all, the same Canadians who reasserted "Haida Gwaii" as the proper name of their islands, symbolically returning the name "Queen Charlotte

Islands" to Premier Gordon Campbell in an empty box. The Haida understood that the Raven Totem was now part of our collective Canadian history and an important symbol of the Haida's relationship with the rest of Canada. Why not replace it with another pole and celebrate the reconciliation that it reflected? And so, we agreed to replace the Raven Totem with a new one that would eventually be carved by the next generation of Haida carvers.

The original Raven Pole was ultimately repatriated to Old Massett, on Haida Gwaii, on National Aboriginal Day in 2010; and as the old pole wound its way home, young Canadian schoolchildren along the route were able to touch it and learn of its history, while young Haida carvers worked on the creation of the new Raven Pole. The new pole was transported to Jasper and raised in July 2011, right near the Jasper train station on Main Street, as a continuing symbol of our history and the uncompleted work of our shared future.

* * *

For me, this story illustrates that we must be confident of ourselves and courageous about our future. We must establish new partnerships, and they must be meaningful, purposeful and respectful of the economic, environmental and cultural aspirations of indigenous peoples. And we must be prepared to dream and to be just a bit audacious about what is possible—which for me is why the Raven Totem is an important national symbol of our shared future.

Canadian prosperity is not a birthright—it must be earned. With better foresight, smart choices and hard work, Canada will be able to fully enjoy the benefits of its national bounty.

ACKNOWLEDGEMENTS

Jean-Sébastien and I dedicate this book to our families, who supported us in countless ways through the long hours spent writing these pages. Writing a book is hard and lonely work, and neither of us would have made it through this enterprise without the love and support of our families.

We also thank Michael Levine for believing that a book on Canada's energy future was important, and for enabling and shepherding our relationship with HarperCollins. Jim Gifford, our senior editor, headed up the team of people with whom we worked at HarperCollins. We thank them for their professionalism. We have been fortunate to work under Jim's expert tutelage as our editor *extraordinaire*. He pushed us relentlessly to continue to improve this book, and the final product reflects his determination and our shared passion for Canada and all things Canadian.

Returning to the notion that writing is hard work, I would like to thank a number of people at the Woodrow Wilson Center in Washington. The center, which was created as a living memorial to Woodrow Wilson, the 28th president of the United States, is a remarkable institution. Its mandate is to support independent global scholarship, and I was invited there to write this book by Gary Doer, the former Canadian ambassador to the United States, and by David Jacobson, the former US ambassador to Canada.

They, together with Hugh MacKinnon, serve as the co-chairs of the Canada Institute at the Woodrow Wilson Center. I would like to thank Laura Dawson, the director of the institute, and Kate Salimi, the program officer, for their help. Both are Canadians— in fact, Albertans. I would also like to thank Janet Spikes, the head librarian at the Wilson Center, and two library technicians, Michelle Kamalich and Katherine Wahler. I have never regarded myself as a scholar, but they treated me like one and I thank them for their help and unfailing kindness.

Jean-Sébastien and I would also like to thank the bright master of public policy students who served as research assistants and helped to gather some of the facts and information used in this book: Curtis McKinney, Lindsay Kline, Brian Conger and Mikaela McQuade. Although some of the facts and figures did not survive the editorial process, you are not forgotten.

As I mention later, I was attending the Copenhagen Climate Change Conference in 2009, the so-called COP 15, when I decided that this book needed to be written. However, it was Jean-Sébastien Rioux, my friend and former chief of staff, who made sure that it did get written. J-S, as he is known to his family and friends, approached me in 2012 after a particularly long-winded speech I delivered in Calgary and convinced me that we should embark on this enterprise together. J-S has been indefatigable in his commitment to this project. Happily, despite a creative and editing process that seemed to have no end, we are now better friends than ever.

NOTES

Introduction
Under the Bins
1   The ERCB's Decision #94-8 on *Whaleback* was handed down in 1994; see: sites. google.com/a/ualberta.ca/wildlife-impacts/home/industrial-development/the-whaleback/excerpts-from-ercb-decision---whaleback-ridge-area

Chapter 1
Canada's Global Opportunity: Our Energy Resources and Markets
1   The US Securities and Exchange Commission (SEC) defines "proved oil and gas reserves" as "those quantities of oil and gas, which, by analysis of geoscience and engineering data, can be estimated with reasonable certainty to be economically producible (...) based on existing economic conditions." See sec.gov/rules/final/2008/33-8995.pdf

2   Canadian Association of Petroleum Producers (CAPP), "Responsible Canadian Energy—2014 Progress Report," capp.ca/publications-and-statistics/publications/255363

3   U.S. Energy Information Administration, July 2015, "U.S.–Canada Electricity Trade Increases," eia.gov/todayinenergy/detail.cfm?id=21992

4   U.S. Energy Information Administration, 2015, "U.S. Field Production of Crude Oil" and "U.S. Natural Gas Gross Withdrawals (Million Cubic Feet)," eia.gov/dnav/ng/hist/n9010us2a.htm

5   U.S. Energy Information Administration, *International Energy Outlook 2013*, eia.gov/forecasts/ieo/pdf/0484(2013).pdf

6   Ibid. See also the International Energy Agency (IEA), *World Energy Outlook 2015* (Paris, 2015), worldenergyoutlook.org

Chapter 2
Canada as a Global Energy Power: The Need for National Leadership
1   Daniel Yergin, "Energy Security and Markets." In *Energy and Security: Strategies for a World in Transition*, edited by Jan H. Kalicki and David L. Goldwyn, 2nd ed. (Washington, DC: Woodrow Wilson Center Press, 2013).

2   Canadian Chamber of Commerce (2013), *50 Million a Day: A Lack of Infrastructure Is Preventing Canadians from Maximizing Their Potential Benefits in Energy Markets*, chamber.ca/media/blog/130917-50-Million-a-Day/1309_50_Million_a_Day.pdf

Chapter 3
A Canadian Global Strategy: What We Need to Do

1   Richard Vietor, *How Countries Compete: Strategy, Structure, and Government in the Global Economy* (Boston: Harvard Business School Press, 2007).

Chapter 4
The Continental Trap: How Canada Unwittingly Lost Its Energy Sovereignty

1   U.S. Energy Information Administration, "Petroleum and Other Liquids—Spot Prices." See eia.gov/dnav/pet/pet_pri_spt_s1_d.htm

2   See Alberta Records Publication Board, David H. Breen, ed., *William Stewart Herron: Father of the Petroleum Industry in Alberta* (Calgary: Historical Society of Alberta, 1984), vol. 5.

3   The owners were lawyer-investors James A. Lougheed and R.B. Bennett; rancher and brewer A.E. Cross; land speculators T.J.S. Skinner and A.J. Sayre, together with driller Archibald W. Dingman.

4   Alberta Records Publication Board, Breen, *William Stewart Herron.*

5   John Herd Thompson and Stephen J. Randall, *Canada and the United States: Ambivalent Allies*, 3rd ed. (Montreal and Kingston: McGill–Queens University Press, 2002), 256.

6   See, for example, section 4 ("Imports from Canada"), Richard Nixon: "Special Message to the Congress on Energy Resources," June 4, 1971. Online by Gerhard Peters and John T. Woolley, *The American Presidency Project,* presidency.ucsb.edu/data.php

7   Thompson and Randall, *Canada and the United States.*

8   See 41.statcan.gc.ca/2008/1741/ceb1741_000-eng.htm

Chapter 5
The Keystone XL Debacle: Canada's Lesson in **Realpolitik**

1   The White House, "Statement by the President on the Keystone XL Pipeline." November 6, 2015, whitehouse.gov/the-press-office/2015/11/06/statement-president-keystone-xl-pipeline

2   The White House, "Remarks by the President in a Town Hall Discussion on Energy in Fairless Hills, Pennsylvania." April 6, 2011, whitehouse.gov/the-press-office/2011/04/06/remarks-president-town-hall-discussion-energy-fairless-hills-pennsylvani

3   The White House, "Remarks by the President on American-Made Energy." Cushing, Oklahoma, March 22, 2012, whitehouse.gov/the-press-office/2012/03/22/remarks-president-american-made-energy

4   Michael R. Bloomberg, "Keystone Solution Runs through Canada," *Bloomberg View*, February 25, 2015: bloombergview.com/articles/2015-02-25/mike-bloomberg-keystone-xl-solution-runs-through-canada

5   NAFTA Secretariat, Legal Text of the NAFTA Agreement, Chapter Six, Energy and Basic Petrochemicals: nafta-sec-alena.org/Home/Legal-Texts/North-American-Free-Trade-Agreement?mvid=1&secid=6ac38ba0-fdf1-4e8b-80ae-8957d3528949

6   See U.S. Department of State Archives, 2008, "Keystone Pipeline Presidential Permit" media note: 2001-2009.state.gov/r/pa/prs/ps/2008/mar/102254.htm

Chapter 6
Hydroelectricity and the North American Electricity Grid:
Canada's Defining Advantage

1   Canadian Hydropower Association, 2008, "Hydropower in Canada: Past, Present and Future," 3, canadahydro.ca/wp-content/uploads/2015/09/2008-hydropower-past-present-future-en.pdf

2   Association québécoise de la production d'énergie renouvelable, "Hydro Power," www.aqper.com/en

3   Canadian Hydropower Association, "Hydropower in Canada."

4   Info Niagara, "Hydro Power Niagara Falls," infoniagara.com/attractions/hydro_power

5   Canadian Hydropower Association, "Hydropower in Canada."

6   IEA Hydropower, "What Is Hydropower's History?" ieahydro.org/faq

7   Ibid.

8   Ibid.

9   Of note is that one of the company's founders was Donald A. Smith, better known as Lord Strathcona, the great Canadian politician, industrialist and philanthropist.

10   Manitoba Hydro, *A History of Electric Power in Manitoba*, hydro.mb.ca/corporate/history/history.shtml

11   National Energy Board, "Annual Canadian Electricity Exports (Sales), 2005–2014," neb-one.gc.ca/nrg/sttstc/lctrct/stt/lctrctysmmr/2014/smmry2014-eng.html

12   Canadian Electricity Association, 2014, "U.S. Department of Energy – Quadrennial Energy Review: Comments of the Canadian Electricity Association," electricity.ca/media/IndustryIssues/USAffairs/CEACommentsQERSept2014.pdf

13   U.S. Department of Energy 2015 Quadrennial Energy Review, 6-2, 6-5, 6-6, energy.gov/sites/prod/files/2015/08/f25/QER%20Chapter%20VI%20North%20America%20April%202015.pdf

Chapter 7
Canada's Bumpy Road from Kyoto to Paris: The Dangers of Signing International Treaties We Cannot Live Up To

1 Eddie Goldenberg, Prime Minister Jean Chrétien's senior adviser for more than two decades, said this during interviews in 2007. See Les Whittington, "Liberals Knew Kyoto a Long Shot," *Toronto Star*, February 23, 2007: thestar.com/news/2007/02/23/ liberals_knew_kyoto_a_long_shot.html; see also Robert C. Paehlke, *Some Like It Cold: The Politics of Climate Change in Canada* (Toronto: Between the Lines, 2008).

2 Major Economies Forum members: Australia, Brazil, Canada, China, the EU, France, Germany, India, Indonesia, Italy, Japan, Malaysia, Mexico, Russia, South Africa, South Korea, the UK and the United States.

3 Umbrella Group countries: Australia, Canada, Iceland, Japan, Kazakhstan, New Zealand, Norway, Ukraine and the United States.

Chapter 8
A Strategic Approach to the Environment: How to Be a Global Environmental Leader

1 Ian Moore, 2011, "Life Cycle Well to Wheels Assessment of GHG Emissions from North American and Imported Crude Oils" (see slide 7 in particular), ceps. eu/system/files/article/2011/03/Jacobs%20Consultancy%20LCA%20Meeting%20 March%2021.pdf

2 See, for example, "First Call for Proposals for Mexico's Energy Ministry with the University of Calgary," UToday, June 10, 2016: ucalgary.ca/utoday/issue/2016-06-10/ first-call-proposals-mexicos-energy-ministry-university-calgary

Chapter 9
Climate Change: An Action Plan That Will Reassert Canadian Leadership

1 This IEA report can be accessed online: iea.org/publications/freepublications/ publication/weo-special-report-2013-redrawing-the-energy-climate-map.html

2 See Environment Canada (2016), *Canada's Second Biennial Report on Climate Change*, February 10, 2016: ec.gc.ca/GES-GHG/default.asp?lang=En&n=02D095CB-1

3 International Energy Agency, 2015, *Energy and Climate Change: World Energy Outlook: Special Report*, 38, iea.org/publications/freepublications/publication/ WEO2015SpecialReportonEnergyandClimateChange.pdf

4 All the figures cited are from the Canadian Electricity Association, electricity.ca

Chapter 10
The Pacific Northwest: Why Canada's Coastal First Nations Are the Key to Canada's Asian Gateway

1   Gerry Angevine, *The Canadian Oil Transport Conundrum*, 26, the Fraser Institute, 2013, fraserinstitute.org/sites/default/files/canadian-oil-transport-conundrum-rev.pdf

Chapter 12
A New Proposal for Oil Exports to Asia: Why First Nations Must Become Economic Partners

1   British Columbia Ministry of Environment, "Information Bulletin" (August 1, 2012), archive.news.gov.bc.ca/releases/news_releases_2009-2013/2012env0049-001120.pdf
2   "B.C. Vows to Block Pipeline Unless Alberta Ponies Up, *Globe and Mail*, July 24, 2012; theglobeandmail.com/news/politics/bc-vows-to-block-pipeline-unless-alberta-ponies-up/article4437308
3   Ibid.
4   National Energy Board, "Trans Mountain Pipeline ULC – Trans Mountain Expansion," neb-one.gc.ca/clf-nsi/rthnb/pplctnsbfrthnb/trnsmntnxpnsn/trnsmntnxpnsn-eng.html#s6
5   Trans Mountain, "Trans Mountain Application Overview," transmountain.com/updates/trans-mountain-application-overview
6   Enbridge, "Northern Gateway Pipelines Project Overview," gatewayfacts.ca/About-The-Project/Project-Overview.aspx
7   Ibid.
8   Canadian Environmental Assessment Agency, "Joint Review Panel Recommends Approving the Enbridge Northern Gateway Project." News release, December 19, 2013, gatewaypanel.review-examen.gc.ca/clf-nsi/nwsrls/2013/nwsrls05-eng.html
9   Douglas R. Eyford, *Forging Partnerships, Building Relationships: Aboriginal Canadians and Energy Development* (Report to the prime minister: executive summary, 2013), nrcan.gc.ca/sites/www.nrcan.gc.ca/files/www/pdf/publications/ForgPart-Online-e.pdf
10 Ibid.
11 Ibid.
12 Ibid.

Chapter 13
Unfinished Business: Energy East and the Importance of Canada's Common Market and the Atlantic Basin

1   Lukas Albrecht and Trevor Tombe, 2015, "Internal Trade, Productivity, and Inter-connected Industries: A Quantitative Analysis." University of Calgary Economics Department: econ.ucalgary.ca/manageprofile/sites/econ.ucalgary.ca.manageprofile/files/unitis/publications/1-6131365/albrecht_tombe_2015_final.pdf

2   Minister Heurtel's conditions, contained in his letter to TransCanada CEO Russ Girling: (1) more consultation with Quebeckers to assess social acceptability issues; (2) conduct a comprehensive environmental review on the Quebec portion of the pipeline; (3) ensure the highest technical standards and permanent monitoring; (4) the project must meet with the approval of First Nations following appropriate consultations; (5) the project must demonstrate job creation, economic and fiscal benefits for Quebec; (6) TransCanada must demonstrate that it has the best emergency response plan, including financial resources, to guarantee an effective response and indemnification; and (7) TransCanada must ensure the security of the supply of natural gas in Quebec once its Mainline is converted. (Translation by J-S Rioux.)

3   See Adrian Morrow, "Premiers Wynne and Couillard Set Seven Criteria for Energy East," *Globe and Mail*, November 21, 2014; theglobeandmail.com/news/politics/premiers-wynne-and-couillard-set-seven-criteria-for-energy-east/article21714915

4   The press conference was viewed on Premier Couillard's Facebook page: video-sea1-1.xx.fbcdn.net/hvideo-xat1/v/t42.17902/10823926_877997778899855_556235977_n.mp4?efg=eyJybHIiOjMwNywicmxhIjo4ODZ9&rl=307&v-abr=171&oh=81dc236e8864fb642537a4ddcd15108a&oe=55E4AECF

5   Quotations are from Robert Benzie's article in the *Toronto Star* on December 3, 2014: "Ontario, Alberta Premiers Agree to 'Work Together' on Energy East Oil Pipeline," thestar.com/news/queenspark/2014/12/03/ontario_alberta_premiers_agree_to_work_together_on_energy_east_oil_pipeline.html

INDEX